U.S.-Cuban Cooperation Past, Present, and Future

CONTEMPORARY CUBA

UNIVERSITY PRESS OF FLORIDA

Florida A&M University, Tallahassee
Florida Atlantic University, Boca Raton
Florida Gulf Coast University, Ft. Myers
Florida International University, Miami
Florida State University, Tallahassee
New College of Florida, Sarasota
University of Central Florida, Orlando
University of Florida, Gainesville
University of North Florida, Jacksonville
University of South Florida, Tampa
University of West Florida, Pensacola

Contemporary Cuba
Edited by John M. Kirk

U.S.-Cuban Cooperation
Past, Present, and Future

Melanie M. Ziegler

University Press of Florida
Gainesville/Tallahassee/Tampa/Boca Raton/Pensacola
Orlando/Miami/Jacksonville/Ft. Myers/Sarasota

12 11 10 09 08 07   6 5 4 3 2 1

Library of Congress Cataloging-in-Publication Data
Ziegler, Melanie M.
U.S.-Cuban cooperation past, present, and future /
by Melanie M. Ziegler.
p. cm. — (Contemporary Cuba)
Includes bibliographical references and index.
ISBN 978-0-8130-3087-6 (alk. paper)
1. United States—Foreign relations—Cuba. 2. Cuba—Foreign
relations—United States. 3. International cooperation. 4. United
States—Foreign relations—1989- 5. National security—United
States. 6. National security—Cuba. I. Title. II. Title: United
States Cuban cooperation past, present, and future.
E183.8.C9Z54   2007
327.730729109'045—dc22   2007004258

The University Press of Florida is the scholarly publishing agency
for the State University System of Florida, comprising Florida
A&M University, Florida Atlantic University, Florida Gulf
Coast University, Florida International University, Florida State
University, New College of Florida, University of Central Florida,
University of Florida, University of North Florida, University
of South Florida, and University of West Florida.

University Press of Florida
15 Northwest 15th Street
Gainesville, FL 32611-2079
http://www.upf.com

In loving memory of my parents,
Don and Ruth C. McClure

Contents

Tables

Preface

U.S.-Cuban Cooperation, Past, Present, and Future describes and analyzes an intriguing pattern of U.S.-Cuban cooperation that emerged during the 1990s. Naked self-interest led the two governments to cooperate in four areas involving illegal migration, drug trafficking, decreasing tensions around Guantánamo Naval Base, and reducing the threat of accidental war. The fact that there has been any cooperation between the United States and Cuba may be surprising to many since the public rhetoric of animosity has always dominated U.S.-Cuban discourse.

This study adds to political science literature on U.S.-Cuban relations, because to date there has been little systematic research on these areas of cooperation. In the introduction I explain how confidence-building measures (CBMs) and quiet diplomacy were used to initiate the cooperation. In chapter 1, I demonstrate how important Cuban exile groups and actors have attempted to undermine all levels of existing cooperation and have pushed to prevent the establishment of any new initiatives. In the next four chapters I present and analyze each of the four cases of U.S.-Cuban cooperation. In the conclusion I summarize the evidence from the cases, review the state of U.S.-Cuban relations under the George W. Bush administration, and argue that CBMs offer the United States and Cuba the best pathway for avoiding future confrontation and for building more normal relations in the twenty-first century.

To the many people who have helped with this book, I extend my sincerest gratitude. I especially want to recognize the superb guidance and professionalism of adviser and friend Laura J. Neack. Laura's timely feedback, scholarly insights, and clearly structured suggestions served to give motivation and momentum to my writing.

I have also benefited from the support of Walt Vanderbush and Pat Haney. Their comments and suggestions were constructive, and their teaching and scholarship on Cuba have both educated and inspired me. Additionally, I am indebted to Walt for graciously sharing his extensive Latin American files with me.

In Washington, D.C., I wish to thank Glenn Baker, Director of the U.S.-Cuba Cooperative Security Project at the Center for Defense Information

(CDI). Early on in my research I came into contact with Glenn and the CDI. Glenn provided me with CDI transcripts of previous meetings between U.S. delegations and Cuban officials. I am especially thankful to Glenn for inviting me to participate as an observer during the CDI trip to Havana, November 3–6, 2003.

For the funding of my trips to Cuba, I wish to thank Ryan Barilleaux, Chair of the Department of Political Science; John Rothgeb Jr., Director of Graduate Studies; and David Francko, Associate Dean of the College of Arts and Science, all of Miami University.

Special thanks go to John M. Kirk, Contemporary Cuba series editor for the University Press of Florida (UPF). John always believed in this project and in my ability to follow through with it. His comments and suggestions for improvement were always focused and direct, and I looked forward to each of his e-mails. Likewise, Amy Gorelick, the acquisitions editor at UPF, was always responsive and helpful when I e-mailed her my many formatting questions, and Susan Albury was an outstanding project editor.

Last, but certainly not least, I wish to thank my friends and family for their interest in this project and for their emotional and financial support. In the Department of Political Science at Miami University, I am grateful for the advice of Dilchoda Berdieva, Sheila Croucher, Adeed Dawisha, and Mark Sachleben. My other dear friends in the Department of Spanish and Portuguese, my neighbors, my sister Marsha, and my best friend Elaine made sure that I took phone breaks, coffee breaks, lunch breaks, and movie breaks from time to time.

I dedicate this book to my beloved parents, Don and Ruth C. McClure. Dad and Mom sadly passed from this life in May 2006, and I deeply feel their loss. Many thanks also go to my Miami University college sweetheart, Rich Ziegler; to my children, Erich and Heidi; and to my in-laws, Gerald and Shirley Ziegler. You all have enriched my life.

Introduction

Although the Cold War has ended, U.S. preoccupation with Cuba certainly has not, and relations between the two countries remain tense and uncertain. For three decades from 1961 to 1991, U.S. policy makers focused on Cuba as the preeminent Communist threat in the hemisphere and accused the Fidel Castro regime of exporting revolution throughout Latin America and the Third World. As such, much of the scholarship during those decades centered on the Cuban revolution, the internationalism of the Castro regime, and the U.S. trade embargo against Cuba.

In the years since the end of the Cold War, relations between the United States and Cuba have remained openly hostile. U.S. presidents George H. W. Bush and Bill Clinton further tightened the geriatric U.S. trade embargo in 1992 and 1996, respectively, and President George W. Bush severely restricted family travel and remittances to the island in 2004. In spite of these more recent attempts by Washington to punish the Castro regime, the two countries have occasionally cooperated on some shared problems. Since the 1990s, bilateral cooperation has been notable in areas of mutual interest involving illegal migration, drug trafficking, decreasing tensions around Guantánamo Naval Base, and reducing of the threat of accidental war. The very fact such cooperative efforts between the United States and Cuba have been undertaken is surprising to many given that the public rhetoric of animosity has always dominated the discourse between these two "closest of enemies" (Smith 1987).

This book covers these four areas of U.S.-Cuban cooperation and seeks to add to our knowledge of post–Cold War relations between the two countries, since to date very little attention has focused on analyzing these efforts. This investigation addresses several questions: What were the factors that motivated these two implacable enemies to put aside their differences in order to cooperate on these four issues? Why was the U.S. government hesitant to publicly acknowledge successful efforts at cooperation? What is the state of these cooperative efforts during the George W. Bush administration? Finally, can these successful efforts at cooperation offer a new model for twenty-first-century U.S.-Cuban relations?

The second part of this introductory chapter reviews the many conflicts and tensions that have plagued U.S.-Cuban relations since the earliest days of the nineteenth century and includes both U.S. and Cuban perspectives as they pertain to the countries' historic mutual distrust. After setting the necessary historical context, the chapter subsequently notes how at the beginning of the 1990s, a small cadre of forward-thinking U.S. and Cuban officials began quietly working behind the scenes on establishing confidence-building measures (CBMs) in order to address bilateral issues of equal concern for both countries.

The next section briefly defines and traces the history and development of CBMs, beginning with the "hotline" that was installed between Moscow and Washington shortly after the Cuban missile crisis in 1962. Although CBMs were born of necessity during the Cold War so as to lessen tensions between the hostile superpowers, in the post–Cold War period they have been utilized effectively by other mutually hostile countries, such as India and Pakistan. Since CBMs involve small, incremental steps at reducing tensions, they are especially applicable when countries exhibit low levels of mutual trust.

The United States and the Soviet Union were forced to establish CBMs because both countries feared mutual assured destruction and nuclear war. In the case of the United States and Cuba, the United States has overwhelming military power, but any conflict with Cuba could result in massive illicit flows of refugees or drugs to U.S. shores. In a worst-case scenario, a U.S.-Cuban conflict could leave Cuba a failed state. Separated by only ninety miles of ocean, the United States and Cuba are quite simply too close for comfort, and the careful implementation of CBMs can help the two countries begin a transition from their conflictive past.

Chapter 1 analyzes the complex political relationship between Washington and the Cuban exile community and focuses on five phases that trace its evolution from the 1960s to the present. The five phases include (1) exile militancy of the 1960s, (2) the moderate exiles' dialogue with the Cuban government and the resulting backlash that occurred during the 1970s, (3) the rise of the lobbying power of the Cuban American National Foundation (CANF) during the 1980s, (4) the rise of the legislative influence of Cuban American members of Congress in the 1990s, and (5) the current phase of retrospection and retrenchment against the Castro regime that began after the public relations fiasco associated with the international custody battle over Elián González. The analysis of the five phases demonstrates that Cuban exile leaders and their

organizations became increasingly influential over the decades, first in a sup-
portive role and later in formulating an inflexible U.S. foreign policy toward
the island. After the end of the Cold War, Cuban exile politics became a serious
obstacle to the reduction of tensions between Cuba and the United States as
well as to the creation and implementation of CBMs, even though Cuba was
no longer perceived to be a national security threat. Nevertheless, U.S. political actors who favored cooperation found ways to circumvent this opposition,
as presented in chapters 2–5, which analyze in detail each of the four cases of
bilateral cooperation that were quietly achieved during the 1990s.

Chapter 2 traces the U.S.-Cuban cooperative efforts that culminated in the
1994–1995 migration agreements that dramatically redefined U.S. immigration policy toward Cubans seeking illegal entry into the United States. The
chapter briefly describes the four major waves of postrevolutionary migrations from Cuba to the United States and analyzes the political and economic
factors that motivated Cubans to leave the island. The chapter subsequently
examines the evolution of the 1994–1995 U.S.-Cuban migration agreements
and explains that the two countries were willing to put aside their hostilities
in order to cooperate on the agreements, because both governments had experienced more pain than gain from their manipulation of illegal migration to
damage the other country. For the United States, the propaganda value gained
from highlighting the failure of the Castro regime each time that waves of
desperate Cubans took to the high seas was no longer worth the financial and
social costs associated with accepting large numbers of illegal migrants. Moreover, during the rafter crisis of 1994, the double standard of U.S. preferential
treatment for admitting lighter-skinned Cuban migrants was uncomfortably
highlighted when the United States refused to accept darker-skinned Haitian
boat people, who were fleeing a country with more serious political and economic problems than Cuba.

Castro had also appeared to be willing to use illegal migration as a political
tool. He was accused by Washington of unleashing waves of migrants whenever political tensions or economic downturns threatened to cause unrest on
the island. By allowing discontented Cubans to depart the island, Castro was
effectively able to export dissent against his regime. Castro was also able to use
illegal migration as a way to call attention to the U.S. embargo and the severe
deprivations that it caused on the island.

By 1994, however, the Castro regime was anxious to negotiate a migration
agreement. The Mariel crisis in 1980 had been especially embarrassing and

chaotic, and the 1994 rafter crisis had resulted in a number of hijackings of government vessels and the tragic loss of life on the high seas. In addition to ferries and fishing vessels, airplanes were also hijacked by Cubans seeking to migrate illegally, but frequently the hijackers were given refuge in the United States and acclaimed as heroes by the Cuban American community. Finally, the Castro regime was anxious for a migration agreement because without the patronage of the Soviet Union, the Castro government could ill afford a confrontation with the United States that might result from any future migration crisis. Therefore, the two countries undertook secret meetings that culminated in the migration agreements of 1994–1995.

The Cuban government continues to push for the United States to rescind the 1966 Cuban Adjustment Act, which encourages Cubans to migrate illegally to the United States, and the Bush administration has canceled the biannual migration talks over Cuba's departure and repatriation requirements. Nevertheless, the two countries manage to cooperate on repatriating illegal migrants who are intercepted at sea.

Chapter 3 traces the cooperative efforts that were undertaken by the two governments during the 1990s as they confronted the enormous challenge of illegal drug trafficking in the Caribbean region. The chapter begins with a brief review of the role of drugs and their criminality in Cuba's prerevolution history and subsequently reviews the Castro regime's drug policies from the early years of the revolution until the fall of the Soviet Union. The chapter focuses closely on the 1990s, paying particular attention to important cases of U.S.-Cuban cooperation on drug interdiction, beginning with the 1996 joint seizure and search of the *Limerick*. U.S. officials credited the discovery of approximately 6.6 tons of cocaine on board to Cuban search efforts once the ship entered into Cuban waters.

In an interesting twist to the events, the U.S. Department of Justice requested that four Cuban officers provide testimony at the trial of the *Limerick*'s captain and chief engineer. In March 1997 the Cubans testified in the U.S. District Court in Miami, and the trial led to the convictions of the accused men. In this particular case the mainstream media reported the cooperation between the U.S. and Cuban governments.

In 1999, with the goal of enhancing joint efforts at drug interdiction by the respective coast guards, the United States made four proposals to Cuba that resulted in an upgrade of an existing fax connection to a telephone connection, coordination of radio frequencies, the stationing of a counternarcotics specialist in Havana, and the provision of technical expertise to assist in joint boarding and searches of commercial vessels on a case-by-case basis.

Cuban American members of Congress and their allies were outraged once they learned of the arrangements, and they argued that Castro was an unfit partner in the war on drugs, because they claimed that Castro himself trafficked in narcotics. The inflammatory charges against Castro were leveled during a contentious congressional hearing and were contested by testimony from the U.S. Coast Guard and the Drug Enforcement Agency (DEA).

Unlike the migration agreements that were signed by both Cuba and the United States, drug cooperation between the two governments has remained limited to a case-by-case basis. Although Castro has repeatedly urged a more formal arrangement between the two countries, to date there has been no further movement at deepening the cooperation with a signed U.S.-Cuba drug agreement. At the same time, the U.S. Coast Guard reports that the information that it receives from Cuba is increasingly reliable.

Chapter 4 deals with cooperation between the U.S. and Cuban military officers regarding operations at Guantánamo Naval Base. Perhaps no issue strikes a more nationalist chord in Cuba than does the presence of U.S. soldiers on Cuban soil. As such, the chapter begins with a history of how and why the United States acquired control of the area, the base's role during and after the Cuban revolution, and its continuing importance to the United States as a holding area for refugees and alleged illegal combatants.

Other sections of chapter 4 explore cooperative efforts between U.S. and Cuban military commanders. Beginning in 1993, the commanders began to give each other advance notification of their military exercises around the base. Other cooperative measures were undertaken in the area of flight safety, and joint meetings were held in order to deal with the complexities of housing a large number of refugees on the base. In response to concerns that Cuban civilians might venture onto the U.S. minefield that surrounded the base if there were another migration crisis or upheaval on the island, the United States quietly removed its mines in 1999. The removal of the mines was also intended as a conciliatory gesture for the international community as well as a signal to Castro.

The chapter also notes how U.S. military officers who returned to the United States after serving on the base have urged more cooperation as being in the best interest of the United States. In the post–Cold War period, high-ranking officers of the Pentagon became concerned that the United States could be drawn into a Cuban civil war or a costly occupation of the island once Castro passed from power. In their view, an established pattern of communication and cooperation would allow the two military establishments to avoid any misperceptions that could draw the United States and Cuba into an unnecessary conflict. The established pattern of consultation and cooperation between U.S. and Cuban military officers helped to pave the way for a smooth transfer of alleged illegal combatants to the base in 2002.

Chapter 5 recounts how, during the 1990s, several hard-line Cuban American organizations began to pursue independent agendas for destabilizing the Castro regime. They felt certain that Castro was in his final days but that the U.S. government was not pushing the regime as hard as it could. As a result, these groups took matters into their own hands. Repeated incursions into Cuban airspace by Hermanos al Rescate (Brothers to the Rescue) planes contributed to the tragic shoot-down in 1996 of one of its planes and led to an international incident in which the United States and Cuba stood on the edge of conflict. As a result of the political crisis caused by the shoot-down, the U.S. and Cuban governments began to work together to avoid being drawn into another conflict provoked by hard-line Cuban American organizations. Both governments set down clear rules for the yearly flotillas organized by exiles that sailed close to Havana harbor. The respective coast guards, supported by the air forces, also established close communications to oversee the flotillas. Moreover, U.S. Coast Guard officers traveled to Havana to discuss how they might coordinate and prevent a provocative incident.

Unofficial visits to Cuba by retired U.S. military officers allowed Cuban military officers to meet with their counterparts in order to openly discuss issues related to migration, drug trafficking, operating procedures at Guantánamo Naval Base, U.S. military maneuvers, and other regional threats. These meetings served as an indirect form of quiet diplomacy whereby the United States and Cuba could overcome the entrenched institutional and historical barriers that kept the two countries divided. These meetings have continued to the present and offer a glimmer of hope that U.S.-Cuban relations will not always be frozen in time.

The book's concluding chapter summarizes the findings of the previous chapters and reviews the overall state of U.S.-Cuban relations during the George W. Bush administration. On the one hand, President George W. Bush generally adhered to the migration agreements and waived enforcement of Title III of the punitive Helms-Burton Act during his first term in office. On the other hand, during his first term Bush nominated several controversial individuals, including Elliot Abrams, Otto Reich, and John Negroponte, to important advisory positions pertaining to Latin America. Abrams, Reich, and Negroponte had been heavily involved in the U.S. interventions in Central America in the 1980s, and many feared a return to the hard-line position of the Ronald Reagan administration with regard to the Castro regime. Inflammatory rhetoric between the two countries increased shortly after the September 11, 2001, terrorist attacks, and in 2002 the Bush administration charged the Castro regime with spying and possessing the capabilities for bioweapons production. The Castro regime responded by claiming that the U.S. Interests Section in Havana provoked illegal hijackings of Cuban vessels and encouraged dissidents in order to foster counterrevolution on the island. The increasing tensions culminated with the incarceration of seventy-five Cuban dissidents and the shocking executions of three Cuban hijackers in the spring of 2003.

After the executions, there was an expectation that the Bush administration would respond with another new punitive policy, and that policy was announced in June 2004 during the height of the presidential campaign. Bush curtailed family visits to the island from once a year to once every three years and reduced by two-thirds the number of dollars that visitors could spend there. A separate rule restricted remittances to members of the immediate family only. With the new restrictions, the Bush administration hoped to deprive the Castro regime of dollars. By November Castro responded by announcing that U.S. dollars would no longer be accepted by Cuban shops and other businesses and that tourists and Cubans exchanging dollars would have to pay a 10 percent commission. U.S.-Cuban relations appeared once again to have deteriorated into a cycle of tit-for-tat retaliatory measures.

At year's end Washington and Havana became embroiled in a nonsensical battle over Christmas decorations after the U.S. Interests Section prominently displayed a large, brightly lit decoration with the number seventy-five, a reference to the seventy-five Cuban dissidents who were jailed in 2003. Cuba's leader of the National Assembly, Ricardo Alarcón, called the sign "rubbish" and told reporters that U.S. Interests Section chief James Cason had erected the sign because he was "desperate to create problems."[1] U.S. State Department spokesman Richard Boucher defended the offensive decoration and said that "it shows our solidarity with Cubans who struggle for democracy and freedom, when we think it's appropriate at the holiday season to remember."[2] Cuba's foreign ministry subsequently demanded that the U.S. mission take down the sign, but Cason said that the decoration would remain. At the end of the week and directly in front of the U.S. Interests Section, Cuba placed two gigantic billboards with photographs of the tortures in the Iraqi Abu Ghraib prison and the word *Fascistas*, together with a Nazi swastika. The billboards also showed Iraqi prisoners bleeding and hooded with a caption that said "Made in USA."

In spite of these mutual recriminations regarding each country's human rights abuses, the prospects and potential for U.S.-Cuban cooperation were not foreclosed. During the very same week of the Christmas decoration feud, Senator Max Baucus (D-Mont.) went to Havana for trade talks between American agribusinesses and the Cuban government. Baucus, the top Democrat on the Senate Finance Committee, struck an optimistic note, affirming, "I just believe that we have a great future ahead of us, both the United States and Cuba, if we just stay on a positive course, and work to build relationships."[3] As this book demonstrates, there are important actors on both sides of the Florida Straits who continue pursuing a cooperative path that may yet offer a new direction for U.S.-Cuban relations in the twenty-first century.

Too Close for Comfort—Differing Perspectives on a Shared History

Unfortunately, the United States and Cuba consider each other to be too close for comfort. A mutually perceived discomfort zone exists with regard to their geographical proximity, their closely intertwined histories, and their strong cultural ties. In the decades since the Cuban revolution, both the U.S. and Cuban governments have emphasized their political differences and have attempted to distance themselves completely from each other's influence. Nevertheless, geography, history, and culture remain unbreakable ties that bind their people together, and like two magnets, the countries seem to alternately attract and repel each other. The essence of the uncomfortable intimacy that exists between the two was articulated by President Bill Clinton, who, in reference to the international custody battle over Elián González, noted that U.S.-Cuban relations had degenerated into a "terrible family feud" (Staten 2003, 3).

As far back as the early nineteenth century, U.S. government officials expressed concerns that Cuba was too close for comfort. Cuba's strategic position at the eastern perimeter of the Gulf of Mexico, only ninety miles south of Key West, Florida, raised serious security issues. There were obvious economic concerns since the island was located alongside key shipping lanes that were important for commerce, but an even more important concern was the fact that Cuba could easily serve as a staging point for European aggression against the young United States. In 1807 Thomas Jefferson wrote to Secretary of State James Madison that should the United States ever go to war with Britain, he would hope to fight Spain as well. Such a conflict would allow the United States to seize Spanish Florida and Mexico, and "probably Cuba would add itself to our confederation" (Schoultz 1998, 48).

U.S. interest in acquiring physical possession of Cuba only increased after the formal acquisition of Spanish Florida in 1821, and subsequent U.S. administrations unsuccessfully offered to purchase the island from Spain. Over the ensuing decades, Cuba was drawn ever closer into the U.S. sphere, and the U.S. goal of annexing the island remained constant until the late 1850s, when the United States became embroiled in the debate over slavery and the admission of new states. In 1859 Senators Jefferson Davis of Mississippi and John Slidell of Louisiana championed a bill that would offer $30 million as a down payment to Madrid. "The fruit is ripe," Davis told his colleagues, "shall we gather it, or shall we permit it to remain on the stem until it decays, under the delusive hope that it may fall into our lap without a struggle? No; I propose we take it now" (Schoultz 1998, 56). Northern opposition to the Southern senators' bill became so heated that the precarious state of the Union itself seemed threatened. In the end, U.S. domestic conflict over slavery precluded the outright annexation of Cuba.

If U.S. government officials thought that Cuba was too close for comfort, Cuban nationalists thought likewise about the United States. Cuban nationalists were interested in obtaining true independence rather than having the island transferred from Spanish to U.S. control. After the Civil War, U.S. strategy regarding Cuba began to shift from outright acquisition or annexation to incorporation of the island into a sphere of influence. Under such an arrangement, the United States would mold the political and economic structures on the island without the financial burden exacted by absolute ownership. One effective way to spread U.S. influence was to establish strong economic ties to the island, and by the 1880s new credit, fresh capital, and new ownership in the Cuban sugar industry originated principally in the United States (Pérez 2006, 103).

Cuban nationalists had already fought a long and unsuccessful war against Spain from 1868 to 1878 and *la Guerra Chiquita*, or the small war, from 1879 to 1880. They reorganized and resumed their struggle for independence in 1895. José Martí, poet and patriot, feared U.S. intervention and warned his compatriots that "to change masters is not to be free" (Pérez 2006, 110). However, when the USS *Maine* mysteriously exploded in Havana Harbor on February 5, 1898, the United States was afforded the perfect pretext to enter the war, and Spain, an empire already in decline and further weakened by the three-year war with the Cuban rebels, was quickly defeated. As part of the peace accord, and bitterly disappointing to Cuban nationalists, Spain transferred control of Cuba to the United States on December 10, 1898.

After the transfer, U.S. armed forces remained too close for comfort, staying on the island until 1902. During its occupation, the U.S. military authority directed the establishment of a new Cuban government that would defer to U.S. tutelage. In order to legitimize the occupation, U.S. military commanders openly discredited the lingering nationalist sentiment for independence by insisting that the Cubans were not prepared for self-government. General Samuel B. M. Young noted that the "insurgents are a lot of degenerates, absolutely devoid of honor or gratitude. They are no more capable of self-government than the savages of Africa" (Pérez 2006, 138).

By 1902, after having endured nearly four years of U.S. occupation, Cuban nationalists were convinced that the United States had participated in liberating Cuba from Spain with an ulterior motive of transforming the island into a U.S. protectorate and in order to showcase the United States as an emerging world power. For them, Cuba's overly close colossal neighbor had hijacked their dream of true sovereignty. Reflecting the Cubans' disillusionment and disappointment, General Máximo Gómez remarked, "It is not the republic we dreamed of" (Baker 1997, 36).

Not only did Cubans fail to achieve their dream of political independence, but they also found themselves in a desperate economic position since the war had damaged much of Cuba's productive capacity. Many Cubans were forced to sell their farms and factories to U.S. companies, and by 1905 an estimated 60 percent of all rural property in Cuba was owned by individuals and corporations from the United States, with another 15 percent controlled by resident Spaniards (Pérez 2006, 151). Foreign firms also controlled the railroads, utilities, and mining, and the 1903 reciprocity treaty between the United States and Cuba increased Cuba's dependency on sugar and further discouraged economic diversification on the island.

Throughout the first two decades of the twentieth century, Cuban nationalists noted that the U.S. armed forces were always too close for comfort, since the United States frequently utilized those forces to intervene in Cuban affairs.

Under orders from Washington to restore political stability on the island, U.S. forces were dispatched to Cuba from 1906 to 1909, in 1912, and then again from 1917 to 1922. Cuban "independence" was marred by both occupation and numerous interventions. The numerous interventions were inconvenient and costly, and the U.S. government had to remain ever prepared until the government of Gerardo Machado was installed in 1924.

Gerardo Machado provided stability through repression, and his dictatorship lasted until 1933, when he was finally forced to depart the island in response to renewed nationalist revolts. Rather than intervene militarily yet again to impose another new and acceptable government, the U.S. administration of Franklin D. Roosevelt instead chose a more indirect path. U.S. ambassador Sumner Welles courted and supported domestic opposition to the reformist government of Ramón Grau San Martín, and Welles's successor as ambassador, Jefferson Caffery, openly encouraged Sergeant Fulgencio Batista to overthrow Grau (Smith 2000, 71).

Unable to overcome the massive political obstacles in his path, Grau was forced to resign, thus paving the way for Batista to seize power. Batista essentially governed Cuba from 1933 to the end of the decade through a series of presidential stooges (Williamson 1992, 442). From 1940 to 1959, Batista ruled Cuba in his own name or wielded power behind the scenes, his loyalty positively impressing Washington (Baker 1997, 39).

When it became obvious that he would not win the 1952 election, Batista staged a bloodless predawn *golpe*, strike against the state. Instead of condemning Batista's illegal power grab, however, the United States responded with military assistance grants of $1.5 million annually from 1954 to 1956 and doubled this figure during the 1957–1958 period (Vanden and Prevost 2002, 331). During the 1950s, Cuba opened up to increased U.S. investment, and Batista cooperated with U.S. mobsters and organized crime interests on the island.

In response to Batista's increasingly repressive and corrupt regime, Fidel Castro, who had been arrested in 1953 and jailed until 1955 for his failed attack on the Moncada barracks, returned in 1956 from exile in Mexico and initiated a three-year guerrilla struggle against the dictatorship. Batista was forced to flee the island on New Year's Day in 1959, and the rebel forces and their supporters celebrated Castro's victory march into Havana on January 8, 1959.

At first U.S. officials watched warily as Castro allowed the Communist Party to operate legally in Cuba, ousted political moderates from positions of authority, and inaugurated trials and executions of some 500 of Batista's supporters (Gilderhus 2000, 166–67). In March 1959 Castro initiated a major land redistribution project in the province of Pinar del Río, and he personally signed over land to the peasants. That same month the U.S.-owned Cuban Telephone Company was nationalized, and rates were reduced. As far as U.S. officials were concerned, political executions, land reform, and nationalizations were all hallmarks of an emergent radical Left, and they began to accuse Castro of being a Communist. During those tense days of the Cold War, the presence of a radical leftist or Communist head of state in the Western Hemisphere was deemed too close for Washington's comfort.

Of even greater concern for the U.S. leaders, however, was the fact that Castro quickly became a symbol and role model for other Latin American nationalists who were searching for a new paradigm for governing in order solve centuries-old issues of social inequality and uneven economic development. When Castro visited the United States in April 1959 but did not request financial aid as was Washington's customary expectation of Latin American leaders, Vice President Richard Nixon, the State Department, and the Central Intelligence Agency (CIA) jointly concluded that Castro was not likely to be a pliable Latin American leader open to direction from Washington. At a press conference on October 28, 1959, President Eisenhower reflected the dominant U.S. perspective when he stated, "Here is a country that you would believe, on the basis of our history, would be one of our real friends" (Gott 2004, 179). Of course, Cuban nationalists like Castro viewed that same history in a much different light. U.S. efforts to overthrow Castro's government were put into the planning stages shortly thereafter.

In April 1961 anti-Castro Cubans, recruited and trained by the CIA, launched a covert invasion designed to topple Castro. The misguided effort at the Bay of Pigs ended in a "perfect failure," and Castro emerged as the great victor against the "imperialist Yankees." In spite of his impressive rout of the invasion, Castro was convinced that the United States and the anti-Castro Cubans remained undeterred by their defeat and that they would regroup, reorganize, refinance, and try again. For Castro, the attempted invasion at the Bay of Pigs had come too close for comfort, and his implacable enemies in Little Havana, Florida, were also too close for comfort.

As history and U.S. declassified records have shown, Castro's instincts that the United States and anti-Castro Cubans would not curtail their efforts to remove him from power were indeed well founded. President John F. Kennedy decided that "there can be no long-term living with Castro as neighbor," and he sent a memorandum to Secretary of State Dean Rusk in which the president stated his decision to "use our available assets . . . to help Cuba overthrow the Communist regime" (Szulc 1986, 563). Meanwhile, in the aftermath of the Bay of Pigs invasion, Castro publicly announced for the first time the socialist nature of the revolution.

On December 1, 1961, Castro informed Cuba and the world that Cuba was officially a Marxist-Leninist state, and the CIA undertook Operation Mongoose, a secret plan to assassinate Castro and to disrupt the Cuban economy through acts of sabotage and terrorism. In order to defend Cuba from another invasion, Castro turned to Soviet Union premier Nikita Khrushchev, and in "one hell of a gamble," Khrushchev offered to secretly install defensive nuclear missiles on the island (Fursenko and Naftali 1997).

In his memoirs, Khrushchev recalled his motives at the time: "The main thing was that the installation of our missiles in Cuba would, I thought, restrain the United States from precipitous military action against Castro's government" (Khrushchev 1971, 547). U.S. overflights of the island produced evidence of the secret missile installation sites, resulting in the worst crisis of the Cold War. For thirteen harrowing days in October 1962, the threat of World War III came too close for comfort for both Kennedy and Khrushchev.

The crisis was finally resolved when the Soviets removed their missiles from Cuba in exchange for a secret U.S. pledge to remove Jupiter missiles from Turkey and Kennedy's implicit promise not to invade Cuba (Gaddis 1997, 271). Nuclear annihilation was averted, and the two chastened superpowers stepped away from the brink.

For the next three decades Cuba's economic and political security depended greatly on its alliance with the Soviet Union. There were some unsuccessful efforts by the Nixon, Ford, and Carter administrations to improve relations with Cuba. Under President Ronald Reagan, however, tensions increased during the 1980s, and hard-line Cuban American groups like CANF were organized and gained political clout and increasing influence over the future course of U.S.-Cuban relations.

Once the Cold War ended following the collapse of the Soviet Union in 1991, the Castro regime was not expected to survive. Without Soviet support, the Cuban economy contracted severely, and there were massive shortages and blackouts, but the shaken Castro regime held on against all odds. In 1992, in order to give Castro the one last push in his "final hour," the United States tightened its decades-old trade embargo by adding extraterritorial measures.

However, to the surprise of Washington and the Cuban exile community, the extreme deprivation on the island did not produce the much anticipated internal revolt against the government. By 1994, the Cuban economy began to stabilize, and Castro was still in control. Cuban Americans consoled themselves by noting that Castro could not live forever—*no hay mal que dure cien años* (nothing so bad lasts 100 years). The widespread assumption was that once Castro died, U.S.-Cuban relations would automatically improve.

In fact, the counterintuitive case has been made that Castro's death is too close for comfort. The reasoning behind this claim is that Castro's passing from power may lead to a dangerous instability on the island. In a 2004 study, González and McCarthy (119) note that Cuba will be at a critical crossroads when the Castro era comes to an end. They also note that the loss of Castro's monumental presence as a revolutionary icon will likely lead to splits among and between the ruling elite and military. In fact, there is evidence that such a split already exists between hard-liners in the Castro regime and well-placed officials and military men who favor a softer line at home and a warmer relationship with the United States.[4] Once Castro has passed from the scene, and if no legitimate successor emerges to fill his void, or if there is civil conflict among competing parties, Cuba could quickly degenerate into a failed state producing internal disorder and a humanitarian crisis on the island. This worst-case scenario would have serious implications for the United States since chaos on the island could very likely result in mass migration and uncontrolled drug flows into the United States.

The Mariel crisis of 1980 and the rafter crisis of 1994 serve as cautionary tales of what can occur when the Cuban government cannot or will not control the exodus of its people. Likewise, historians can point to Cuba's pre-revolutionary past for evidence of the island having served as a transshipment center for contraband. Since the most important national security issue facing the United States in the post-9/11 world is the war on terror, the possibility of a failed or failing state too close to the U.S. mainland has serious and sobering implications. In order to prevent terrorists attacks at home, U.S. officials have argued that the United States must work to eliminate illegal border crossings and to disrupt the terrorists' financial networks, which have been linked to drug trafficking. In fact, limited bilateral efforts to establish cooperation on these issues have already been quietly undertaken by U.S. and Cuban officials.

Throughout the 1990s certain sectors of the U.S. government recognized the importance of establishing a level of cooperation between the United

States and Cuba on post–Cold War issues of mutual concern related to migration, drug trafficking, decreasing tensions around Guantánamo Naval Base, and reducing the threat of accidental war. Since the United States and Cuba do not maintain diplomatic relations or bilateral trade, it was a challenge to find the appropriate mechanism for addressing these issues, and as a result, U.S. and Cuban officials came to rely on CBMs in order to initiate the cooperative efforts. Before proceeding, it is important to define and trace the evolution and implementation of CBMs so as to clearly demonstrate why U.S. and Cuban officials would turn to them as tools for avoiding conflicts and building trust between the two countries.

Confidence-Building Measures (CBMs)

CBMs are bilateral and multilateral actions specifically designed to prevent situations of crisis and conflict. They seek to strengthen communication between actors and to create a favorable atmosphere for establishing a framework of understanding in order to lessen the perception of immediate threat and to prevent the element of surprise. CBMs recognize the existence of differences of interests and of mutually low confidence in the relations between hostile parties. Their application is crucial when the attainment or defense of differing ideas might result in the use of force. In those situations, misinterpretation can result in unwanted conflict (Rojas Aravena 1998, 130). In other words, CBMs include unilateral, tacit, or negotiated steps that improve cooperation or decrease tensions between states. In the post–Cold War period, CBMs have become an important means of preventing accidental wars and unintended escalation in strife-ridden regions around the world (Krepon et al. 1999, 1).

Forerunners of modern-day CBMs were proposed at the 1958 Surprise Attack Conference in Geneva and at the 1962 Eighteen Nation Disarmament Committee, where the United States first proposed the ideas of a Washington-Moscow hotline and an agreement to ban nuclear testing in the atmosphere (Darilek 1999, 276). During the 1970s most of the European states, the United States, and Canada participated in meetings that culminated in 1975 with the signing of the Helsinki Final Act, which included notification and access agreements for reducing the risk of surprise attacks, increased restraints on military maneuvers, and the regulation of dangerous nuclear activities.

The purpose of the first generation of CBMs was not to limit military capabilities or to control the military forces of the hostile states. Instead, they were aimed at increasing openness in order to reduce the secrecy that generally surrounded military activities. Greater transparency was deemed necessary in order to reduce mutual suspicion and to minimize the chances of misunderstandings or miscalculations that could lead into war.

A new generation of CBMs was developed in the wake of the Soviet invasion of Afghanistan in 1979 and Soviet threats to Poland in the early 1980s. The 1986 Stockholm Agreement of Confidence-and Security-Building Measures and Disarmament in Europe not only required even greater transparency, but it also relied on measures that required observation and inspection of certain military activities. The key for success was the provision of independent means for verification of compliance and intent, such as mandatory on-site inspections of military activities.

A third generation of CBMs was made possible after Soviet president Mikhail Gorbachev's 1988 speech to the United Nations in which he clearly placed conventional arms control high on the list of East-West priorities. These newest measures promised to set limits on conventional military forces that were much tighter and more direct than any previously negotiated. The tougher constraints in the North Atlantic Treaty Organization (NATO) package called for the outright prohibition of specified activities. For example, they called for placing various types of military equipment (tanks, artillery, troop carriers, and bridging equipment) in monitored storage sites. Additionally, they included limiting the amount of this equipment that could be removed from storage at any given time (Darilek 1999, 282). Finally, 1990 negotiations in Vienna further strengthened the constraints on military activities and the provisions on notification and observation.

This short review of the initiation and development of CBMs during the Cold War illustrates their value as pragmatic steps with ideal objectives. The CBM process begins by identifying common interests and developing cooperation over time. It makes sense to start the process modestly, with steps that are likely to be successful, and then to build on those steps. CBMs can be designed to fit multiple needs that range from avoiding unintended escalation to making new wars unthinkable.

In the post–Cold War period, CBMs have generated increasing interest since they are flexible tools that allow national leaders to adapt more easily to the new and less predicable international environment. Political and military leaders can utilize CBMs to prevent conflict, to warn the various parties

Table 1.1. Major Components of CBMs

Goals of CBMs	Conflict Avoidance
Implementation of CBMs	Quiet/Unofficial Diplomacy
Outcome of CBMs	Political Agreements
Issues of CBMs	High Politics
Scope of CBMs	Incremental, Small Steps

of troubling developments, and to negotiate and/or strengthen agreements. Mutually hostile countries, such as India and Pakistan, have been able to implement CBMs in order to reduce the threat of conflict (Devabhaktuni et al. 1999, 196). It therefore makes sense to promote CBMs in regions of high tension. Table 1.1 summarizes the major components of CBMs.

Intense U.S.-Cuban hostilities have persisted since the early years of the Cuban revolution, and the two countries have never reestablished the diplomatic relations that were severed during the Eisenhower administration. Given the nearly five decades of perceived threat and hostile rhetoric, U.S.-Cuban relations certainly exhibit mutual low confidence and a lack of trust. CBMs offer a crack in the door, an entry point for minimizing tensions, because they begin with small, incremental steps. Rather than simply wait for Castro to depart the world stage before making serious attempts at stabilizing bilateral relations, pragmatic officials on both sides of the Florida Straits have determined that the establishment of CBMs between the United States and Cuba serves as a necessary safeguard against an unpredictable and dangerous future.

Given the post-9/11 reorientation of U.S. foreign policy from fighting Communism to fighting terror, CBMs between the United States and Cuba are arguably in the national interest of each country. Illegal migration and drug trafficking have both been identified as illicit flows that are conducive to the spread of terrorism. Therefore, in the post-9/11 world, the United States has made the security of its borders a primary focus in its war on terrorism and has sought to dry up terrorist funding obtained through drug trafficking.

The Castro regime has been willing to cooperate with the United States in the areas of migration and drug trafficking, because both are considered threats to the future security of the Cuban revolution. Cuba sits in the middle of the Caribbean drug transit area, and when drug runners miss their rendezvous or the Cuban Coast Guard intervenes, some of the illicit goods float inland

(Corbett 2002, 219). Economically strapped Cubans who come across the contraband are less and less inclined to report it to Cuban officials and instead sell it themselves. Moreover, the increase in tourism on the island has also increased the overall availability of drugs in Cuba. In addition to the dangers that drugs pose to Cuba's social fabric, the Cuban government is fully aware of their threat to national security. Beginning in the 1980s, Cuba went on full military alert, because it feared that the United States might launch an invasion of the island using the war on drugs as a pretext.

Cuban officials also have expressed concern that another migration crisis might likewise trigger a U.S. invasion. According to the Helms-Burton Act of 1996 (Title I, Sec. 101), a massive exodus, similar to the crisis of August 1994, would be considered a direct attack on U.S. national security and a sufficient motive for a military response. It is therefore in the best interest of the Castro regime to push for greater levels of cooperation between the two countries in these areas so as to dispel any perception that the Cuban government is actively involved in fostering the illicit flow of drugs or people. In other words, Washington needs policies that reflect the new reality of the post–Cold War era, in which terrorism is a greater threat than Cuban Communism.

As to Cuba's willingness to support the U.S. war on terror, the Castro regime has noted that since 1959, Cuba has often experienced the devastating effects of terrorist attacks on its own soil. Castro has frequently spoken at length about the numerous acts of terrorism that have been inflicted on the island by Cuban exile groups based in the United States. For concrete evidence of these activities, the Castro regime points to the 1984 U.S. trial of leaders of the Cuban exile group Omega 7, when the accused admitted that they had transferred swine fever germs to the island, causing an epidemic. The Cuban government further maintains that the 1984 epidemics of dengue fever and hemorrhagic conjunctivitis on the island were also purposely spread (Hernández 2002, 21). Therefore it appears that the Castro regime would be willing to cooperate with the United States in the areas related to the war on terror, with an implicit expectation that the U.S. government would likewise reciprocate by closely regulating the terrorist activities of Cuban exile groups based on U.S. soil.

Another motivation for establishing CBMs with the Cuban government reflects the pragmatic need of U.S. policy makers to plan for the future of U.S.-Cuban relations in a post-Castro period. Once Castro has passed from power, established CBMs would give the U.S. government a preexisting relationship with the new leadership on the island. A failure to develop a respectful relationship with the next generation of Cuban leaders might contribute to a dangerous destabilization of the island during the uncertain post-Castro transition. An ensuing power vacuum on the island could result in civil conflict or chaos, and a failed or failing state so close to U.S. borders could easily provide safe harbor for terrorist organizations or networks. Moreover, if the United States decides to maintain its holding cells on Guantánamo Naval Base, a secure surrounding area will be essential to future operations. With the establishment of U.S.-Cuban cooperation in all of these areas, the U.S. government not only would begin to lay the necessary groundwork for a safer transition to a post-Castro Cuba, but it would also further its own goals in the war on terror.

This book examines and analyzes the post–Cold War CBMs that have been undertaken by the United States and Cuba in the areas of migration, drug trafficking, lessening tensions around Guantánamo Naval Base, and reducing the threat of accidental war. Since both the U.S. and Cuban governments realized that cooperation on these four areas was in their best interest, they were motivated to put aside their long-standing animosity in order to establish CBMs. In other words, Cuba and the United States had to put aside the long-held idea that they were simply too close for each other's comfort, and the implementation of CBMs has made them strange bedfellows instead. The two countries may not be comfortable with each other after such a long period of estrangement. Nevertheless, they still share a common goal of maintaining the overall security and stability of the area. However, as the specific case studies in chapters 2–5 demonstrate, deeper stages of CBMs have been seriously limited by hard-line Cuban American organizations and/or Cuban American members of the U.S. Congress who consistently use their considerable political clout to push for punitive measures rather than CBMs.

In order to better understand the political atmosphere and constraints that face U.S. and Cuban officials interested in implementing CBMs, the next chapter covers basic background information on Cuban exile politics. The chapter gives a brief history of Cuban exile politics, with a particular focus on the role of some of the major exile organizations and exile leaders who have had a significant impact on the debate and direction of U.S. policy decisions with regard to Cuba.

The largest Cuban American community is concentrated in Florida, an important swing state in U.S. presidential elections, with twenty-seven electoral votes. Candidates for the U.S. presidency have found that they can ill afford to alienate the large numbers of Cuban American voters whose passions run deep about the Castro regime. As such, U.S.-Cuba relations have become an important domestic issue as well as an international issue. Therefore it is necessary to consider U.S.-Florida-Cuban relations in order to better understand the complications that present themselves whenever U.S. officials formulate foreign policy or work to establish CBMs.

1

Cuban Exile Politics

In many ways the Cubans who fled to the United States after the triumph of the 1959 revolution were not unlike the exiles of the previous century. Disillusioned with or threatened by the current leadership on the island, they opted to leave, as had their predecessors. As so many others had done in the past, post-1959 exiles expected to wait out the new regime in Havana, and they spoke longingly of how they dreamed of returning home. However, the months of waiting turned into years and finally into decades. As a result, many exiles remained concentrated in the Miami metropolitan area located close to their homeland, and the city transformed itself to mirror the impact of the Cuban community (Torres 1999). Indeed, Miami became so imbued with Cuban culture that many Cuban exiles eventually admitted that "the pain of the lost country is much reduced by the sensation that one lives in a city conquered peacefully" (Pérez 1999, 503). Today Miami retains its position as the U.S. city with the largest population of Cuban residents, and Cuban American voting power in local, state, and national elections has been influential, especially given the fact that Florida is an important swing state during presidential elections.

If there were similarities between the Cubans who fled the Castro regime and Cuban exiles from previous political upheavals, there were striking contrasts as well. During the nineteenth century, U.S. officials had initially supported the exiles' goals for independence but ultimately withheld backing for their cause. Racist attitudes about the island's population, hopes for U.S. acquisition of the island, and economic interests on the island were all intervening factors that convinced U.S. officials that a truly independent Cuba was not desirable. However, after the triumph of Castro's revolution, U.S. officials' and exiles' attitudes coincided and mutually reinforced each other, given both groups' shared revulsion at the revolution. On the economic level, the revolution was seen by exiles and U.S. officials as a threat to private property, business, and investment. On the geopolitical level, Castro's revolution played into larger Cold War fears of a Communist penetration of the entire hemisphere. The intersection of these political and economic fears motivated many exiles and U.S. leaders to resort to the expediency of violent tactics in order to topple Castro from power. Unfortunately, the lasting legacy from this tacit acceptance of violence and intimidation would come to haunt the exile community and Washington in the ensuing decades. From its very inception, U.S. foreign policy toward Castro's Cuba included high levels of violence and sabotage, and since many hard-line Cuban exiles participated in U.S. covert operations that utilized these tactics, their approach toward politics in general often included physical and/or vocal intimidation of their opponents.

This chapter traces the complex political relationship between Washington and the Cuban exile community and demonstrates how, over the decades, Cuban exile leaders and their organizations became increasingly influential in first supporting and later formulating an inflexible U.S. foreign policy toward the island. After the end of the Cold War, their political activism became a serious obstacle to the reduction of tensions between Cuba and the United States and to the creation and implementation of confidence-building measures (CBMs), even though Cuba was no longer perceived to be a national security threat. In order to better understand how exile politicians gained enough influence to be able to hamper the development and implementation of CBMs as well as other more moderate foreign policy initiatives, this chapter analyzes exile politics over the years and focuses on five major phases of its evolution: militancy—1960s; dialogue and backlash—1970s; the rise of the Cuban American National Foundation (CANF)—1980s; the rise of Cuban American legislative power—1990s; and reevaluation and retrenchment in the new millennium.

Militancy—1960s

The earliest collaboration between the U.S. government and the exiles was the covert planning for the ill-fated Bay of Pigs invasion in 1961. In fact, the operation itself exhibited many problematic patterns that would persist into the future with regard to the intense disagreements between the various exile groups and with regard to the ambivalent attitude of the U.S. government concerning exile plots against Castro. From the early days of planning the invasion, sharp differences of opinion were evident between the rival exile factions of *Batistianos*, anti-Batista exiles, and "left-wing" exiles who had initially supported Castro. It was only when the Central Intelligence Agency (CIA) threatened to close down the entire project that the various factions finally stopped their internecine bickering and began to work together (Wyden 1979, 116). Likewise, the exiles complained of U.S. governmental high-handedness, claiming that the CIA planned every aspect of the invasion without placing any real value on exile input (Antón and Hernández 2002, 155).

Once the mission failed, many exiles were embittered and felt betrayed by the United States. They responded by forming their own paramilitary organizations and commando units, such as Alpha 66, which launched raids against the island in the hope of inciting a popular insurrection. Members of Alpha 66 employed terrorist tactics, and by 1970 the organization had established a complete underground network on the island that made it possible to carry out a series of devastating attacks that included bombings in Havana and the burning of sugar warehouses, cane fields, tobacco houses, and factories.

Over time, the CIA and the Federal Bureau of Investigation (FBI) became concerned about militant exiles striking out on their own, even though both U.S. government agencies shared the exiles' goal of ousting Castro. For the most part, however, the FBI and the CIA ignored militant exile activities, because exiles served as useful proxies for U.S. interests while giving the U.S. government the convenient cover of plausible deniability. Only when the exiles publicly flaunted their illegal activities against the Castro regime were they arrested on arms violations. González-Pando notes that the most controversial by-product of the exiles' holy war against Castro was their glorification of violence as an acceptable political tactic (González-Pando 1998, 143). A brief look at the early career of Luis Posada Carriles, a self-declared would-be assassin of Fidel Castro, serves as an illustrative case of the extreme measures that militant exiles undertook in their campaign to oust Castro.

Posada began bombing Cuban government targets barely six months after the 1959 revolution. Subsequently Posada was recruited by the CIA in Havana in 1960 and later trained as part of the Bay of Pigs exile force. After the failure of the invasion, he entered the U.S. Army and was dispatched to Fort Benning, Georgia, where he was trained along with other members of the exile elite and given specialized instruction in clandestine operations and intelligence gathering. Posada described the training in a lengthy 1998 interview with Ann Louise Bardach, saying, "The CIA taught us everything. They taught us explosives, how to kill, bomb, trained us in acts of sabotage" (Bardach 2002, 175–76).

By the late 1960s Posada's relationship with the CIA became tenuous because of his independent involvement in clandestine sabotage activities, and at one point he even planned to blow up a Soviet or Cuban freighter in Veracruz, Mexico.[1] Finally, in 1967 Posada left Miami for Caracas, Venezuela, where he began working for the Venezuelan intelligence service, eventually rising through the ranks to become the head of counterintelligence. Nevertheless, throughout the years Posada maintained close contacts with the CIA, continuing to serve as an informer and actively collaborating with the CIA during the Central American wars of the 1980s.

In spite of participating in the Bay of Pigs invasion and other raids against the island, during the 1960s the political role that Cuban exiles played in the formulation of U.S. foreign policy was little more than that of pawns in the larger context of the Cold War. Exiles were deemed to be most useful as symbols, and they served the ideological function of providing living evidence that Communism was a repressive system (Torres 1999, 59). Washington recruited militant exiles to participate in efforts at destabilizing the Castro government as well as other leftist movements in the region. Nevertheless, Washington made the big political decisions and called the shots, while exiles served as dutiful foot soldiers.

Dialogue and Backlash—1970s

In the early 1970s a debate developed within the exile community over whether Cuban exiles should initiate a dialogue with the government whose policies and ideology had driven them from the island. There were several factors that contributed to the momentum for shifting from militancy to a more moderate stance. Within the exile community, a younger generation of Cuban Americans came of age, and many were inquisitive about their island roots. Others, radicalized by the civil rights and antiwar movements, were interested in pushing for rapprochement with Cuba. For many of these young people, permission to travel to the forbidden island became a cause célèbre (Torres 1999, 90).

By the 1970s the political climate in Washington had changed as well. The Nixon administration had lessened tensions between the United States, the Soviet Union, and China, and it now seemed reasonable to apply the lessons of détente to Cuba. In 1973 Cuba and the United States signed an antihijacking treaty that seemed to clear a path for further rapprochement. The next year Secretary of State Henry Kissinger undertook a series of secret talks with the Cuban government, but after Castro dispatched Cuban troops to Angola in late 1975, Kissinger decided to halt the process.

Early in his first term, President Jimmy Carter resumed the process of improving relations between the two countries, and in 1977 successful negotiations resulted in an agreement between the United States and Cuba on fishing rights and maritime boundaries. In the absence of diplomatic relations, Cuba and the United States also agreed to establish interest sections in each other's countries to serve as unofficial embassies hosted by third countries. Finally, certain restrictions of the trade embargo were relaxed, and travel to Cuba was permitted for the first time in nearly twenty years.

In mid-1977 the Cuban government made its own quiet overture to the Cuban exile community. Cuban government representatives approached Bernardo Benes, a successful Miami banker and prominent member of the exile community, during a family vacation in Panama. Since Benes hoped to bridge the gap between the exile community and Cubans on the island, he and his business partner, Carlos Dascal, undertook negotiations for the release of political prisoners and for permission to arrange family visits to the island.

In mid-1978 David Aaron, the principal deputy of National Security Advisor Zbigniew Brzezinski, met in New York with one of Castro's closest aides, José Luis Padrón. Padrón indicated that the Castro government was considering the release of several thousand political prisoners. At this juncture, the Carter administration asked Benes to continue confidential negotiations with the Castro regime (Levine 2002). Benes's efforts helped pave the way for Castro's announcement in 1978 of his willingness to conduct discussions with representatives of the Cuban exile community. Eventually, these discussions, referred to as "the dialogue," resulted in the release of 3,600 Cuban political prisoners and established the right for Cuban exiles to return to visit family members on the island.

Instead of being hailed as a hero, however, Benes suffered an extreme backlash from other hard-line exiles for having negotiated personally with Castro. As a result of the backlash, the Miami Continental Bank where Benes worked was bombed, his career was ruined, and he became a pariah in the community. The case of Bernardo Benes clearly underscored the great personal risks that moderate exiles who dared to work for reconciliation faced, and Benes himself noted with irony, "I feel sorry for the Cuban community in Miami. Because they have imposed on themselves, by way of the Right, the same condition that Castro has imposed on Cuba. Total intolerance. And ours is worse, because ours is totally voluntary" (Didion 1987, 113).

Another member of the exile community, who suffered a violent backlash for advocating dialogue was the popular Miami radio commentator Emilio Milián. Milián frequently denounced Communism on his radio program, but he also spoke against exiles who used terrorist tactics to achieve their goals. Because he dared to openly criticize the extremists, Milián tragically lost both legs in a car bombing in 1976. The backlash of exile violence against other exiles was indeed shocking. Whereas the paramilitary organizations of the 1960s had limited their hostile actions to Cuba and its allies, exile extremist groups like Omega 7 targeted all those they perceived to be their enemies, including members of their own community (García 1996, 141).

Within the exile community, Omega 7 claimed responsibility for assassinating Carlos Muñiz Varela, a young man who had worked at a travel agency that arranged travel to Cuba. Omega 7 also took credit for more than twenty bombings that were aimed at the homes and businesses of participants in the dialogue. Eventually, after being pressured by more moderate members of the exile community, a special FBI task force named Omega 7 the most dangerous terrorist group in the United States (Torres 1999, 100–101).

Dialogue not only provoked backlash within the exile community in the United States, it also heightened tensions inside Cuba as well. As part of the agreements made possible by dialogue, Castro opened the doors for the exile community to return to the island for family visits. Many Cubans on the island, however, were shocked to learn first-hand how well their relatives had fared living in the United States. The family visits motivated many Cubans to decide to leave the island in search of a more prosperous life in the United States, and this contributed to a massive exodus from the port of Mariel. The unexpected migration crisis increased tensions between the Carter administration and the Castro government, and the dialogue came to an ignominious end, as did Carter's equally damaged presidency.

The Rise of CANF—1980s

By the 1980s a new phase began as the exile community became politically organized and learned to flex its own muscle to influence and shape U.S. policy toward the Castro government. The community embraced the idea of mainstream political involvement as the result of two linked changes in attitude. The desire of returning to the island had been gradually diminished by greater integration into the United States, and that change was coupled with the unhappy realization that Castro's regime was not about to fall (Molyneaux 1999,

294). Therefore the majority of Cubans eventually sought and acquired U.S. citizenship, and since they were already a highly politicized community, they soon became equally committed to voting. This high level of political activism was made possible to a large degree through the establishment of well-financed conservative lobbying groups, most notably CANF. Before the appearance of CANF, the exile community had never presented an organized political voice in Washington. Whereas exiles had taken their marching orders from Washington in the past, with the establishment of a Cuban American lobby, they now had the opportunity to actually influence those Washington politicians who were responsible for formulating Cuba policy.

CANF was founded in 1981 by Jorge Mas Canosa, Raúl Masvidal, and Carlos Salman, prominent and wealthy businessmen who wanted to establish a fund-raising and lobbying organization that would have political clout in Washington. The idea originated from the brainstorming of Richard Allen, Reagan's first national security adviser, who told the influential exiles, "There will be a new opportunity for Cuban Americans. I suggest you copy the Israeli lobby, and I will help you. You should lobby both branches of government" (Newhouse 1992, 76). The timing could not have been more fortuitous, since the ideological interests of the Reagan administration and those of hard-line Cuban Americans coincided perfectly with regard to Castro, Communism, and the revolutionary movements in Nicaragua and El Salvador. CANF also set up its own political action committee, Free Cuba. Its other arm, the Cuban American Foundation, served as a lobby for dispensing money and information designed to convince lawmakers to continue a hard-line stance against Castro.

Jorge Mas Canosa eventually came to dominate CANF as its most important leader. His own stance against Castro had hardened when he trained as a member of the exile invasion's Brigade 2506, although his launch never actually landed at the Bay of Pigs. Another of Mas Canosa's early ties with the U.S. government was forged when he became a commentator on Radio Swan, which broadcast CIA anti-Castro propaganda into Cuba. Not surprisingly, Mas Canosa later joined the private sector as a commentator on two Spanish-language stations in Miami, Radio WQBA and Radio Mambí. From his CIA experience at Radio Swan, he was quick to recognize the value of the media for disseminating his political ideas, and he pushed successfully for CANF to receive taxpayer funding for Radio Martí in 1981 and TV Martí in 1987. The foundation also owned its own radio station called La Voz de la Fundación, which not only attacked Castro but moderate voices within the exile community as well.

Along with effective use of the media, Mas Canosa and CANF soon amassed large amounts of money. Foundation funds were collected from wealthy members, who contributed from $5,000 to $50,000 per year. CANF also received hundreds of thousands of dollars from the National Endowment for Democracy, which was created by the U.S. Congress in order to support the development of democracy in the world. In addition, CANF received government grants for its sponsorship of exiles entering the United States from third countries. In a real sense, CANF received funds from Congress and then used those same funds to further lobby Congress in support of its anti-Castro agenda.

Over the years Mas Canosa and CANF made strategic donations to politicians who supported anti-Castro measures and legislation. Some of the largest recipients of CANF largesse included Florida representatives Ileana Ros-Lehtinen (R) and Lincoln Díaz-Balart (R), New Jersey representative Robert Menéndez (D), and New Jersey senator Robert Torricelli (D). Senator Torricelli eventually became the darling of CANF after he sponsored the controversial 1992 Cuban Democracy Act (CDA/Torricelli Bill).

The CDA called for free elections in Cuba and further tightened the economic embargo of the island by prohibiting U.S. companies based outside the United States from conducting business with Cuba. The George H. W. Bush administration recognized the international repercussions that would be caused by the extraterritorial nature of the legislation and initially did not lend its support to the bill. However, CANF members were certain that the time was right to pounce on a weakened Castro, and the interest group demonstrated its enormous political influence by continuing to lobby for the CDA even after the legislation failed to receive the blessing of the White House. To counteract executive resistance, CANF formed a bipartisan congressional support group that included representatives from Florida and New Jersey.

For Torricelli, a junior senator, lending his name and support to the bill greatly helped his standing with New Jersey's sizable conservative Cuban community, which had become convinced that a tightened embargo would topple the Castro regime since it could no longer depend on the external support of the Soviet Union. In short, the end of the Cold War had left Castro out in the cold, and the CDA would serve to give him a final push into the dustbin of history. The larger international concerns of the White House mattered not to the proponents of the CDA.

In the heat of the 1992 presidential election, both Bush and Clinton wanted to improve their chances in the pivotal electoral race in Florida, and both were acutely aware of the need for CANF political and financial support in order to carry the state. On April 23, Clinton endorsed the controversial legislation at a fund-raising banquet in Miami hosted by CANF, and he insinuated that President Bush had missed the chance to "put the hammer down on Castro." President Bush quickly responded to Clinton's challenge and signed the bill into law on October 23, 1992. The pressures of electoral politics had trumped the wider considerations of flaws related to the extraterritorial measures in the legislation.

As expected, the international reaction to the CDA was one of outrage over the extraterritorial provisions, and the legislation especially infuriated the United States' closest trading partners. Both Mexico and the European Union threatened to file formal protests and accused the United States of undermining global free trade. Moderate Cuban Americans and anti-Castro human rights groups within Cuba argued that the bill violated Cuba's sovereignty. The bill's detractors went so far as to compare it to the infamous Platt Amendment of the 1902 Cuban constitution that gave the United States the right to intervene in Cuba's internal affairs. In fact, the passage of the CDA illustrated how CANF and its supporters managed to profoundly influence U.S. foreign policy. In the process, CANF successfully expanded its tactics beyond the White House to include the building of its own alliance on Capitol Hill. In the end, CANF used its money and votes to influence a sitting president to support a policy that he had previously argued was unnecessary, if not harmful to U.S. interests, as well as constitutionally problematic (Vanderbush and Haney 1999, 395).

When the *Miami Herald* ran an editorial opposing the harsh measures of the CDA, Mas Canosa became outraged, and he used his own radio powers of persuasion to denounce the newspaper by comparing it to Cuba's state paper, *Granma*. What followed next was a campaign of intimidation against the newspaper and its editors. Newsstands were destroyed or smeared with feces, and death threats were sent to *Miami Herald* executives. Like Fidel Castro, the man whom he most hated, Mas Canosa found it hard to deal with critics or opponents, and his autocratic ways eventually led to the departure of several of the foundation's directors. The veteran of the Bay of Pigs and Fort Benning was quick to resort to violence and intimidation in order to achieve his political goals.

On the heels of the passage of the CDA, in 1993 CANF decided that Mario Baeza, the Clinton administration's nominee for assistant secretary of inter-American affairs at the Department of State, did not exhibit proper anti-Castro credentials. Baeza, a black Cuban American lawyer, had visited Cuba as part of a Mexican conference on investment prospects on the island and was presumed to be anti-embargo (Vanderbush and Haney 1999, 396). Once CANF determined that Baeza was an unacceptable addition to the Department of State, the interest group moved quickly to undermine the nomination, and when the final list of nominees was sent to the Congress, Baeza's name had been removed from consideration.

During the decade from 1982 to 1992, CANF donated $1.1 million in campaign contributions, and Mas Canosa himself alone was the biggest Hispanic contributor nationwide (Booth 1992, 57). By the 1990s the power of Mas Canosa and CANF had grown to such a degree that the foundation was no longer limited simply to influencing U.S. politicians. Mas Canosa also ventured forth as an international player and traveled the world urging other governments to isolate the Castro regime. As a direct result of Mas Canosa's actions, the Czech government stopped representing Cuba in Washington. Moreover, as encouragement for Moscow to cut its remaining ties to Cuba, Mas Canosa offered the foundation's help in subsidizing Russia's sugar purchases elsewhere (Booth 1992, 56).

Mas Canosa was largely successful in his efforts to exclude the more moderate voices within the exile community itself. As a result, CANF presented itself as the national and international voice of the exile movement. Bardach notes that during these years, Mas Canosa set the tone and the agenda for America's foreign policy with Cuba: no compromise and no negotiation—a policy of slow strangulation (Bardach 2002, 169–70). In short, CANF, headed by its own autocratic leader, was poised to replace the bearded, autocratic leader in Havana. Critics were quick to note that Mas Canosa and Fidel were, in many respects, *la misma cosa* (the same thing).

The Rise of Cuban American Legislative Power—1990s

After its creation in 1981, CANF benefited politically and financially from maintaining its close association with the Republican administrations of Ronald Reagan and George H. W. Bush. With the 1992 election of Democrat Bill Clinton, however, moderate exiles saw a window of opportunity to challenge the dominance of CANF that had been closed to them during the previous twelve years. In 1993 new moderate exile organizations, such as the Cuban Committee for Democracy (CCD) and Cambio Cubano (Cuban Change), were founded, and they announced their opposition to the harsh provisions of the CANF-sponsored CDA. Nonetheless, hopes for a sustained momentum for moderation of Cuba policy were dashed once again after the midterm elections in 1994 gave Republicans the majorities in both houses of Congress. The House now had three Cuban American members, and they assumed many of the duties that CANF had previously performed. These duties included watching over the appropriations for Radio Martí and TV Martí, drafting Cuba policy legislation, and lobbying other members of the Senate (Vanderbush and Haney 1999, 401). The fact that a small number of Cuban American members of Congress became influential in shaping U.S. policy toward Cuba was not unlike the trajectory of other foreign policy issues where various members of Congress had prevailed "by virtue of their persistence, expertise, or cleverness" (Tierney 1994, 111).

The persistence, expertise, and cleverness of Representative Díaz-Balart became especially evident during the final stages of the crafting of the Helms-Burton Act. Officially known as the Cuban Liberty and Democratic Solidarity Act, the bill had been introduced by Senator Jesse Helms (R-N.C.) and Representative Dan Burton (R-Ind.) on February 9, 1995. The legislation consisted of four parts. In brief, Title I prohibited Cuba's participation in international financial organizations and threatened sanctions against countries that provided "economic assistance" to Cuba. Title II laid down a series of conditions demanded by the United States for reengagement with a future Cuban government. In order to be recognized, the Cuban government had to be democratically elected and could not be headed by either Fidel Castro or his brother, Raúl. Title III would give U.S. citizens the right to sue in U.S. courts foreign companies "trafficking" in stolen property in Cuba. The Clinton administration originally withheld support for the highly controversial bill, noting that Title III would cause problems with U.S. allies. Finally, Title IV barred executives of foreign countries said to be "trafficking" in those expropriated U.S.

properties from entering the United States. If passed, Helms-Burton would certainly provoke an even greater outpouring of international protest and retaliatory actions than had the CDA in 1992. President Clinton argued against the bill, stating that it was unnecessary since the CDA already was in force.

After the tragic shoot-down of two Cuban American planes by the Cuban air force on February 24, 1996, the bill was resurrected as a punitive payback for the deaths of the four Cuban American pilots. The Clinton administration suddenly found itself under pressure to react forcefully to the tragedy, and Representative Díaz-Balart seized the opportunity to add a new measure to the bill, which codified the embargo law and ended presidential prerogative on the future lifting of the embargo. Thus the Cuban American legislator cleverly influenced the policy track of a sitting president, who lacked other viable options in the midst of the crisis. Representative Charles Rangel (D-N.Y.) succinctly summed up the impact of Cuban American politics on the formulation of Cuba policy in the 1990s when he quipped on CNN, "We don't have a foreign policy toward Cuba. We have a Florida policy." As the 1990s drew to a close, Cuban American legislative persistence, expertise, and cleverness had paid off with the codification of the embargo and new harsh measures against Cuba firmly in place.

Retrospection and Retrenchment in the New Millennium

On November 23, 1997, Jorge Mas Canosa died of cancer, and CANF entered a "protracted and tortured midlife crisis" (Bardach 2002, 323). Although rumors of his illness had circulated for over a year, Mas Canosa's family had never confirmed them, and the exile community was rocked by the news. Mas Canosa's son, Jorge Mas Santos, stepped in to fill the void left by his father's passing, but he quickly discovered that it would be very difficult to fill his father's shoes.

First of all, Mas Santos and CANF fared badly in their handling of the Elián González affair that began in November 1999. In the beginning, after Elián miraculously survived the tragic crossing of the Florida Straits in which his mother and nine others drowned, CANF quickly took the lead in setting the agenda. The foundation produced posters with Elián's face and the heading, "Another Child Victim of Fidel Castro."[2] Later it would be noted that the posters began the transformation of Elián into a political and ideological tool. Hard-liners for the most part dominated the television coverage by protesting around the clock outside the home of Elián's relatives. Americans who had paid little attention to the policy debate over Cuba came to regard the struggle as a father's rights to custody of his young son, and they were disgusted by images of exiles blocking traffic and flying American flags upside down in protest. By the end of the crisis, the exile community had alienated large segments of the U.S. population, who considered the exiles to have manipulated the tragedy of a young boy for political gain. Moreover, the exiles had defied U.S. custody laws throughout the process.

The negative reaction of most non-Cubans with regard to the stance of hard-liners during the Elián González controversy convinced Jorge Mas Santos and other influential exile leaders that CANF needed to moderate its tactics. To that effort, he worked to bring the Latin Grammys award show to Miami and to include performances by artists from Cuba. The whole concept held great appeal for many Miamians since it would help the city's image and bring in millions of dollars. However, older members of CANF and other hard-line exile groups were outraged by the prospect of Cuban artist participation or attendance at the event. The threat of protests and disruptions ultimately led the organizers of the Latin Grammys to move the event out of Miami entirely and to locate it in Los Angeles instead.

A few days later a full-page ad appeared in the *Miami Herald* urging the exile community to remain strong in their opposition to Fidel Castro and his regime. Diego Suárez, a former senior official of CANF, said, "It is a message that fixes our view that there should not be any kind of deviation in the exile community from the position of never compromising with the Castro regime or any other type of alternative of toleration that only serves to send mixed signals to the Communist regime" (De la Torre 2003, 133–34). Whereas Jorge Mas Canosa had effectively pushed his hard-line agenda, his son was unable to unite CANF behind a push for a more moderate stance.

In the summer of 2001 at least eighteen members of CANF's board of directors resigned, saying they were angry about not being consulted, particularly on the decision by the group's leaders to support moving the Latin Grammy award show to Miami. By the end of the year the CANF internecine conflict resulted in the creation of two new splinter groups. The Cuban Liberty Council was headed by former CANF hard-liners like Ninoska Pérez, and the Cuba Study Group was organized as a moderate organization committed to seeking more practical, proactive, and consensual approaches toward Cuba.

In the aftermath of the death of Jorge Mas Canosa and the struggles of his son to modernize CANF, the leadership vacuum was filled by Representative Díaz-Balart. Díaz-Balart, a nephew of Castro's first wife, Mirta Balart, injected a personal hatred of Castro into his politics. The congressman was widely regarded by the community as a formidable legislator for his codification of the embargo and his successful stewardship of the punitive Helms-Burton Act. Díaz-Balart now replaced Mas Canosa on the national stage and appeared frequently on network and cable news programs as the spokesperson for the hard-line agenda. Moreover, he enjoyed strong ties to Florida governor Jeb Bush and the Bush family. In the 1980s Jeb Bush himself had convinced Díaz-Balart to switch his party affiliation from that of Democrat to Republican.

Along with the stepped-up presence of Díaz-Balart, a new political action committee, Cuba Democracy PAC, was created in August 2003 by the Cuban American lobbyist and former U.S. Treasury lawyer Mauricio Claver-Carone. Claver-Carone contacted more than 120 lawmakers, donated money to their campaigns, and urged them to reject any easing of the trade and travel sanctions.[3] Additionally, first-term congresswoman Debbie Wasserman Schultz (D-Fla.) helped to convince other members in Congress to vote against initiatives to weaken the sanctions. As a result in large part of the efforts of Claver-Carone and Wasserman Schultz, the five-year trend toward softening the sanctions was reversed, and in June 2005 the House rejected four initiatives that would have relaxed restrictions.

The death of Mas Canosa in 1997 contributed to an identity crisis within CANF and a split that resulted in the departure from the organization of many hard-line members. At first it appeared that the weakening of CANF might open the way for a moderation of exile politics. Nevertheless, the intense and successful lobbying efforts by Cuba Democracy PAC in 2005 demonstrated that hard-line Cuban Americans had retrenched and still wielded considerable clout within the legislative branch of the U.S. government.

The Evolution of Exile Politics

The Washington-Cuban exile relationship now spans nearly five decades and has passed through several distinct phases. The first phase encompassed the years immediately following the triumph of the revolution and is best understood in terms of its militancy. During this first phase, many exiles participated in the Bay of Pigs invasion, organized counterrevolutionary activities, launched other violent attacks against the Castro government, and even struck targets inside the United States that were deemed sympathetic to the revolution.

By the mid-1970s both Republican and Democratic administrations, in conjunction with the emerging influence of moderate exile leaders, changed directions and initiated a dialogue with the Castro government. Since the Castro regime had successfully consolidated its control on the island, it no longer seemed likely that the revolutionary government could be easily toppled. Therefore it now seemed pragmatic that some level of contact between Washington and Havana be established. During this stage, the Cuban and U.S. governments improved communication by opening interest sections that functioned as unofficial embassies. Not surprisingly, this second phase was met with backlash by militant exiles, and it also had the unanticipated effect of increasing illegal migration from the island after the Cuban and U.S. governments agreed to allow family visits. The dialogue between the two governments was essentially halted after the chaotic Mariel migration crisis in 1980. Renewed suspicions and recriminations between Washington and Havana made a continuation of the dialogue impossible.

During the third phase, Cuban exile politics visibly entered the mainstream of the U.S. political system, beginning with the 1981 creation of CANF. Washington and CANF established a type of political symbiosis whereby CANF publicly supported Washington's wars against revolutionary movements in Central America, and in return CANF received federal funding that the organization used to further its own anti-Castro agenda. This phase marked the political maturation of the exile community, with CANF initially playing an important supporting role in Washington's efforts at public diplomacy.

The demise of the Soviet Union once again changed the dynamics of the relationship between Washington and the Cuban exile community. When Cuba lost its Soviet subsidization, many exiles felt certain that Castro could finally be ousted, and they began to push their own legislative agenda to accelerate his fall from power. The Cuban Democracy Act of 1992 marked the high point of the influence of members of CANF and Jorge Mas Canosa, who were no longer content to follow Washington's lead in pressuring the Castro regime.

Once control of the Congress passed to the Republicans in 1994, Cuban American legislators began to take on a highly visible role in Congress with regard to Cuba policy. After the Cuban army shot down two Cuban American planes in February 1996, Representative Lincoln Díaz-Balart succeeded in adding codification of the embargo to the controversial Helms-Burton Act. By the end of the 1990s a small group of Cuban American legislators wielded considerable political clout by virtue of their "persistence, expertise, and cleverness" (Tierney 1994, 111).

The death of Mas Canosa in 1997 and the mishandling of the Elián González affair in 1999 led to a shake-up within the community. There were splits within CANF as a result of differences over whether to seek a more moderate stance after the public relations fiasco that resulted from vociferous Cuban American protests about little Elián. Retrospection was followed by retrenchment, as Díaz-Balart moved to center stage as national spokesperson for Cuban policy. Moreover, renewed efforts to relax the embargo in 2005 were thwarted by the new Cuban Democracy PAC. Given the continued impact of exile politics on both elections and legislation, U.S. and Cuban officials who were interested in developing cooperative efforts with regard to migration, drug trafficking, lessening tensions around Guantánamo Naval Base, and reducing the threat of accidental war had to tread carefully.

The Migration Agreements of 1994–1995

On September 9, 1994, the United States and Cuba reached a migration agreement designed to stop the illegal wave of Cuban *balseros*, or rafters, who had been steadily washing up on Florida shores since 1993. The two governments announced that the agreement was designed "to ensure that migration between the two governments is safe, legal, and orderly" (Peters 2001, 2). On May 2, 1995, a more comprehensive agreement was signed as an additional deterrence to the illegal migration. White House press secretary Mike McCurry explained, "The big difference is that in the past [the rafters] may have presumed that they would wind up in Guantánamo. And now they know . . . they will be returned directly to Cuba" (Peters 2001, 3). The two historic agreements were notable in that the Cuban and U.S. governments worked together to reverse over three decades of U.S. immigration policy toward Cuba. As a result of the agreements, the Cuban migrants who reached the United States "in irregular ways" would no longer be granted "parole" (Peters 2001, 3). In other words, illegal Cuban immigrants would not be automatically given entrance into the United States as had been routinely done in the past.

In order to place the 1994–1995 agreements into their proper historical perspective, the first four sections of this chapter briefly describe the four waves of postrevolutionary migrations from Cuba to the United States and include an analysis of the political and economic factors that motivated Cubans to leave the island. Once the necessary background is established, the rest of the chapter examines specifically the evolution of the 1994–1995 U.S.-Cuban migration agreements and examines why the United States and Cuba were willing to put aside their hostilities in order to cooperate on fashioning agreements to curb illegal migration. The chapter ends with an update on the status of the agreements during the George W. Bush administration.

The First Wave: Cuba's Elite, 1959–1962

It has been noted that, overall, an inverse relationship between date of departure and social class best describes the postrevolutionary migration from Cuba to the United States (Pedraza 1996, 264). As such, the Cuban upper and upper-middle classes participated in the very first wave that departed Cuba soon after the defeat and exodus of President Fulgencio Batista and his supporters. These upper classes were bound to a political and economic structure that was completely interpenetrated by the demands and initiative of American capital, and once economic and diplomatic war ensued between Cuba and the United States, they opted to leave the island (Pedraza 1996, 264). The first wave was largely comprised of landowners, industrialists, and managers of expropriated U.S. enterprises. They brought with them enormous social resources, such as class standing, education, training, values, and expertise consistent with those of capitalism, as well as knowledge of U.S. society. As the revolution radicalized and further transformed the Cuban class structure, this early group was soon joined by a large number of professionals and merchants. Approximately 215,000 Cubans came to the United States during this first exodus (Portes and Bach 1985, 85–86).

Many Cubans of the first wave clung tightly to the belief that the United States would eventually lose patience with the new regime in Cuba and would intervene in order to oust Fidel Castro from power. They had strong ties to North American ways, since many had studied in U.S. schools or had lived for extended periods on the U.S. mainland. Mindful of U.S. past interventions, they were fully convinced that Washington would soon rid their homeland of Castro. As Louis Pérez has aptly noted, these Cubans could not have appreciated at the time that North American hegemony depended on their presence inside Cuba since they both shared and spread U.S. values and interests (Pérez 1999, 500–501). These were Cubans who had thoroughly embraced U.S. ways, and whenever they defended their own interests, they also defended and promoted U.S. interests. Ironically, their emigration all but guaranteed the internal success of the revolution.

The Kennedy administration's policy toward Cuban migration of the first wave reflected its ideological and strategic orientation. Ideologically, the United States aspired to welcome any immigrant who landed on its shores "yearning to breathe free" (Domínguez 1992, 38). However, U.S. immigration laws since 1924 had become increasingly restrictive, and there was little public support for a more open policy. Therefore, in order to suspend immigration law for Cubans, the Kennedy administration framed an ideological argument based on anti-Communism. Since Cuban migration called attention to the Castro regime's failure and since Castro was a Communist and a Soviet ally, mass exodus from Cuba served as proof of the superiority of the U.S. political system (Domínguez 1992, 38).

The concentration of large numbers of anti-Castro Cubans in the United States was considered to be strategically important as well since they were seen as valuable assets for organizing and participating in the overthrow of the Castro government. At the same time, it was expected that they would return to their homeland once they had rid Cuba of Castro (Domínguez 1992, 39). In the early years, both the first-wave Cubans and the U.S. government fully expected that their stay in the United States would be temporary and not a permanent exile. However, after the strategic failure of the 1961 Bay of Pigs invasion, the Cuban revolution became more entrenched and radicalized, and it appeared more likely that the émigrés were in for a longer stay. The Kennedy administration resorted again to anti-Communist ideology in order to shape preferential policies for easing the settlement of the Cubans into life in the United States. The unintended consequence was that once the policies were in place, they enticed future waves of Cubans as well.

Within a month of the failure of the Bay of Pigs invasion, the revolutionary government in Cuba moved to secularize the schools. The rumor quickly spread that Castro planned to indoctrinate Cuban schoolchildren in Marxist-Leninism by sending them to the Soviet Union. The groundwork for such a rumor had been laid earlier in October and November 1960. Radio Swan, based on Swan Island near Honduras, had strong ties to the Central Intelligence Agency (CIA) and had reported night after night that the Cuban government had plans to abolish parental rights and take children away from their mothers (Torres 2003, 89). Frightened parents feared that they were about to lose legal authority over their own children, and they began looking for ways to send their children out of the country.

Many Cubans had heard rumors that it was possible to get U.S. visa waivers signed by Monsignor Byran Walsh, director of Catholic Charities in Miami. In fact, Walsh had received a State Department mandate to help arrange the safe departure of approximately 200 children of underground agents. After the Bay of Pigs fiasco, Walsh was extended blanket authority to issue visa waivers to any Cuban child under the age of sixteen.[1] Diplomats smuggled the visa waivers into the country, and Ramón Grau, nephew of the former president, distributed them to the families.[2]

As a result of the combined efforts of the Catholic Church and the U.S. State Department, some 14,000 Cuban children migrated to the United States without their parents from 1960 to 1962. Pan Am flights took the children to Miami, Florida, which was referred to as "Never-Never Land," and the children became known as the "Peter Pans," thus giving rise to the project's name, Operation Peter Pan.

The 1952 Immigration and Nationality Act, which provided for visa waivers, had meant for them to be used only on a selective, case-by-case basis. The massive application to thousands of Cubans essentially transformed the policy so as to meet larger U.S. foreign policy objectives of undermining Castro by luring away large numbers of Cuba's next generation. It was a dramatic plan that would ensure that the 14,000 Peter Pans would never grow up to be revolutionaries.

Cubans who were already in the United States could also request a waiver for Cubans living on the island by contacting the State Department's Visa Office in Washington, D.C. In order to make it possible for Cubans to remain indefinitely in the United States, the entrants with waivers were then encouraged to apply for indefinite voluntary departure or parole. By 1962 the United States had issued approximately 400,000 visa waivers to Cuban nationals (Engstrom 1997, 17). The arrival in the United States of so many Cubans who were visibly fleeing the repression of Communism served as valuable anti-Castro propaganda.

Established in 1961, the Cuban Refugee Program had as one of its primary goals the relocation of Cubans out of Florida in order to lessen the strain on the resources of the state. This resettlement program provided the means by which Cubans were to be dispersed throughout the United States. Besides reception and resettlement, the program included financial assistance, food stamps, health care, job training, and education paid for by federal and state governments (Engstrom 1997, 17). These benefits surpassed those that were available at the time to other migrants to the United States or to U.S. citizens for that matter. Domínguez argues that ideology best explains both the preferential treatment and wide scope of the program (Domínguez 1992, 39). As part of the ideological war, Cubans were heralded as "golden exiles," because they were able to prosper within just a few years of their arrival in the United

States (Torres 1999, 75). In reality, U.S. government grants and other subsidies facilitated much of the early economic security of the exile community.

Passed in early 1962, the Migration and Refugee Assistance Act conferred upon most of the Cubans living in the United States the status of "political refugee." However, as a result of the October 1962 Cuban missile crisis, President Kennedy suspended all direct flights between the United States and Cuba, and tens of thousands of people who had hoped to immigrate legally to the United States were suddenly left stranded. Among those stranded were many parents who had planned to be reunited with their children who had already left Cuba via Operation Peter Pan (Arboleya 1996, 13). As many as 8,000 of the 14,000 Peter Pan children were forced to stay in foster homes or orphanages.[3]

The only alternative for migration to the United States in the aftermath of the missile crisis was to get visas for travel to a third country. Once there, the relocated Cubans could subsequently request entry into the United States. Specifically, they would have to meet the same conditions as other potential immigrants, who faced the limitations of country quotas set by U.S. law. However, those who emigrated from Cuba illegally and entered the United States without complying with the laws were still granted the status of "political refugee," and some 30,000 people emigrated in that way between 1962 and 1965 (Arboleya 1996, 14). In other words, since the U.S. government did not provide the physical or practical legal means for Cuban migrants to enter the country directly, the result was a tremendous incentive for illegal immigration.

The Second Wave and the Freedom Flights, 1965–1973

From 1962 to 1965 internal pressures for migration increased steadily on the island. During this period the Castro regime unsuccessfully attempted to break the country's dependence on sugar and to increase industrial development. A painful irony soon became evident, because the first wave of migration had resulted in the loss of many skilled Cubans; that loss now compounded the difficulty of transforming the economic structure. Other major economic planning problems were exacerbated by the overly ideological and overconfident revolutionary leaders who set unrealistic goals. The resulting economic downturn and shortages during that period were further aggravated by the U.S. trade embargo, which President Kennedy broadened in February 1962 to include all trade with Cuba, except for nonsubsidized sale of foods and medicines.

On September 28, 1965, after three years of mounting internal pressures, Castro announced his plan to reopen emigration, and he invited Cubans living in the United States to travel to the port of Camarioca to pick up their relatives. Castro probably intended, by this action, to rid the island of malcontents with close ties to the earlier exiles. In one clean sweep, he would release the internal pressure of "closet counterrevolutionaries" who stood ready to undermine his regime (González-Pando 1998, 44). By unleashing a new wave of migrants, Castro also showed Washington how easily he could create an immigration crisis.

The sudden opening of Camarioca on October 10 demonstrated to the United States that Havana, and not Washington, exercised control over how many Cubans could enter Florida's seacoast borders. Accepting large numbers of refugees required an orderly screening process, and the arrival of thousands of small boats within a short period of time presented the Johnson administration with a logistics nightmare. Nevertheless, refusal to accept any Cuban fleeing the oppression of Communism would seriously undercut U.S. foreign policy objectives.

During October and November 1965, approximately 160 boats left South Florida and picked up 2,866 Cubans awaiting departure from Camarioca. The Johnson administration realized that it was important to deter large numbers of Cubans living in Florida from heading to Camarioca. The State Department announced, "There is no need for a hasty, disorganized and dangerous resort to small boats."[4] The Johnson administration threatened to intercept and fine boat operators, yet it continued to admit Cubans who arrived illegally. After years of waiting to reunify their families, Cuban Americans, who were accustomed to preferential treatment, simply ignored the federal government's warnings.

The critical situation that resulted from Castro's unilateral decision to open Camarioca essentially forced the United States into a negotiation process that resulted in the signing of a Memorandum of Understanding in December 1965. This document was the first in which the two governments established an agreement for handling migration in an orderly way. The U.S. government pledged to transport between 3,000 and 4,000 Cubans a month to the United States and to give priority to those Cubans with close relatives already in the country. The United States requested and received permission to screen the refugees on Cuban soil in order to eliminate the suspicion that the Cuban government might try to infiltrate the groups of refugees with spies. For its part, the Cuban government placed tight restrictions on the departure of people considered indispensable to the economy and young men of military age between fifteen and twenty-six years old (Masud-Piloto 1988, 62).

During the second wave of migration, the Cuban and U.S. governments also agreed to jointly administer an orderly air bridge. Castro closed the port of Camarioca on November 3, and beginning December 1, 1965, Vuelos de Libertad, or Freedom Flights, began transporting Cubans from Varadero to Miami on a daily basis. During the eight years from 1965 to 1973, some 250,000 people emigrated from Cuba to the United States, and 90 percent had relatives in the United States (Bach 1987, 113). The second wave consisted largely of the working class, including employees, independent craftsmen, small merchants, and skilled and semiskilled workers. Amaro and Portes (1972, 13) have noted that, over time, political exiles had increasingly become economic exiles. The first wave was comprised of Cubans who had left the island because of their political opposition to Castro, and because of their departure, they incurred great financial and property loss. Their political orientation and identification with the U.S. system had been primary factors in deciding to leave Cuba. The second wave, however, included many Cubans who were searching for greater economic opportunities than were available in a revolutionary society, with its focus on forgoing individual consumption so as to achieve collective goals. For these migrants, economic factors were of primary concern, and political issues were secondary.

A complete review of U.S. immigration policy was undertaken in 1965 in order to cut the costs of the Cuban Refugee Program and to make it legal for the émigrés to remain permanently in the United States. On November 2, 1966, President Johnson signed into law the Cuban Adjustment Act, which exempted Cubans from general U.S. immigration laws. The act permitted any Cuban who had reached U.S. territory since January 1, 1959, to be eligible for permanent residency after residing in the United States for two years, a requirement that was later shortened to one year. In other words, Cubans already in the United States were given the opportunity to "adjust" their legal status so that they could become American citizens without having to go through the cumbersome process required for refugees from other countries, since the adjustment required no review and very little waiting time. The program also included other benefits, such as food and cash allotments that were not extended to local residents (Torres 1999, 80). In other words, the adjusted status allowed illegal Cuban immigrants the opportunity to work legally and to receive government welfare, unemployment benefits, and free medical care. This preferential treatment of Cuban immigrants in effect created a double standard (González-Pando 1998, 45). Whereas an illegal Mexican immigrant feared arrest and deportation, an illegal Cuban immigrant found refuge and a welcome mat.

The United States therefore both encouraged and facilitated the entry of Cubans into the country, and those Cubans who were among the first to arrive after the revolution erected economic and social networks that helped cushion the adjustment of subsequent Cuban migrants (Engstrom 1997, 18–19). The exile community maintained close contacts with family members and friends on the island, and the emotional and social ties served as yet another stimulus that motivated continued migration to the United States. For some Cubans, politics was actually secondary to personal and emotional ties, and family reunification was the major force that drove them to decide to leave the island.

Throughout this period there had been tensions in Washington as to how to assess the impact of U.S. immigration policy on Cuba. As early as 1963 Representative Michael Feighan (D-Ohio), chairman of the House Subcommittee on Immigration, voiced his concern that the dispersal of Cubans through resettlement programs out of Florida reduced their ability "to contribute to the emancipation of their homeland" (Domínguez 1992, 42–43). Representative Arch Moore Jr. (R-W.Va.) further argued that by systematically dispersing the Cuban refugees, the U.S. government was sending a message to the world that once and for all the United States had surrendered Cuba to the thugs who had gotten hold of it (Domínguez 1992, 43).

Domínguez (1992, 43) argues that the critics of resettlement were correct on ideological and strategic grounds. The resettlement program, which was created to reduce the burden on Miami and to incorporate Cubans into U.S. society, reduced the incentives for Cuban émigrés to continue their struggle against the Cuban government. Resettlement was subsequently made permanent with the Cuban Adjustment Act. Pedraza further posits that to the extent that the Cuban and U.S. governments organized, concerted, and facilitated the exodus (1996, 268), they set into motion a system of political migration that for many years proved politically beneficial to both. The loss of the educated, professional middle classes was damaging to the Cuban revolution, but it also produced the positive result of externalizing dissent. At the same time, the arrival in the United States of so many refugees who "voted with their feet" also served to provide the legitimacy necessary for foreign policy actions during the tense years of the Cold War (Pedraza 1996, 268).

The Third Wave: The *Marielitos*, 1979–1984

As early as 1970 the consensus on Cuban immigration had begun to crumble, and members of the U.S. Congress argued that whereas U.S. policy toward Cuban refugees had originally been instituted as an emergency measure, the emergency no longer existed. On June 4, 1970, Representative William Clay (D-Mo.) called for an end to the airlift, stating that the expenditure was "wasteful and unnecessary" (Engstrom 1997, 31). On June 29, 1971, Senator Allen Ellender (D-La.), Appropriations Committee chairman, moved to cut off all funding for the airlift and noted, "It is time to halt the program, not because we are against the Cubans, but because they ought to come through the regular channels. I really believe that we have done enough" (Domínguez 1992, 71). In March 1972 no funds were requested for the airlift's continuation, and in 1973 President Nixon suspended all agreements that had given rise to the airlift in 1965 (Arboleya 1996, 16). Between 1973 and 1979 there was a significant drop in Cuban emigration as a result of the suspension of the airlift but also because the Cuban economy was more sound (Masud-Piloto 1988, 3). In these years, the United States received an average of 5,000 Cubans annually, compared with an average of 38,000 between 1966 and 1973 (Engstrom 1997, 43).

Late in 1978 and five years after the end of the airlift, the Cuban government invited a group of exiles from around the world to attend a series of constructive talks to be held in Havana. As a result of that dialogue, the Cuban government agreed to release over 3,000 political prisoners, to promote the reunification of families, and to allow Cuban émigrés in the United States to visit their families and their homeland (Pedraza 1996, 269). The atmosphere that helped promote the dialogue was made possible in part because tensions between the Carter administration and Cuba had lessened, and counterrevolutionary activity within Cuba had also diminished (Arboleya 1996, 23).

In 1979 thousands of Miami Cubans, bearing gifts for families and friends, ignored threats from hard-line exiles in the United States, who opposed any dialogue with Castro, and visited the island. The returning Cubans, whose lifestyle symbolized the affluence available in the United States, rekindled in many Cubans on the island a desire to go to the United States and become a part of the "Cuban American success story" (Torres 1999, 98). As such, the returning Cubans became instrumental in putting into motion events that would culminate in yet another migration crisis.

The Cuban economy had suffered a period of stagnation during the late 1970s, and the visiting Cuban Americans injected much-needed hard currency into the system but at a cost to stability on the island. Discontent among the Cuban population increased when Cubans began to question the value of their sacrifice and struggle after hearing how easy life was for Cuban Americans. Likewise, the release of political prisoners increased the numbers of dissidents on Cuban streets, and anti-Castro leaflets and posters appeared in Havana in late 1979.

In October 1979 several hijackings of Cuban vessels occurred, but the United States paroled the hijackers after they arrived in Florida instead of arresting them for the hijacking. The Castro regime voiced displeasure with the United States for not prosecuting the crime, which violated the terms of the 1973 hijacking treaty. Vice President Carlos Rafael Rodríguez complained to Wayne Smith, head of the U.S. Interests Section, "You turn people away everyday in the Interest Section when they apply for entry documents, but if they enter illegally you greet them with open arms" (Engstrom 1997, 49). Smith alerted Washington that the Cuban government might resort to a repeat of the Camarioca boatlift, but Washington failed to heed the warning.

For the Carter administration, "Cuba was not on the radar screen," since the president's attention was focused on foreign policy crises in Iran and Afghanistan (Engstrom 1997, 51). Meanwhile pressures were building in Cuba that would soon result in a crisis. On January 30, 1980, a sand dredge was hijacked in Varadero, and sixty-six Cubans on board were granted asylum after landing on Miami Beach thirty-two hours later. On February 16, eight Cubans hijacked a Liberian freighter and sailed it to Key West. Finally, on February 26 twenty-six Cubans seized a government pleasure craft, and they also headed for the Keys.[5]

In addition to the hijackings, in early 1980 small groups of Cubans broke into several Latin American embassies with the hopes of obtaining visas for emigration to the United States through third countries. In a March 8 speech, Castro suggested that massive emigration was a possibility, saying: "We hope they will adopt measures so they will not encourage the illegal departures from the country, because we might also have to take our own measures.[6] On April 1 six Cubans in search of asylum crashed a Havana city bus into the gates of the Peruvian embassy. Cuban guards opened fire, and one guard was killed in the crossfire. The Cuban government, citing the lack of cooperation shown by Peruvian authorities, withdrew protection from the embassy and allowed anyone who wanted to immigrate to that country to enter the embassy's grounds. Within three days approximately 10,000 people had crowded into the embassy's grounds (Arboleya 1996, 27). On April 5 the Cuban government announced that it would permit Cubans to leave if another country would take them, and the Carter administration agreed to accept up to 3,500 refugees.

As its next move, the Carter administration urged an international response in order to avoid turning the incident into solely a U.S.-Cuban problem. Costa Rica offered to set up camps to help process the embassy Cubans, but on April 18 the Cuban government suddenly ended the air bridge from Cuba to Costa Rica, effectively keeping the pressure on the U.S. government. The April 19 edition of *Granma* announced that Cuban Americans could travel to Cuba to pick up friends and relatives, and within days over 1,000 boats sailed from Florida to the port of Mariel.

The Carter administration had hoped to be able to screen and process the Cubans on Costa Rican soil and to avoid the chaos of a boatlift, but the sudden halt of the Costa Rican airlift left the administration without viable options for averting an immigration crisis. The State Department and the Immigration and Naturalization Service (INS) threatened to prosecute anyone who transported aliens without valid visas, but Cuban Americans ignored the warnings since the INS had never fined or prosecuted boat operators in the past when they transported Cuban nationals to U.S. territory.

The Carter administration's initial response to the Mariel exodus was indeed slow, with the president waiting until May 6 to declare an emergency. Domínguez (1992, 73) explains that the slow response was partially related to the inopportune enactment on April 1, 1980, of the Refugee Act. Prior to the act, those emigrating from Communist countries had been automatically treated as refugees and given rapid entry into the United States. The act required a case-by-case decision based on a well-founded fear of persecution, and group parole was not permitted. This contributed to the slow response since the act severely limited the options available to President Carter during the height of the crisis (Domínguez 1992, 73).

Senator Edward Kennedy (D-Mass.), an author of the 1980 Refugee Act, argued that the act did allow for the president to admit a fixed number of refugees in the case of an unanticipated emergency. However, the White House rejected Kennedy's interpretation, and the crisis continued. In the end, President Carter paid dearly for rejecting Kennedy's interpretation, and his reelection bid was seriously damaged by charges that he was incompetent in dealing with Castro and the *Marielitos* (Torres 1999, 107).

The approximately 125,000 Cuban nationals who subsequently arrived in Florida via the Mariel boatlift overwhelmed the capabilities of the INS. A further political complication arose when it was rumored that the *Marielitos* differed greatly from the previous two waves of Cuban immigrants. This new wave reportedly included many of Cuba's social undesirables: those who had been in prison, mental patients, and homosexuals (Pedraza 1996, 269). Many *Marielitos* were young men, single or without their families, and there was a visibly higher proportion of blacks than in the past. Close to 71 percent were blue-collar workers. Mechanics, heavy equipment and factory machine operators, carpenters, masons, and bus, taxi, and truck drivers led the list of occupations (Bach et al. 1981/82, 34).

The Mariel exodus coincided with an economic downturn in the United States, a fact that aggravated anti-immigrant sentiments among the general U.S. population. Zucker and Zucker (1996, 60–61) have noted that U.S. citizens voiced several concerns about the *Marielitos*. First, many believed that it was unfair to give jobs to Cubans when local residents were unemployed. Second, there was a fear that the refugees would strain social services and that this would lead to tax increases. Yet another fear was related to the news reports that there were many criminals and social deviants among the refugees. As a result, many in the United States began to argue that the country no longer needed immigrants as it had in the past.

The Mariel exodus was chaotic, disorderly, and traumatic for Cuba as well as for the United States. The distraction caused by the boatlift added to Cuba's economic problems, because the country stopped working for several weeks as thousands of Cubans left the island. On May 2 Cuban security agents clashed with a group of some 800 former political prisoners, and a riot broke out. On September 25 Castro closed Mariel, thus ending the 159-day exodus of 125,266 Cubans.

Ronald Reagan was elected to the U.S. presidency in 1980, and the new administration immediately hardened U.S. policies toward Cuba and sought ways to limit contact with the island. One way in which this was accomplished was by establishing regulations in 1982 that prohibited the transfer of U.S. currency to Cuba. The administration also became involved in the creation of the Cuban American National Foundation (CANF) (Torres 1999, 115, 117). However, the Reagan administration differed from CANF on immigration policy and entered into a landmark accord with Cuba in 1984. The United States was motivated to push for an accord because it did not want another country to decide who entered its territory, as had happened during the Mariel crisis. It wanted a guarantee that if someone entered the United States without permission, that person could be deported. Cuba wanted to have a way by which people who wanted to emigrate could do so in a timely and orderly manner (Torres 1999:117). The 1984 migration agreement therefore provided that 3,000 former political prisoners could go to the United States and that normal migration could accept 20,000 persons per year, as well as arranging for the deportation of 2,746 excludable *Marielitos* back to Cuba. Domínguez (1992: 81–82) notes that the State Department and the INS worked well together in helping to bring about the agreement. Both agencies shared a restrictive attitude toward Cuban migration, and together they led the Reagan administration to negotiate with Castro's government as an equal partner at the cost to anti-Communist ideology. The Department of State, the INS, and the Cuban government worked in a friendly and professional manner to implement the agreement during its six months in operation. The agreement broke down, however, once ideology was reinserted into the scheme. Radio Martí, the pet project of CANF, went on the air on May 20, 1985. It beamed a strong anti-Castro, pro-American message into Cuba, and the Cuban government showed its anger by suspending the migration agreement.

The United States reacted to the suspension by refusing to grant any immigrant visas to Cubans (Domínguez 1992, 51). It also suspended the entry of officials and employees of the Cuban government and of the Cuban Communist Party, thereby inhibiting travel sought by the Cuban authorities. In 1986 it further suspended entry into the United States of Cuban nationals located in any country in order to stop the practice of emigrating from Cuba to third countries and from there to the United States. It also made clear that it would not cancel Radio Martí. In other words, the United States refused to allow Cuba to link other issues to migration agreements.

U.S. tactics and an economic downturn on the island successfully pressured the Cuban government, and on November 20, 1987, the agreement was reinstated. However, its implementation proceeded quite slowly, and the number of Cuban immigrants accepted by the United States each year after 1987 always remained well below 5,000, instead of the 20,000 mentioned in the terms of the agreement (Domínguez 1997, 68). The agreement remained in effect during the term of President George H. W. Bush, but many Cubans who were not issued visas continued coming to the United States illegally, and they continued to be treated as heroes both by the Cuban American community and by U.S. officials (Torres 1999, 132). The fact that the United States failed to accept up to 20,000 Cubans coupled with an economic meltdown on the island resulted in a new crisis.

The Fourth Wave: Rafters, 1990–1994

When Communism collapsed in the Soviet Union and Eastern Europe, Cuba was plunged into an unprecedented economic crisis. The impact from the loss of trade and the loss of subsidies from the former Soviet Union was truly devastating. Economic activity in Cuba contracted by about 40 percent, and Castro himself declared that the country was in "a special period in a time of peace" (Baker 1997, 56). In 1992 the United States further damaged the struggling Cuban economy when it enacted the Cuban Democracy Act (Torricelli Bill), which severely tightened the thirty-year-old U.S. trade embargo. Given the double shocks of the loss of Soviet subsidies and the tightening of the U.S. embargo, the number of Cubans who departed the island clandestinely on rafts and small boats increased dramatically after 1990. Whereas in 1990 the U.S. Coast Guard picked up approximately 500 rafters, by 1991 that number had risen to 1,722, and in 1993 the number climbed to 2,882 (Peters 2001, 2). During the summer of 1994, Florida braced itself for even more rafters as fears of a repeat of the Mariel crisis grew among the U.S. authorities (García 1996, 78).

On July 26, 1994, a group of Cubans planning to flee to Florida hijacked two Havana ferries, and a Cuban police officer, who happened to be a passenger, was killed (Arboleya 1996, 56). There were several other hijacking incidents, and tensions mounted. On August 5 the largest antigovernment demonstrations since Castro came to power took place on the streets of Havana. Many Cubans gathered along the seawall area of the Malecón, the main waterfront boulevard, after hearing rumors that a fleet had departed the United States and was en route to pick up anyone who wanted to leave Cuba (Fernández 2000, 33). When some of the rioters began to shout, "Down with Fidel!" the demonstration was quickly halted, but the rioters' angry message was not lost on Castro. Within hours, he let it be known publicly that his police would no longer arrest or even try to stop Cubans attempting to flee by makeshift boat or raft (Gibbs 1994, 32).

Washington, however, believed that Castro was reacting to domestic unrest by deciding to play a risky game with the United States, whereby he hoped to force the United States to reconsider its policies on the Cuban trade embargo and immigration. One State Department official argued that Castro's ultimate goal was "to force us to negotiate the embargo" (Church 1994, 30). By threatening to swamp South Florida with another wave of refugees, Castro was gambling that he could wring concessions out of the United States without destroying his own regime in the process. The official noted, "What [Castro] is always good at is flipping things so his problem becomes someone else's. This is his last card. He knows this is the one thing he can do to get our attention and inflict some measure of cost on us" (Church 1994, 30). The U.S. reply from Clinton White House chief Leon Panetta was that Castro would not dictate U.S. immigration policy and that the U.S. government would not allow another Mariel (Arboleya 1996, 57).

On August 12 the Cuban government subsequently decided to remove restrictions on illegal departures and to allow ships from other countries to come and pick up waiting Cuban emigrants. One week later the Clinton administration suddenly reversed nearly thirty years of Cuban policy by declaring that Cuban émigrés would henceforth be treated just like the Haitian refugees, who had also taken to rafts to escape economic and political misery at home. Any Cuban who reached U.S. soil would thereafter be sent to the Krome Detention Center in Miami, and Cuban rafters intercepted at sea would be interned at the Guantánamo Naval Base.

The Cuban government was quick to react to the Clinton administration's announcement and accused the United States of converting the base into a "concentration camp" first for Haitians and now for Cubans. A Foreign Ministry statement said Cuba strongly objected to the U.S. use of the base to house Cuban refugees. Washington had decided to add to a "dangerous situation," the statement said, referring to the approximately 15,000 Haitian boat people already camped at the base.[7] Moreover, no one knew at the time how long the Cubans would have to remain at Guantánamo, and General Mike Williams, military chief of the base, INS officials, and President Clinton had no answer when posed the question (Fernández 2000, 92). The detainees at Guantánamo were in limbo, and the naval base soon expanded its accommodations to eventually house up to 65,000 refugees (Baker 1997, 57).

During August and September 1994 more than 37,000 Cubans were intercepted at sea (Pedraza 1996, 273). The temporary solution of detaining the Cubans at Guantánamo created other serious problems for the Clinton administration. There were concerns about hygiene and the possibility of epidemics and endless protests from Cuban and Haitian detainees. The base itself was surrounded by thousands of mines, and when three Cubans tried to sneak across the field onto the base, they were seriously wounded. Senator Bob Graham (D-Fla.) reported that fifty Cubans per day had arrived at the base by land or by sea (Fernández 2000, 95–96). The Clinton administration needed to find a new measure for dealing with the mounting crisis.

Clinton first contacted Mexico's president Carlos Salinas de Gortari, because Salinas and Castro were on good terms. Salinas contacted Castro, who in turn procured his dear friend, the Colombian writer Gabriel García Márquez, to be Castro's mediator with Clinton (Esteban and Panichelli 2004, 237). In his memoirs Clinton recounts the steps that were taken next to address the crisis. Late that summer while on vacation at Martha's Vineyard, the Clinton family attended a dinner hosted by William and Rose Styron, where the guests of honor were Mexican writer Carlos Fuentes and Gabriel García Márquez. Clinton asked García Márquez to tell Castro that if the influx of Cubans continued, he would get a very different response from the United States than he had received in 1980 from President Carter (Clinton 2004, 615). Clinton was well aware of the political damage that an immigration crisis with Cuba could inflict. He blamed his 1980 reelection loss as governor of Arkansas on *Marielitos* who rioted at Arkansas's Fort Chaffee relocation center. Clinton reminded García Márquez of his prior experience by stating, "Castro has cost me one election. He can't have two" (Clinton 2004, 615). Shortly after, former president Jimmy Carter quietly contacted Castro, and crucial talks were initiated between the two governments.

A Cuban delegation headed by former foreign minister Ricardo Alarcón arrived in New York on September 1, 1994.[8] The Cubans wanted to include discussions on the trade embargo, which they blamed for causing economic hardship and prompting Cubans to flee to the United States. The U.S. delegation refused to accept the linkage and made clear that they would only discuss the joint implementation of an orderly, legal process for immigration.

According to the *Caribbean and Central American Report*, another major stumbling block was the number of legal Cuban immigrants the United States would accept. The United States offered to take up to 20,000 a year.[9] It was pointed out that under a long-standing authority, the United States could accept up to 27,500 legal immigrants a year from Cuba but had rarely issued more than 3,000 visas. The Cubans said that the United States should clear up the backlog of many tens of thousands of applications for legal entry. The U.S. negotiators countered that, allowing for those who had died, emigrated illegally, or changed their minds, there were really only a few thousand remaining on the waiting list.

The United States prevailed on allowing only 20,000 per year but did agree to admit the Cubans currently on the waiting list for U.S. visas. The Cuban government agreed to take firm measures to halt the flow, but announced that the crackdown would not begin until September 14. That resulted in a rush by Cubans to beat the deadline, and 1,004 Cubans were intercepted in the Florida Straits on September 11.

The agreement contained several major provisions. First, it declared that both governments held a "common interest in preventing unsafe departures from Cuba." It also included a U.S. statement that "migrants rescued at sea" would be brought to "safe haven facilities outside the United States" and that Cuban migrants who reached the United States "in irregular ways" would no longer be granted "parole." The agreement further declared that "Cuba will take effective measures in every way it possibly can to prevent unsafe departures using mainly persuasive methods." The two governments pledged cooperation in stopping human smuggling, the trafficking of migrants for financial gain usually via go-fast speedboats. Another important provision stated that "the United States ensures that total legal migration [from Cuba] will be a minimum of 20,000 per year." Finally, Cuba and the United States agreed to schedule meetings to review the implementation of the agreement (Peters 2001, 2–3).

Peter Tarnoff, assistant political affairs secretary at the State Department, and Ricardo Alarcón secretly negotiated the companion agreement in New York and Toronto. The secret negotiations were begun during the fourth round of immigration talks in mid-April 1995. Of the 1995 agreement, State Department political adviser Richard Nuccio said, "The agreement involves an unprecedented level of cooperation. This is a recognition that, in order to resolve some problems, it is necessary to negotiate with the Cuban government." For his part, Alarcón added, "As in all good agreements, both sides win" (Fernández 2000, 186).

The joint agreement was announced on May 2, 1995, by Attorney General

Janet Reno, who stated, "Cubans must understand that the only way to enter the United States is by applying for entry from Cuba" (Fernández 2000, 185). The new agreement facilitated the entry into the United States of most of the 20,916 migrants still housed temporarily at Guantánamo Naval Base. It provided that Cubans picked up at sea would be returned promptly to Cuba. The agreement also contained a joint commitment "to ensure that no action is taken against those migrants returned to Cuba as a consequence of their attempt to immigrate illegally" (Peters 2001, 3).

In short, the migration agreements of 1994–1995 discouraged dangerous illegal migration by making it more difficult and also by providing more opportunities for legal migration. The main disincentive was the direct repatriation of those migrants picked up at sea. The agreements have been judged to be successful in that there has been no recurrence of the massive departures of 1994.

An Analysis of Illegal Migration, 1962–1994

As previously noted, President Kennedy suspended direct flights between the United States and Cuba after the Cuban missile crisis. With no legal direct entry into the United States and virtually no access to visas, many Cubans subsequently resorted to illegal migration. However, those Cubans who entered the United States illegally were welcomed nonetheless and immediately granted the status of political refugees. Therefore beginning in 1962, there was a great incentive for Cubans to emigrate illegally.

The two governments did sign the Memorandum of Understanding in December 1965 in order to handle the exodus of the second wave. The Freedom Flights were established to give transportation out of Cuba, but the Memorandum of Understanding did not distinguish between legal and illegal immigration. During that same period, around 10,500 Cubans entered U.S. territory illegally, and they were given the same preferential treatment as earlier (Arboleya 1996, 15).

The next formal agreement between the two countries did not occur until the Migration Agreement of 1984, because both countries were motivated to avoid the chaos of another Mariel boatlift. This was the first real attempt at cooperation to reduce the incentive for illegal immigration. As previously noted, the two countries negotiated as equals and reached an agreement whereby the United States would allow up to 20,000 Cubans to immigrate legally to the

United States. In return, Cuba would accept the return of some 2,746 *excludables* (Arboleya 1996, 33). Some of these were *Marielitos* who were judged as unacceptable after their arrival in the United States, and they had been sitting in U.S. jails since 1980. Others had been arrested after being released from Mariel processing camps.

Although the Migration Agreement did mark a historic attempt at cooperation between the two governments, its implementation failed to lessen the incentive for illegal emigration given that the United States never granted legal entry to more than 5,000 Cubans. U.S. authorities pointed out that the agreement had stated "up to 20,000," and that figure was an upper limit and not a firm promise. The end result was that pressures for illegal migration remained and continued to grow as Cuba entered into "a special period in a time of peace." To summarize, before 1994 there was no lasting, successful cooperation between the two governments that resulted in an effective agreement to jointly control illegal migration.

U.S.-Cuban Cooperation in Forging the 1994–1995 Immigration Agreements

The 1994–1995 migration agreements merit close examination since they were the first agreements between the United States and Cuba that effectively resulted in a reduction of illegal immigration to the United States. Previously, the United States had not repatriated those Cubans who were intercepted off U.S. shores. Nor had the United States truly lived up to the spirit of the 1984 agreement by allowing 20,000 Cubans to enter the United States legally each year. The 1994–1995 agreements marked a dramatic change in U.S. immigration policy toward Cuba, and their negotiation was made possible because of the cooperative efforts of both countries.

The most apparent goals of the United States and Cuba with respect to the migration of the fourth wave were that the U.S. government wanted to stop the illegal rafters from washing up on Florida shores, and the Cuban government wanted to stop the numerous thefts and hijackings that had been part of the increased attempts to leave the island. These goals focused on domestic concerns within each country and might suggest that the Cuban migration issue in 1994 was one of "low politics," since "low politics" involves issues that do not strike at the core security concerns of states. However, the historical context of each major wave of postrevolutionary migration from Cuba to the United States points away from assigning migration issues between the United States and Cuba to the sphere of "low politics." The historical evidence shows clearly that both Cuba and the United States used migration as a potent weapon against each other. The United States used Cuban migration as a political tool in its propaganda war to discredit the legitimacy of the Castro regime. As evidence, Cuban officials pointed to the Cuban Adjustment Act, which they described as "murderous and genocidal," because it actually encouraged Cubans to make the dangerous crossing of the Florida Straits. In spite of provoking migration from Cuba, the United States granted Cubans very few visas, with only approximately 2,000 given per year instead of the 20,000 that the United States had set as a goal (Pedraza 1996, 272).

Cuba also used migration as a weapon against the United States. The Cuban government linked the migration issue to the economic hardships caused on the island by the continued existence of U.S. trade embargo. In order to pressure the United States to weaken or lift the embargo, Castro was willing to unleash waves of desperate Cubans. In so doing, Castro was also able to export his opposition. Both countries linked the migration issue to their competing ideologies. For all of these reasons, migration was an issue of "high politics," which both Cuba and the United States used in order to create conflict in the other country.

In 1994–1995 the coinciding of interests among influential sectors of the White House and the Pentagon led to secret talks between U.S. and Cuban officials in New York City, which in turn led to the migration agreements. Morton Halperin and Tony Lake, members of the National Security Council who, along with Peter Tarnoff, assistant political affairs secretary at the Department of State, favored a normalization of relations with Cuba, found strong support for their position among high-ranking Pentagon officials. Pentagon officials sought to avoid U.S. military involvement in Cuba at all costs. They thought that such an involvement could be provoked either by mass exodus or a civil conflict, and both were possible consequences of a deepening political and economic crisis on the island (Fernández 2000, 187).

Although the negotiations between the two countries were held in secret, the Castro regime did manage to score a major victory by getting U.S. de facto recognition as the effective government in Cuba (Klepak 2000, 17). This was a goal that the regime had long hoped to achieve. The United States was also successful in limiting the scope of the agreements when it refused the Cuban government's request to consider the trade embargo as an issue affecting immigration. The resulting document established a precedent. While not formally called a treaty, it was included in the 1994 volume of *Consolidated Treaties and Agreements of the United States* (Klepak 2000, 17).

The Need for "Quiet Diplomacy"

One reason that the United States resorted to quiet diplomacy with Cuba was that it hoped to avoid an immediate confrontation with the politically active and vocal Cuban American community. Beginning with the break-up of the Soviet Union, Cuban American lobbies had become convinced that Castro was in his final hour, and they pushed hard to tighten the embargo via the Cuban Democracy Act, which they hoped would hasten Castro's demise. Many Cuban American groups did not want to see any cooperation or lessening of tensions between the two governments. For them, there could be no coexistence with Castro, and they would only accept Castro's complete capitulation. This was in diametric opposition to the position within the White House and the Pentagon, where officials were concerned about a potential mass exodus from Cuba that would likely result from a power vacuum or violent overthrow of the regime.

One Cuban American group that was especially dismayed by the signing of the migration agreements was Hermanos al Rescate (Brothers to the Rescue). Beginning in 1991, Brothers had begun flying single-engine planes over the Straits of Florida in search of Cuban rafters. Upon sighting any rafters, the group subsequently notified the U.S. Coast Guard so that rescue operations could be undertaken (Franklin 1997, 278). José Basulto, veteran of the Bay of Pigs invasion and a founder of Brothers to the Rescue, described the group's original purpose as humanitarian: "The absolute failure of Cuba's communist regime generated deep disappointment among Cubans in the island. This caused the exodus of more than 50,000 Cubans who took to sea in search of a better future. *Hermanos al Rescate* was founded with the idea of saving those who, risking their lives, boarded fragile rafts and vessels" (González-Pando 1998, 76).

On May 6, 1995, shortly after the signing of the second immigration accord, four Brothers to the Rescue planes set out in search of rafters and also to see if they could witness the U.S. Coast Guard in the actual process of handing over intercepted rafters to Cuban patrol boats. "From now on, we will be the eyes of the community. Even if we have to enter Cuban air space," declared Basulto

(Fernández 2000, 188). In a meeting with his pilots, Basulto proposed the idea of entering Cuban air space to detect detentions of rafters. It was optional, but if they agreed to do it, they would then bring back proof of violations (Fernández 2000, 188). One unintended consequence of the migration agreements therefore was the radicalization of Brothers to the Rescue away from its original purpose as a humanitarian organization. In time, Brothers to the Rescue would provoke an even greater crisis between the United States and Cuba than the migration crisis.

The Current State of the Immigration Agreements

The case of the 1994–1995 migration agreements shows how Cuba and the United States cooperated effectively to avoid future conflicts related to illegal migration. For over thirty years the migration issue between the two countries had been one of "high politics," which both sides had used as a weapon against the other. When both sides determined that illegal migration was causing more pain than gain, secret negotiations were initiated. This quiet diplomacy culminated in two political agreements that dramatically redirected U.S. immigration policy toward Cuba. The scope of the agreements, however, was limited to the migration issue alone and did not address the deeper problems related to the U.S. trade embargo and U.S.-Cuban hostilities. Whereas the two countries had both benefited in the past from not having an effective agreement, by the 1990s both countries had been significantly hurt by illegal migration and were therefore compelled to temporarily put aside their mutual hostility in order to deal with a shared problem.

The George W. Bush administration adhered to the immigration agreements during its first three years in office. However, the administration postponed migration talks that were scheduled to take place in Cuba in January 2004. Biannual meetings had taken place after the signing of the migration agreements of 1994–1995. State Department spokesman Richard Boucher said that U.S. officials declined to attend, because the Cubans were unwilling to discuss five key issues that were on the U.S. agenda. These issues were Cuba's obligation to issue exit permits to all qualified migrants, Cuba's cooperation in holding a new registration for the lottery from which two-thirds of all legal migrants are chosen, a deeper port in Cuba for repatriations by the U.S. Coast Guard, permission for U.S. diplomatic personnel to monitor the government's treatment of repatriated Cubans, and Cuba's obligation under international law to accept the return of Cuban nationals that the United States wished to deport.[10]

The deportation of Cuban nationals was an especially pressing concern for U.S. officials since approximately 1,000 Cuban refugees from the 1980 Mariel boatlift were awaiting release from jails after having served sentences for crimes committed in the United States. Illegal immigrants convicted of crimes while residing in the United States were usually deported to their home countries, but since the United States and Cuba did not maintain diplomatic relations, the federal government had continued to detain the Cubans even after they had completed their prison sentences. A case was pending before the U.S. Supreme Court as to the constitutionality of indefinite detention of illegal migrants, and a ruling that declared their detention to be unconstitutional would allow the Cubans back into U.S. society if Cuba did not agree to repatriate them.

Dagoberto Rodríguez, chief of the Cuban Interests Section in Washington, remarked that the administration's position was surprising, because Cuban officials had sought to widen the scope of the talks in the past, while the Americans had adhered strictly to the agreements as written. Cuban officials had long argued that the "wet foot, dry-foot" policy still encouraged Cubans to make the dangerous crossing by sea, and they had urged the United States to extend the talks to address the mixed signals of such a policy.[11]

The timing of the postponement during a presidential election year also brought a strong rebuke from the Cuban government. "What they're doing is a political maneuver to calm the insatiable demands of the extreme right in Miami," Rodríguez said in an interview.[12] The Cuban Foreign Ministry released a statement noting that the U.S. stance "means that Cuba should be willing to make all necessary unilateral concessions and accept all demands and whims from the U.S. authorities."[13]

In April 2004, during a United Nations (UN) meeting convened in Geneva and dedicated to a discussion on the human rights of migrants, Jorge Ferrer Rodríguez, from the Cuban delegation, made an impassioned argument against the historic framing of illegal migration from Cuba to the United States. He noted that 900,000 Mexicans were arrested each year for illegally crossing into the United States and that tens of thousands of Central Americans likewise attempted to make the illegal crossing. In comparison, Cuban illegal migration was quite small, and yet it received intense media focus because of its propaganda value, whereby Cubans were always referred to as refugees who were escaping to freedom. He further argued that Cuban migrants were received as heroes in the United States even when they had hijacked vessels. Finally, he noted that many Cubans illegally migrated for economic reasons exacerbated by the U.S. blockade of the island. Ferrer Rodríguez contended that the hard-line members of the U.S. government and the Cuban American community in Miami were actively working to undermine the 1994–1995 migration agreements.

In fact, growing numbers of Cuban Americans had become involved with human smuggling after the 1994–1995 migration agreements tightened the U.S. interdiction policy at sea. As previously noted, under the agreements those Cubans who were intercepted on the high seas were returned to Cuba if they could not prove that they had a "well-founded fear of persecution." Instead of loading onto aging boats and make-shift rafts, growing numbers of illegal migrants turned to profit-seeking smugglers with speedboats in order to make a rapid crossing.

By late summer 2001 the *Miami Herald* reported that virtually all Cubans who now came to the United States by sea were doing so as part of human smuggling rings. Smugglers generally charged the migrants or their families in the United States as much as $8,000 to $10,000 per person. Some eighty people, most of them Cuban Americans, were placed behind bars on charges of trafficking human cargo out of the island by means of go-fast boats outfitted to elude pursuit by Cuban and U.S. authorities. Coast Guard officials noted that many migrants perished at sea because smugglers, who were motivated by profit, often ignored safety precautions by packing their boats with large numbers of migrants. On yet another front, U.S. authorities worried that al-Qaida could easily establish ties to the smuggling rings and position operatives inside the United States. The increase in human smuggling was the unintended and unsavory result of the contradictions inherent in the "wet-foot, dry-foot" policy.

In June 2005 an incident involving a makeshift Cuban watercraft that had been fashioned from a 1948 Mercury taxi served to dramatically illustrate both countries' contention that the other country was violating the spirit of the 1994–1995 migration agreements. The floating taxi intercepted by the U.S. Coast Guard contained thirteen Cuban passengers, and four of the thirteen held valid visas from the U.S. government. Ramón Saúl Sánchez, head of the Movimiento Democracia (Democracy Movement), a hard-line Cuban exile group, was quick to note that Cuba had refused to allow the migrants with U.S.

visas to leave the island.[14] That action by the Cuban government appeared to confirm the U.S. complaint that Cuba was not issuing exit permits.

The four U.S. visa-holding Cubans were members of the same family. The mother, a doctor, had not been allowed to leave the island because the Cuban government requires five years of service from its medical personnel to compensate for their free schooling. The eldest son was of military age and likewise prohibited by Cuban law from leaving. From the perspective of the Cuban government, the family members were in breech of long-standing Cuban laws, and the Cuban government therefore could not be accused of manipulating or evading the provisos of the 1994–1995 migration agreements.

The incident in 2005 illustrates the continuing challenge that illegal migration poses for both countries. It also underscores that there are major disagreements between the two governments as to how to address the remaining contentious issues related to visas. By backing out of the scheduled talks the George W. Bush administration has halted further progress at cooperating to find solutions to these issues. On the other hand, the administration has not withdrawn from the agreements. In adherence to the 1994–1995 migration agreements, the Bush administration continues to repatriate illegal migrants intercepted at sea, and the passengers of the floating taxi, who did not possess valid visas, were dutifully returned to Cuba.

U.S.-Cuban Cooperative Efforts
on Drug Interdiction

From the perspective of drug traffickers, Cuba occupies a strategic position, since the island is located approximately ninety miles south of Key West, Florida, placing it on a direct flight path between Colombia's Caribbean coast and numerous entry points into the United States. Cuba has more than 42,000 square miles of territorial water containing some 4,195 islands and small keys, providing drug traffickers potential areas in which to hide themselves or their contraband from detection. In fact, Cuba has always been a haven for contraband and smugglers, dating back to the days of pirates and gunrunners in the eighteenth and nineteenth centuries (Corbett 2002, 219). During the U.S. Civil War, blockade runners evaded Union warships by hiding in the waters, shoals, and sandbars around Cuba, and rumrunners also escaped capture during the years of Prohibition (Kitfield 2002, 2698).

Cuban officials have often noted that their resources to watch and patrol this vast area are quite limited (Smith 1998, 3). Even with Cuba's limited resources, the head of the National Anti-Drug Task Force at the Ministry of the Interior (MININT) has reported that from 1994 to July 2004, seventy-five tons of drugs were seized, of which more than forty-eight tons were packets that washed ashore.[1] The government had initially counted on Cuban citizens to turn in all such contraband, but even Fidel Castro admitted that some Cubans retained the packets found on the beaches instead of turning them over to the police. Today an incipient problem of drug use on the island, along with a resurgence of prostitution, the distortions of the black market, and an internationally isolated economy, intersect each other and increasingly threaten the stability of the revolutionary order. It stands to reason therefore that the U.S. and Cuban governments could mutually benefit by joining in cooperative efforts to reduce the flow of drugs through Caribbean waters.

This chapter examines and analyzes cooperative efforts that were initiated by the two governments during the 1990s as they confronted the enormous challenge of illegal drug trafficking in the Caribbean region. It begins with a brief review of the role of drugs and their criminality in Cuba's prerevolution history. The next section reviews the Castro government's drug policies from the early years of the revolution until the fall of the Soviet Union. The third section focuses closely on the 1990s, paying particular attention to important cases of U.S.-Cuban cooperation on drug interdiction. The concluding section offers an analysis of U.S.-Cuban cooperative efforts and considers the state of cooperation during the George W. Bush administration.

Drugs in Cuba before the Revolution

North American mobsters first penetrated Cuba in 1933, the same year that the Gerardo Machado dictatorship and U.S. Prohibition ceased to exist. During that year, Meyer Lansky, a Jewish mobster with strong ties to the Italian Mafia, came to Cuba and met with Fulgencio Batista, Cuba's new leader. At the time, Lansky came representing New York bootleggers, who were interested in building rum factories on the island. As an additional goal of his visit, Lansky was interested in seeking out other new profitable criminal ventures. After an amicable meeting with Batista, during which the two men connected on a personal level, Lansky decided that Cuba offered not only a beautiful tropical location for gambling casinos but also an accommodating host government.

Over the next decades the Mafia began to construct a massive criminal empire in which gambling, drugs, tourism, gaming, and financing all interacted and reinforced each other. In *The Mafia in Havana*, Enrique Cirules describes those early years:

> The Mafia began to operate in the race track, where horse races, tourism, and betting converged. Popular gaming likewise came under the control of the Mafia. In the same way they controlled banks, the Mafia founded airline companies (allowing the age of cocaine to begin in Cuba). They also set up financial bodies, insurance companies, and import and export houses. Many deals took place in an unusual pyramid scheme in the Spheres of commerce, industry, transportation, communications—press, radio and television—and, of course, political leadership. (Cirules 2004, 22)

During World War II, the mobster Charles "Lucky" Luciano, notorious for his organization of Mafia criminal operations into a corporate-like structure, cooperated with the U.S. government from inside his prison cell. Luciano, who was serving a thirty-to-fifty-year sentence, put out the word to the underworld to help U.S. military intelligence uncover Nazi spies and to help with the invasion plans for Sicily. After the war, Luciano received clemency for his assistance in defeating the Axis, was released from prison, and was immediately deported to Sicily. In 1946 he secretly arrived in Cuba and was met at the Havana airport by his old childhood chum and criminal cohort, Meyer Lansky. By December of that year, the two mobsters helped to host one of the largest Mafia meetings ever held, using the public pretext of gathering at the Hotel Nacional to honor Frank Sinatra (Cirules 2004, 40).

In the months that followed, Luciano moved to the exclusive Miramar neighborhood in Havana and established Cuba as the midway point for drug shipments, since the island was conveniently located between his heroin suppliers and consumer markets in the United States (Cirules 2004, 32). Since heroin was the most consumed illegal drug in the United States and Luciano already had the corner on that market, the Mafia in Cuba decided to introduce South American cocaine into the Cuban market. As such, the cocaine era in Cuba began thirty years before the drug became widely popular in the United States (Cirules 2004, 32).

Living glamorously and attracting publicity, Luciano operated openly in Cuba. As a result, his presence on the island soon drew the attention of the U.S. Federal Bureau of Narcotics. U.S. authorities claimed that Luciano was planning to headquarter a worldwide drug-smuggling operation in Cuba, and in 1947 the U.S. government issued Luciano an ultimatum, forcing him to leave Cuba and return to Sicily. Before leaving, however, Luciano passed control of his Mafia interests in Cuba to the capable hands of Meyer Lansky.

Mafia activities at the end of the 1940s slowed in Cuba, because Mafia businesses in Las Vegas and Florida were increasingly lucrative. However, when Florida voters rejected legalized gambling, Lansky redirected his sights to Cuba. Following Batista's 1952 coup, Cuban laws were crafted to facilitate mobster business and investment. Eventually, Lansky, along with Santos Trafficante Jr., the Tampa, Florida, Mafia boss, controlled at least ten hotel-casinos in Havana. With the support of Batista, Cuba was completely converted into a "mobster's paradise" (Coe 1995, 134).

It has been noted that the Mafia's Cuban adventure was essentially an experiment in nation-building whereby the Mafia mobsters constructed a state so corrupt that they had no need to break the laws in order to pursue their profits (Coe 1995, 134). For important partners in legalized crime, the Mafia relied on Batista and members of the Cuban political elite who were connected to Batista's government. Batista began his financial association with the mob by initially charging a flat fee, but when he saw the spectacular profits, he demanded and eventually received 50 percent of Lansky's slot machine net. The bagman for Batista's wife nightly collected 10 percent of the profits in Trafficante's casinos (Coe 1995, 138). The casino trade attracted large numbers of tourists, which also generated profits for related businesses such as prostitution and drugs. In fact, prostitution was widespread in the hotels and cabarets owned by the mob.

Cocaine consumption was rampant among both the foreign tourists and the Cuban nationals who participated in the tourist economy. According to one account, cocaine produced in Medellín, Colombia, was flown to Cuba by a private Cuban airline controlled by the Mafia (Lee 1997, 50). The company's operations reputedly relied on pilots, spare parts, maintenance service, fuel, and airfields provided by the Cuban air force.

During these years, Cuba also played a role in the international heroin trade. Most of the heroin that entered Cuba was not sold inside the country but instead was transshipped to its final destination in the United States. Marijuana was also cultivated in Cuba, since the island's mountainous regions provided excellent growing conditions. The market for marijuana was confined mainly to the poorer classes of Cubans rather than sold for consumption by the foreign tourists.

While the Mafia and the Cuban elite flourished in Havana, the roots of revolution took hold in the countryside, where the majority of the rural population lived in appalling poverty. Few people in the rural areas had running water, electricity, or access to health care or education, and the country was rife with corruption, oppression, and inequality. On December 2, 1956, a band of rebels under the leadership of Fidel Castro set out to oust Batista from power. After three years of guerrilla warfare against the government, Castro and his rebels finally forced Batista and his supporters to flee the island.

Drugs after the Revolution

On January 1, 1959, Cubans celebrated the revolutionary victory, and many took to the streets of Havana. Soon they began attacking the symbols of the mob and the decadent Batista dictatorship by smashing parking meters, slot machines, and roulette wheels. One of the Castro government's very first actions was to close down all casinos, lotteries, and games of chance. Trafficante and Lansky held on for several months, hoping for a counterrevolution or a modification of Castro's attitude (Coe 1995, 139). By June, however, Trafficante and Lansky were both arrested and deported, and in October 1960 the Castro government struck the final blow when it nationalized all foreign-owned businesses. Lansky, when asked later about his dealings in Cuba, simply stated, "I crapped out" (Coe 1995, 139).

Revolutionary Cuba ceased to be a world capital for the smuggling and peddling of cocaine and other illegal substances. Castro claimed that "the very first thing the revolution did was to eradicate the [drug] problem. Stern measures were taken to destroy marijuana fields and to strongly punish all forms of drug production and trafficking" (Lee 1997, 50). However, the high moral ground of Castro's early revolutionary moral stance against drugs would be called into question in the following decades.

Oppenheimer (1992, 41) has written that by the 1970s, Castro ordered his intelligence services to penetrate the Colombian drug-trafficking rings, because he wanted to have first-hand knowledge of what was rapidly becoming one of Latin America's most powerful economic and political forces. After collecting the necessary intelligence, he would decide later exactly how to best to use it. Since the U.S. government was increasingly interested in fighting drugs, Cuba's intelligence on the cartels might prove useful in order to convince U.S. officials to normalize relations with Cuba so that they could gain access to the intelligence. In fact, when the Carter administration launched an exploratory dialogue with the Castro regime in the 1970s, one of the carrots that the Cubans offered was to help stop drug smuggling through the Caribbean region. Talks between the two countries in 1978 and 1979 resulted in the Cubans agreeing to help U.S. efforts against drug smugglers. When the Reagan administration further restricted travel to Cuba, however, the Castro government renounced the agreement.[2]

Castro subsequently developed an association with Colombian drug barons based purely on political convenience and self-interest. In the early 1980s Castro fostered and used Medellín cartel contacts to fly weapons to the M-19, an urban guerrilla movement attempting to destabilize the Colombian government. The planes flew over Cuban airspace with no questions asked and picked up the weapons on improvised runways in various Caribbean islands and occasionally in Cuba itself (Oppenheimer 1992, 42).

The extent of Cuban government ties to the drug business became a focus of U.S. investigation, and on November 5, 1982, the Reagan administration leveled charges of drug trafficking against four top Cuban officials. The charges did not gain traction, however, and were generally seen as politically motivated since the administration had a record of leveling accusations against the Castro regime. At home, Castro used the Reagan administration's charges to warn all Cubans against compromising national security by bringing drugs onto the island.

According to its critics, the Castro regime became actively involved in the drug trade to earn hard currency for the revolution and to demoralize and destabilize U.S. society. In 1986 Castro countered those accusations in an interview with Representative Mervyn Dymally (D-Calif.). Castro declared that Cuba was "the place most feared by drug smugglers" and that the country "had stood sentinel against the drug traffic in the Caribbean." Yet he also suggested that Cuba was under much pressure to participate in the traffic: "More than once Cuba has been offered fabulous amounts of money if we would cooperate in drug deals. Although we are blockaded by the United States, we have never accepted a single drug deal" (Lee 1997, 51). Ann Louise Bardach writes that Castro's personal repugnance for drugs is well known (Bardach 2002, 271). However, one military source has offered another explanation: "It is true that Cuba has no interest in drugs, but Fidel is always shopping for more and better weapons. And in this hemisphere, the arms business is controlled by the narcotraffickers. You cannot buy arms without dealing with the cartels or their companies" (Bardach 2002, 271). By the end of the 1980s, Castro's claim of noninvolvement would be challenged in a Miami courtroom, and the Cuban government would face its greatest scandal since the revolution.

On February 23, 1988, a seventeen-member Miami-based drug ring was indicted for smuggling cocaine into the United States by way of Cuba. Testimony presented at the trial maintained that Cuban "government facilities" had been utilized during the smuggling and that a drug plane had landed at least once at a military base in Varadero. In a plea bargain with U.S. authorities, the ringleader of the group, Reinaldo Ruíz, a Cuban exile resident in Miami, identified his principal collaborators in Cuba. These included Colonel Antonio de la Guardia Font, head of the Moneda Convertible (MC) Department of the Ministry of Interior, a department charged with circumventing the U.S. economic blockade of Cuba, and two officials of the department, Amado Padrón Trujullo and Miguel Ruíz Poo, a cousin of Ruíz's who worked in MC's

Panama office. In Cuba, Fidel Castro initially denounced the revelations as "lies from top to bottom," but he later authorized an internal investigation (Oppenheimer 1992, 52). The investigation was headed by Raúl Castro of the Defense Ministry (MINFAR), who mistrusted the past statements and behavior of officials in the rival MININT. The investigation culminated in the public trials in 1989 of several Cuban military and government officials. The trials televised to the nation ultimately led to the conviction and execution of four of the accused, the most famous of whom was General Arnaldo Ochoa Sánchez, hero of the revolution and commanding officer of the Angolan War.[3]

At his trial, Ochoa characterized his motives as altruistic and patriotic: "My main concern in this has not been for myself but for the revolution," he told the military tribunal. The general's stated intention regarding his connection to the drug ring was to use the proceeds from narcotics trafficking to invest in tourist enterprises in Cuba. "If tourism develops, Cuba benefits," he said. This economic rationale brought forth a blistering response from Fidel Castro. In a speech to the State Council, he said pointedly: "A revolution that must depend on drug trafficking is not viable. Even if millions of dollars were involved, a revolution here in the hemisphere, 90 miles from the United States, that maintains itself on its principles, its morality and its serious interest could not sustain itself on this basis" (Lee 1997, 52).

On July 13, 1989, General Ochoa, Colonel Antonio (Tony) de la Guardia, and their two aides were executed for their crimes. A number of other Cuban officials, including de la Guardia's brother, Patricio, and Interior Minister José Abrantes, were given long jail sentences. Castro himself has discussed the crimes of the two principal figures, Ochoa and de la Guardia. For Castro, de la Guardia was the more contemptible of the two, and he noted, "Tony was the organizer, an irresponsible individual who risked his country's security." Castro further noted that Ochoa let himself be carried away by crazy ideas about converting drug money into a resource for the country (Bardach 2002, 270).

Numerous analysts have maintained that the execution of Ochoa was not so much the result of his connection to drug-trafficking schemes but was more directly related to Castro's desire to eliminate a possible political rival, given that Ochoa had voiced his concerns about Cuba's need to reform its economic policies and to resurrect its tourism industry in order to bring currency to the island. Oppenheimer argues that by executing Ochoa and his friends, and by purging all disaffected officers from the government, Castro sent a strong warning to the armed forces, the Cuban people, and the outside world that

Cuba would not tolerate the "new thinking" that had brought about the fall of Poland and that was threatening to shake East Germany, Hungary, and the rest of the Soviet bloc (Oppenheimer 1992, 129).

In the view of other U.S. observers, the highly visible trials and executions were a signal that the Cuban regime intended to disengage itself from any connections to the narcotics business and instead to seek improved relations with the United States (Lee 1997, 52). Such an analysis is highly plausible given the near concurrence of the Ochoa case to the fall from power of General Manuel Noriega, Panama's strongman. As previously mentioned, one of the figures in the Ochoa drug scandal was Miguel Ruíz Poo, a midlevel Cuban government official who operated out of a station in Panama, and his involvement put the Cuban regime in a dangerous predicament.

With the Cold War cooling down and Communism fading, the United States reheated the war on drugs as justification for armed intervention in Latin America. Ochoa may have been executed so that the United States would not be able to directly tie Castro to drug-trafficking schemes connected to Panama or Colombia. A quick review of the Noriega case and Noriega's connection to Cuba provides some additional insight into the Castro regime's motives for steering clear of drug trafficking.

As a junior officer in Panama's National Guard, Noriega had trained at Fort Bragg, North Carolina, in 1966 and was recruited as an agent by the Central Intelligence Agency (CIA). By 1983 he had risen to command the Panamanian guard, and soon he began to cooperate closely with the Reagan administration by allowing the United States to use Panama as a staging area for its military operations in Nicaragua and El Salvador. In addition, he assisted the CIA in its efforts to strengthen the Contras, the U.S.-backed Nicaraguan counterrevolutionaries who opposed the leftist Sandinista government. As late as 1987, Noriega received a letter of commendation from Attorney General Edwin Meese III.

That Noriega cooperated with the Reagan administration is true, but he also maintained close contacts with Cuban intelligence agents and the Soviet KGB. In many respects, Noriega was a double agent who played all sides and was trusted by no one. Additionally, Noriega established links with the Medellín cartel of Colombia and allowed the cartel to use Panama as a transit route and for laundering its drug money in the Bank of Credit and Commerce International (BCCI). For years, Washington had appeared to be willing to ignore Noriega's ties to the Colombian cartel as long as he furthered U.S. goals in the wars of Central America. Once Noriega was no longer seen as a necessary evil, his relationship with the U.S. government was drastically altered. In February 1988 U.S. federal prosecutors unexpectedly indicted Noriega on charges that he had participated in drug shipments and money laundering and for accepting a $4 million payoff to shelter and protect the Medellín cartel (Smith 2000, 294).

In May 1988 President Reagan announced that the United States needed to remove Noriega from power, and during his campaign for the presidency that year, Vice President George H. W. Bush promised to protect U.S. interests in Panama. In late 1989 the CIA attempted to seize Noriega covertly, and President Bush banned all ships of Panamanian registry from U.S. ports. The Panama National Assembly responded by declaring that the country was in a "state of war." The next day, Panamanian Defense Forces opened fire on a car carrying four U.S. military officers when the car failed to stop at a roadblock, and one of the officers was killed. Another nearby confrontation resulted in the beating of a U.S. Navy lieutenant, and an outraged President Bush approved an invasion.

The U.S. invasion of Panama at the end of December 1989 was the largest military operation since the Vietnam War and played out on a changing world stage, where the United States was no longer restrained by Cold War bipolarity. An intense search for Noriega accompanied the invasion, and it was rumored that he was hiding in the residence of the Cuban ambassador, Lázaro Mora. Cuban diplomats, including the ambassador himself, were detained and questioned by U.S. soldiers. Now it was Castro's turn to be outraged. He wrote to the United Nations (UN) secretary general and the president of the UN Security Council urging a condemnation of the invasion, which Castro argued was a "reconquest of the Panama Canal" (Furiati 2003, 561). Moreover, Castro demanded guarantees that Cuban embassy personnel would not be subjected to continuing U.S. provocations (Furiati 2003, 561).

Cuba and Drugs in the 1990s

In the end, the lesson of Manuel Noriega's ouster from power in Panama in December 1989 was somberly noted by Cuban officials, who believed that the demise of the regime was brought about, at least in part, by Noriega's international narcotics links. As the decade of the 1990s began, Havana tried very hard to engage Washington on the issue of drugs. Havana's overall policy goal was to deny the United States any excuse for an invasion justified by claims of a Cuban connection to drugs.

As Klepak (2000, 19) has noted, only a very reckless or foolish Cuban government would dare to risk the anger of Washington on the drug issue once the Soviet Union no longer was able to offer support to the regime. As a result, the Cuban government stepped up its own drug war. Besides seizing more that thirty-one tons of drugs from 1994 to the beginning of 1998, some 188 foreigners and many more Cubans were arrested during the same period for attempting to use Cuba as a point of transit. And while Cuba probably exaggerated its claim that it seized over 90 percent of drugs landing on its coasts, the Cuban record was by international standards very good indeed (Klepak 2000, 19).

Cuban officials pointed to their record of cooperation with European governments as further evidence of their commitment to fighting drugs. "Cuba does not have a drug problem in the sense of large-scale domestic production and consumption and trafficking," a Havana-based European diplomat explained. "Cuba's problem arises because of where it is—a crossroads between North and South America and Europe. In 1995 when we discovered that people were traveling through Cuba for transit, we recognized that Cuba could become a very important transit point to Europe" (Peters 2001, 10).

Cuba eventually signed thirty-three antidrug agreements with foreign countries. These pacts stressed four aspects of mutual assistance with regard to investigative technology, cooperation in training, formulation of joint strategies, and exchange of information on current cases. In some instances, these agencies helped Cuba to develop selected law enforcement capabilities, such as investigative techniques, searching ships, and airport control.

Peters (2001, 10–11) has summarized Cuba's cooperative efforts with other governments and has noted that France's discussions with Cuba began in the early 1990s. Customs officer training programs began in France and Cuba in 1992. More recent French-Cuban efforts have focused on airport security and include training in passenger profiling and the provision of trained dogs for roaming the passenger lounges and luggage areas in Cuban airports and hotels (Peters 2001, 10–11).

Since 1995 Britain has also assisted Cuba in similar efforts, and in March 1999 the two governments signed a Memorandum of Understanding on operational cooperation. Subsequently, the two governments signed a letter of intent for a future prisoner exchange agreement that would allow prisoners convicted in one country to serve their terms in the other's prisons. It was also announced that British customs officials would spend three months assisting and training Cuban law enforcement authorities at the Havana and Varadero airports (Peters 2001, 10–11).

Cuba and Spain signed an antidrug accord in 1997 and created a joint commission of government officials to coordinate their efforts. Cooperation included education to prevent drug use, police training courses, and law enforcement efforts on specific cases. A Spanish Interior Ministry officer posted at Spain's embassy in Havana was established as liaison for drug cases and other law enforcement matters (Peters 2001, 10–11).

A Cuba-Canada Memorandum of Understanding that was signed in January 1999 contained a framework for joint efforts to fight drug cultivation and trafficking and associated crimes. It provided for exchange of evidence and information on specific shipments, routes, and criminal suspects. The agreement also established liaison officers and procedures for consultations, for requesting the other side's collaboration, and for evaluating the results of cooperative efforts (Peters 2001, 10–11).

In contrast to Cuba's increasing cooperation with other countries, throughout the 1990s the United States prevented Cuba from fully cooperating with three important regional organizations. First, the United States blocked Cuba from becoming a full member in the Caribbean Customs and Law Enforcement Commission, based in Saint Lucia. Second, Cuba was a participating member of the World Customs Union, but since the organization's Caribbean chapter was located in San Juan, Puerto Rico, Cuba had no access to its intelligence facilities. Third, the most important regional effort of counternarcotics was conjoined with the Caribbean Drug Initiative. Intelligence sharing for this organization was coordinated through the Inter-American Commission against Drug Abuse, an agency of the Organization of American States (OAS). However, since Cuba was not an active member of the OAS, it could not take part.[4] "You would think that if there were any area in which we [Cuba and the United States] could work together, this would be it," said Ricardo Alarcón, president of Cuba's legislative assembly and the government's point man on relations with the United States. "It shows a lack of will by the United States. Both sides would benefit from broader systematic cooperation."[5] Although the United States severely restricted Cuban efforts at regional cooperation, and although the United States refused to consider Cuba's expressed interest in an official U.S.-Cuban accord to formalize collaboration on counternarcotics, the

Clinton administration did authorize small, limited steps toward cooperation on a case-by-case basis.

The watershed case of U.S.-Cuban cooperation on drugs occurred on October 1, 1996, with the seizure and search of the *Limerick*, a vessel that had departed from Barranquilla, Colombia, and was headed to Miami. U.S. Coast Guard officials boarded the *Limerick* in the international waters close to Cuba. When the officials began to search for smuggled drugs, the ship's crew opened bilge valves and attempted to scuttle the Honduran-registered vessel. Soon after, the *Limerick* drifted into Cuban waters. After the U.S. Coast Guard faxed a description of the situation to the Cuban authorities, the Cuban Border Guard intervened and towed the ship to Santiago de Cuba, where the Cubans began a lengthy search. U.S. Drug Enforcement Agency (DEA) personnel traveled to the site and joined the search operation. U.S. officials credited the discovery of approximately 6.6 tons of cocaine to Cuban search efforts (Peters 2001, 12).

Kornbluh (2000, 1) has noted that U.S.-Cuban cooperation on the *Limerick* yielded one of the largest cocaine drug busts in the history of counternarcotics operations. In what became the first joint U.S.-Cuban drug-smuggling investigation, U.S. officials were invited to inspect the ship in order to verify and gather evidence for prosecuting the smugglers. The U.S. Department of Justice requested that four Cuban officers provide testimony at the Miami trial of the *Limerick*'s captain and chief engineer. In March 1997 a Cuban intelligence officer and three border guards appeared in U.S. District Court in Miami to testify at the trial of the captain and chief engineer, both of whom were subsequently convicted on two narcotics-trafficking counts. Law enforcement officers told the press that such cooperation between the two governments was unusual but not unprecedented.[6]

The DEA, the U.S. Coast Guard, and European authorities have recognized several other major achievements of the Cuban authorities. First, Cubans intercepted a go-fast boat en route from Colombia to Haiti in February 1996, which led to the confiscation of 360 kilograms of cocaine. Also in February 1996 Cubans seized the freighter *Spiritus* and confiscated 180 kilograms of cocaine. In November 1998 Cubans broke up an international smuggling ring of eighteen foreigners trafficking in drugs from Jamaica to Britain through Havana. In June 1999 a Cuban air patrol forced a smuggling plane to jettison 449 kilograms of cocaine. The drugs and the go-fast boats waiting to transport them were then captured by the Cuban Border Guard (Kornbluh 2000, 5).

In May 1999 Barry McCaffrey, the Clinton administration's director of national drug control policy, said that the United States "probably ought to be willing to encourage" dialogue with Cuban authorities on counterdrug cooperation. McCaffrey had been under attack by Cuban American lawmakers and their allies in Congress, who contended that Castro's government was not fighting drug smugglers but assisting them. In a December 30, 1998, letter, House Republicans Lincoln Díaz-Balart (R.-Fla.), Ileana Ros-Lehtinen (R-Fla.), and Dan Burton (R-Ind.) demanded that McCaffrey address "the issue of the Cuban government's participation in narco-trafficking and take all necessary actions to end the Clinton administration's cover-up of that reality." On January 28 McCaffrey, a retired army general, said that he was "insulted" by the tone of the letter, and he "categorically" denied a cover-up, saying that there is "no conclusive evidence to indicate that the Cuban leadership is currently involved in this criminal activity."[7] McCaffrey has more recently reiterated his position:

> It is my own view that charges that the Cuban leadership actively condones or supports drug criminal activity are without merit. The evidence seems convincing that in the past several years the Cubans have actively cooperated with regional partners to conduct air and sea interdiction of drugs starting with the October 1996 seizure of seven tons of cocaine off the freighter *Limerick* in response to U.S. intelligence reports. They are also determined to minimize the growing exposure of their own workers and families to the increasing availability of drugs generated by the hundreds of kilograms of cocaine and marijuana that wash up on Cuban beaches as well as the growing tourist involvement in drugs.
>
> On a case-by-case basis, the U.S. actively cooperates with Cuban authorities by providing intelligence through our U.S. Coast Guard LNO [liaison officer] in Havana. In my judgment, more needs to be done in law enforcement, intelligence, and scientific cooperation on drug treatment and prevention. (McCaffrey 2002, 4)

Coast Guard officials offered a number of specific suggestions to the White House to improve U.S.-Cuban counternarcotics operations. As a result, a meeting of quiet diplomacy was held in Havana on June 21, 1999. Robert Witajewski, Department of State deputy Cuba desk officer, led the U.S. delegation. Other participants were Michael Kozak, head of the U.S. Interests Section in Havana; Steven Peterson, a Department of State drug specialist; and two Coast Guard officials. The Cuban delegation consisted of Dagoberto

Rodríguez, head of the Ministry of Foreign Affairs U.S. section, and Fuerzas Armadas Revolucionarias (FAR)(Revolutionary Armed Forces) colonel Oliverio Montalvo (Kornbluh 2000, 8).

The proposals were to upgrade the fax connection to a telephone connection, to coordinate radio frequencies, to station a counternarcotics specialist in Havana to coordinate with Cuban law enforcement, and to provide technical expertise to assist in joint boarding and searches of commercial vessels on a case-by-case basis. Within two weeks the Cuban government passed a diplomatic note through the U.S. Interests Section in Havana saying that it accepted the proposals. The negotiations were referred to as "conversations," and the delegation was referred to as "low-level" (Kornbluh 2000, 8).

Michael Ranneberger, head of the State Department's office of Cuban affairs, clarified the U.S. position by stating that the meeting was not a change in U.S. policy and that the meeting was taking place within existing guidelines for law enforcement efforts on counternarcotics. Although the meeting was aimed at elevating communications on counternarcotics issues, the U.S. team had no plans to offer assistance to Cuba, to share intelligence, or to discuss joint operations.[8]

Cuban officials stated that they would be willing to expand cooperation. One Ministry of Justice official offered, "We would be interested in a true cooperation that permits an effective effort" in the fight against drugs. He explained that this would include expanded maritime cooperation with the U.S. Coast Guard, expanded information exchange, transfer of resources and technology, and training. "The problem is not the technical preparation of a discussion, but rather the political will to have this discussion take place. In spite of all the conflicts, we are prepared to collaborate with no preconditions" (Peters 2001, 12).

On June 25, 1999, Representative Charles Rangel (D-N.Y.) sponsored House Bill 2365. The bill would authorize the director of the Office of National Drug Control Policy to enter into negotiations with representatives of the government of Cuba to provide for increased cooperation between Cuba and the United States on drug interdiction efforts. By July 1, however, opponents of Rangel's bill had crafted one as well. Representatives Benjamin Gilman (R-N.Y.) and Dan Burton (R-Ind.) introduced House Bill 2422, which provided for the determination that Cuba was a major drug transit country and that the country should be subject to annual certification procedures.

A few weeks later, Castro entered the fray and used the occasion of his annual July 26 speech to launch a fierce attack against Cuban American leaders and conservative U.S. politicians in the United States, whom he blamed for blocking closer cooperation between the two countries against drug trafficking. Before a rally of 100,000 people, Castro argued that U.S. reluctance to sign an antidrug agreement with the island was politically motivated "foolishness."[9] He further claimed that Cuban Americans and right-wing senators were, in effect, supporting drug traffickers by sabotaging a closer deal with President Clinton:

> By sabotaging an agreement between Cuba and the United States to fight international drug trafficking—similar to the one established against the trafficking of immigrants—Senator Helms, Representatives Burton, Gilman, and Smith and 10 or 12 other lawmakers associated with the Cuban American National Foundation objectively become drug trafficking's greatest allies. That is the truth. Whose interest does it hurt? Who does it harm? They are largely accountable for the hundreds of tons of various drugs that end up in the hands of millions of adolescents and young people in the United States, or people who suffer the terrible scourge of drugs. A major part of such drugs could be intercepted through serious, responsible and efficient cooperation between Cuba and the United States.[10]

Castro further argued that closer ties "would benefit the United States 50 times more than it would Cuba." Moreover, he noted that Cuba had recently toughened sentences for drug offences and that drug traffickers would be tried "without a single exception." Finally, Castro warned that the island would quickly become a crime and drug center if his government were ever unseated:

> It is also understandable, as many intelligent people in the United States are beginning to discern, that with the destruction of the Cuban revolution and the moral values it has brought to the country—which would be impossible, in any event—this island would become the most dangerous center of corruption, gambling, drug trafficking and crime in the world, something much worse than a political, economic and social system so despised by the extreme right in the United States.[11]

Within a few months of Castro's speech, Washington became embroiled in a politically charged battle over whether Cuba should be included on the "majors" list, which identified major transit points for U.S.-bound narcotics. The "majors" list had been created in 1986 after the U.S. Congress amended the Foreign Assistance Act of 1961 to include a provision barring countries from receiving several forms of aid if they were not certified by the president as cooperating in the war on drugs. Congress created the mechanism in an effort to pressure other countries into cooperating with its antidrug programs. The law dictated that before November 1 of each year, the president was required to send to Congress a list of all the countries that were considered "major illicit drug producing countries" and "major drug transit countries." From this came the name, the "majors" list.

Since 1986 major drug-producing countries were designated as those countries that cultivated over 1,000 hectares of opium poppy, 1,000 hectares of coca, or 5,000 hectares of cannabis. Major drug-transit countries were those through which drugs were transported into the United States. Twenty-four countries worldwide currently meet one or both of these criteria, including Colombia, Bolivia, Peru, Ecuador, and Mexico.[12]

By March 1 of the year following placement on the "majors" list, the president was required to announce which countries on the list he had "certified" as cooperating in the war on drugs. Congress then was given thirty days to overturn the president's decision by approving a joint resolution, and if no congressional action was taken, the president's decision would stand.

Major drug-producing and drug-trafficking countries that were denied certification as a result of this process faced a range of sanctions. With the exception of humanitarian and antidrug aid, the U.S. government would cut all other forms of economic assistance. U.S. representatives to multilateral banks (such as the World Bank and the Inter-American Development Bank) would automatically vote against all loans or grants to a "decertified" country. The president could also exercise discretionary trade sanctions by removing trade preferences and suspending import quotas for a "decertified" country. If the president believed that these sanctions could jeopardize other U.S. interests, he could issue a national interest waiver for those countries that he would otherwise deny certification.

Until recent years, the certification process had been fairly predictable. The only countries that were denied certification under Presidents Reagan and George H. W. Bush were the ones with which the United States had limited or no relations. Under President Clinton, certification was denied more broadly, but the policy was applied in a less consistent manner than earlier.

For example, in 1997 Clinton denied certification to Colombia for the second year in a row on the basis of presidential corruption charges. Nonetheless, he certified Mexico despite evidence of high-level drug-related corruption within the Mexican government. Clinton's decision was most likely based on the U.S. economic relationship with Mexico under the North American Free Trade Agreement (NAFTA) and not on Mexico's performance in the drug war. This created a great deal of debate in the United States surrounding certification, and many Latin American nations subsequently began to express their dislike of the policy more openly.[13] In fact, few U.S. policies irritated Latin Americans more, because they considered the U.S. approach to illicit narcotics to be a largely unilateral, punitive, and counterproductive strategy that had long failed to acknowledge properly the overwhelming demand and consumption of drugs in the United States (Shifter 1998, 54).

Although Cuba had never been included among the "majors" since the creation of the list in 1986, anti-Castro members of Congress now became vociferous in pushing to have Cuba added. This push for placing Cuba on the "majors" list resulted in part from an earlier letter written on May 27, 1999, by Barry McCaffrey. In the letter, McCaffrey had informed Representative Dan Burton, chairman of the House International Relations and Government Reform Committee, that "detected drug over-flights of Cuba, although still not as numerous as in other parts of the Caribbean, increased 50 percent last year [1998]."[14] McCaffrey would later state at a news conference on November 4 that there was little reason to believe that the Cuban government was complicit in the trafficking, but Representative Burton cited the letter as evidence for including Cuba on the "majors" list.

Cuban American and conservative members of Congress demanded that the White House put Cuba on the "majors" list since smugglers' planes and boats had passed through Cuban airspace and waters on their way to the United States. This was an embarrassing spotlight that President Clinton had hoped to avoid, because it would complicate his policy of quietly working to increase U.S.-Cuban counternarcotics cooperation. In order to bolster the administration's position, U.S. government lawyers argued that the wording of the law did not include countries that had only a collateral connection to the drug routes.[15]

Representatives Burton and Gilman also released a statement shortly before Clinton was to make his yearly announcement of the "majors" list. In it, they maintained that evidence existed that Cuba should be included on the list.[16]

They noted that on December 3, 1998, the Colombian National Police seized six shipping containers with over seven tons of cocaine in hidden compartments that were destined for shipping to Havana. The shipment belonged to a joint-venture company owned by the Cuban government and two Spanish partners. Although Castro blamed the Spaniards for operating a drug-trafficking ring, Representatives Burton and Gilman argued that Castro himself must have been part of the illegal operation.

On November 10, 1999, President Clinton announced that he had decided not to include Cuba on the "majors" list. In a letter to Congress, Clinton recognized Cuba as an "area of concern" but stated that recent evidence showed that the flow of U.S.-bound drugs through Cuban airspace and waters had actually "decreased significantly since last year."[17] Representative Gilman, as chairman of the House International Relations Committee, blasted the decision and said that he would hold a hearing to consider legislation that would force Cuba's inclusion on the list. "Clear evidence shows that massive amounts of illegal narcotics bound for the United States transit the Cuban land mass, Cuban airspace and Cuban waters," Gillman said.[18]

Just one week later, on November 17, 1999, a meeting of the Criminal Justice, Drug Policy, and Human Resources Subcommittee of the U.S. House of Representatives was convened in order to consider Cuba's link to drug trafficking and to decide whether Cuba should have been placed on the "majors" list. As the deliberations began, Representative Patsy Mink (D-Hawaii) noted that the countries that were placed on the "majors" list were denied 50 percent of their current U.S. assistance, except humanitarian or counternarcotics aid, until a certification decision was made. However, because Cuba was not a recipient of U.S. assistance, the designation would in essence have no practical effect even if Cuba were to meet the statutory criteria for inclusion on the list.

Representative Ros-Lehtinen responded by arguing that the Clinton administration had a larger political agenda, which was to establish and normalize relations with Castro and to undermine the U.S. trade embargo. She maintained that cooperating with the Castro regime was naïve and dangerous:

> Castro is clearly part of the problem. He is not the solution. But, after all, this administration sent United States Chamber of Commerce officials to Cuba to talk to those hordes of nonexistent small businessmen in Cuba and a Cuban Chamber of Commerce, as if there is such a thing, as if there are small businesses in Cuba and a Cuban Chamber of

Commerce. And if you are naïve enough to believe that, then I guess you could believe that Castro is not involved in drug trafficking. It fits the pattern very well.

And Castro, by the way, also says that he has no political prisoners. Castro says he is not a dictator. And, of course, the jails are full of political opposition leaders, and it is actually illegal in Cuba to have any other political party except the Communist party to operate in Cuba. There is no freedom of expression, and I suppose that we should believe Castro . . .

And this is not just naïve. It is dangerous. It endangers our young people for us to believe that Castro is a willing partner in stamping out drugs. In treating Castro as a cooperative agent, this could mean that the United States will look the other way when faced with even more clear evidence of Castro's involvement in trafficking, which would mean then more drugs coming to the United States. It is not naïve. It is dangerous for us to assume this position. (U.S. Congress 1999)

Representative Burton accused the Clinton administration of ignoring the facts in order "to proceed down the trail of normalization with the murderous drug-running Castro dictatorship." He further accused the Clinton administration of "turning its back to American children in order to normalize relations with a brutal dictator who is flooding American streets and schoolyards with deadly drugs" (U.S. Congress 1999).

The committee called together a panel that included three U.S. government witnesses from the Department of State, the DEA, and the navy. The first witness, Rand Beers, the assistant secretary of International Narcotics and Law Enforcement Affairs with the Department of State, noted that only nine suspected smuggling flights crossed Cuba in 1999 as compared to twenty-seven in 1998, which had been the year cited by General McCaffrey in his letter to Representative Burton. Drug overflights had actually decreased in 1999. Beers explained his position on cooperative efforts between the United States and Cuba:

We believe that it is in our interest to work more closely with Cuba in maritime interdiction operations, including operations that disrupt the retrieval of air-dropped drugs. Cuba's principal drug interdiction organization, the Border Guard, appears committed to supporting maritime drug interdiction efforts when it has enough resources and information to operate effectively. For instance, the Coast Guard and the Cuban Border Guard have exchanged dozens of telexes this year in an attempt to identify suspect smuggling operations and make seizures. Such exchanges resulted in at least two seizures we are aware of by the Government of Cuba earlier this year, the seizure of a 3,300 pound marijuana suspect vessel and the arrest of three smugglers in January; the seizure of 1,200 pounds of marijuana from a go-fast boat in March.

Our counternarcotics objective is to facilitate drug interdiction efforts around Cuba and to prevent the island from becoming a major drug transit center to the United States. As members of this committee are aware, we are currently exploring some modest steps to achieve these goals.

For instance, we have proposed to the Government of Cuba that we upgrade the current telex link between the United States Coast Guard district Headquarters in Miami and the Cuban Border Guard to a voice link to facilitate more timely exchanges of information. We have also proposed adding extra frequencies for safety and security purposes over which Coast Guard and Cuban Border Guard boats can communicate when conducting coincidental counternarcotics and search and rescue operations in the region. (U.S. Congress 1999)

William Ledwith, the chief of International Operations of the DEA, testified about the recent controversial case in which the Colombian National Police had seized a shipment of 7.2 metric tons of cocaine in Cartagena, Colombia, on December 3, 1998. The shipment was discovered on a vessel jointly owned by the Cuban government and two Spanish businessmen. Ledwith stated that the DEA was certain that the shipment was headed for Cuba as an intermediary stop en route to its final destination in Spain. The DEA had not uncovered any evidence to indicate that high-ranking officials in the Cuban government were complicit in the smuggling operation.

The final witness was Admiral Ed Barrett, the director of the Joint Interagency Task Force East, who reported that his agency had seen little indication that cocaine traffickers were using Cuba as a transshipment point. What his agency had seen was noncommercial air and maritime suspect tracks flying over Cuba or skirting the territorial waters en route to the Bahamas and the southeast United States. Admiral Barrett also confirmed the statistics that whereas there had been an increase in drug overflights between 1997 and 1998, in 1999 there had been a significant drop-off to only ten.

In short, the three U.S. officials addressed the major points of concern regarding Cuba's connection to drug trafficking that had led to calls for Cuba's inclusion on the "majors" list. According to the U.S. government information, overflights had decreased from 1998 to 1999, and there was no evidence to connect Cuban government officials to the December 3, 1998, incident of smuggling.

Explaining U.S.-Cuban Cooperative Efforts on Drugs

As the 1990s began, Cuba found itself ever more isolated and vulnerable. It had lost the political and economic support of the Soviet Union, which had resulted in a weakening of the Castro regime. Gillian Gunn Clissold has underscored the threat to the regime:

> Now Castro is far less secure. His people are facing severe shortages of many basic necessities. His allies in the Soviet Union have long since disappeared. His security officials do not have the resources to effectively patrol Cuba's air and seas. Corruption and criminality, while not out of control, are increasingly straining Cuba's social fabric. Under current conditions, organized crime could provide high remuneration for simple services and could evolve into an alternative power base with the wealth, international connections, management skills, technical resources and the will to undermine the Cuban state.[19]

As Klepak (2000, 19) notes, only a very daring or reckless Cuban government would risk the anger of the United States during the 1990s. No matter what Castro's position regarding drug trafficking had been in the past, by the 1990s he realized that in order to maintain power in Cuba, he could not even afford the perception of Cuban softness on the subject of drugs. Castro's major concern therefore was to avoid conflict with the United States. Likewise, U.S. officials became concerned in the 1990s that a power vacuum in Cuba could result in Cuba becoming a major transit area of illegal narcotics. Given Cuba's geographic location, it could be seen as key to sharply reducing the flow of drugs. Indeed, Castro himself recognized the importance of Cuba to U.S. national interest and noted that should he fall from power, Cuba could easily become a crime and drug center. U.S. agencies like the Coast Guard and the DEA observed that Cuba was making a greater effort at fighting drugs than were many countries that enjoyed U.S. favor (Klepak 2000, 20). In spite of the poor relations between the U.S. and Cuba, when it came to drugs, the United States decided to avoid conflict with the Castro regime. Given the proximity of Cuba to the United States and the long history of poor relations, any interaction between the two countries takes on the air of high politics.

The four proposals that the United States made to Cuba in 1999 resulted in an upgrade of the fax connection to a telephone connection, a coordination of radio frequencies, the stationing of a counternarcotics specialist in Havana, and the provision of technical expertise on a case-by-case basis. The proposals were exceedingly modest and represented small steps at cooperation. The negotiations were held in Havana and were referred to as "conversations," and the delegation was referred to as "low-level." The careful wording was necessary since the proposals resulted from quiet diplomacy. Even though the Cuban government accepted the delegation's proposals in writing, no references were made at any time by either side to agreements or accords.

Kornbluh (2000, 9) has noted that even a low-level approach to Cuba has generated high-level protests from the anti-Castro members of Congress and the Cuban American National Foundation (CANF). Given this strong resistance to cooperation with Cuba, it was necessary to resort to quiet diplomacy. The measures that were ultimately decided upon by the two governments can best be described as confidence-building measures (CBMs). In fact, it may be more apt to describe them as mini-CBMs, since they were not as formalized as were the CBMs related to migration, which resulted in signed agreements and public acknowledgment. The CBMs related to drug cooperation did not produce a formal agreement. Moreover, given the strong resistance of the anti-Castro members of Congress and CANF, it is not surprising that the U.S. government did not publicly acknowledge the existence of CBMs in drug trafficking.

The State of Cooperation during the George W. Bush Administration

Hard-line anti-Castro members of Congress, who were furious with the Clinton administration's limited cooperation with Cuba on drugs, looked for new ways to voice their opposition. Within weeks of the November 1999 congressional hearing on Cuba's link to drug trafficking, five Republican members of the committee, along with Representative Díaz-Balart, convened another hearing in Sweetwater City Hall, Miami. Representative Burton called the hearing a historic event since it was the first congressional hearing of the new millennium, and it was being broadcast live into Cuba via Radio Martí.

The first day of the hearing added no new material to the previous information brought forth in November 1999. Congressional members focused instead on making inflammatory accusations and rehashing well-covered cases from the 1970s and 1980s and included testimony from the daughter of Tony de la Guardia. Díaz-Balart accused the Clinton administration of "covering up Castro's crimes in a wrongheaded effort to improve relations with Havana," and Burton charged that Castro was "allowing drug traffickers to use Cuba as a syringe for injecting drugs into American streets and schoolyards."[20]

On the second day of testimony, John Varrone from the U.S. Customs Service noted that there was no evidence or intelligence that the use of Cuban waters to thwart interdiction efforts was promoted, supported, or coordinated in any way by Cuban government forces.[21] In other words, drug smugglers used Cuban waters and airspace to conduct airdrop operations because they believed themselves to be safe from U.S. interdiction. However, the smugglers did not coordinate with or seek permission from Cuban authorities, and Cuban forces were simply unwilling or too slow to respond to the smugglers' incursions.

In spite of the harsh attacks by critics of the Clinton administration's limited cooperation with Cuba, President George W. Bush maintained the new channels, and in a January 27, 2002, editorial in the *Boston Herald*, William Delahunt and Phillip Peters argued that the continuation of the cooperation between Cuba and the United States had begun to pay off. They noted that in 2001, Cuba mounted a special three-month drug enforcement operation during which time the Cuban authorities and the U.S. Coast Guard exchanged intelligence on nine shipments passing through Cuban waters and airspace. Moreover, the joint operation yielded seven sizable seizures of marijuana and cocaine.[22]

On October 10, 2001, the Cuban government detained Jesse James Bell, a fugitive from the United States with fifteen outstanding drug charges. Within two weeks the United States requested his extradition, and the Cuban government responded positively. Bell's transfer took place on January 12, 2002, which, according to a Cuban foreign ministry statement, occurred "as a goodwill gesture that shows clearly the commitment of our government to cooperate with all nations in fighting drug trafficking."[23]

The Bell case was a significant accomplishment, but it was eclipsed in the months that followed when the Cuban government apprehended two important Colombian drug traffickers. On March 6, 2002, Rafael Miguel Bustamante Bolaños was arrested along with a Bahamian drug trafficker after the U.S. Marshals Service relayed the news that the Colombian was in Cuba. Bustamante Bolaños had escaped from prison in Santa Marta, Colombia, where he was serving a sentence for money laundering. He was wanted by the United States for also having escaped from a federal prison in Alabama, where he had been serving a sentence for trafficking in cocaine and money laundering.

On March 21, 2002, after the Cuban government's public statement about the arrest of Bustamante Bolaños, Cuban television held a roundtable discussion of the event. Brigadier General Lázaro Román Rodríguez spoke of the ties between drug smuggling, illegal immigration, and terrorism and the importance of Cuban-U.S. cooperation in these areas:

> I'd like to mention that since drug traffickers use the same *modus operandi* as the human smugglers and the terrorists, who often share other common characteristics, there has therefore also been an important flow of information with the Miami Coast Guard Service in the battle against illegal immigration. This amounts to 970 faxes sent, 28 telephone conversations on our part, and we have received in turn 463 faxed and 19 telephone calls. This also demonstrates Cuba's willingness to cooperate in this area.[24]

In addition to cooperating with the international community on the war on drugs, Cuban authorities also intensified efforts to eradicate their own emerging domestic drug problem. In 2003 Cuban officials admitted publicly that domestic drug consumption, although limited, was becoming a problem on the island. Until 2003, Cuban authorities had referred to drug consumption as a "capitalist ill" that existed in Cuba only as a result of the influx of foreign tourists. Prior to that date, the Cuban government had merely acknowledged that some of its citizens cultivated small amounts of marijuana or sold drugs that washed up on the shore.

The government fought this "incipient market" with a vengeance. In January 2003 it began conducting early morning raids with drug-sniffing dogs on the homes of suspects. When drugs were found, special Interior Ministry police units confiscated the entire contents of the residence. Meanwhile, Cuba's already stiff penalties for drug trafficking were made even more stringent.[25]

On July 2, 2004, Cuban government authorities reported that they had detained Luis Hernando Gómez Bustamante, kingpin of Colombia's large and powerful Norte del Valle drug cartel suspected of having smuggled more than $10 billion worth of cocaine into the United States. The importance of Gómez Bustamante's arrest was underscored by the fact that the United States had offered a $5 million reward for his apprehension. Gómez Bustamante, alias Rasguño, had entered Cuba using a false passport. Reports were circulated that Colombian authorities were planning to head to Cuba in order to retrieve Rasguño and to subsequently extradite him to the United States for trial since he stood accused of controlling between 30 and 50 percent of the cocaine that made it to the U.S. market.

After the arrest of Bustamante Bolaños, the Cuban government publicly called on the Bush administration to negotiate agreements on drugs and terrorism.[26] There had been earlier calls for bilateral agreements as early as November 29, 2001, when the Cuban government proposed U.S.-Cuban cooperation in the fight against illegal migration, drug trafficking, and terrorism. When Ricardo Alarcón resubmitted the three proposals at the biannual talks on migration on December 3, 2001, the U.S. delegation refused to consider them, stating that the proposals went beyond the agreed-upon framework for the talks.

In response to the Cuban proposals in March 2002, a U.S. State Department official said that contacts on law enforcement and human smuggling would continue on a case-by-case basis only. Senator Arlen Spector (R-Pa.), who had met with Castro for more than six hours earlier in the year, expressed support for working more closely with Cuba. "If we can stop the flow of drugs with Castro's assistance, we ought to take him up on that offer," he argued.[27]

After successfully apprehending major drug figures, the Cuban government had clearly shown its ability and willingness to fight the war on drugs. In spite of these efforts, a formalized drug agreement with the United States still remained elusive. It is therefore not surprising to learn that the Cuban government hedged on handing Rasguño over to the Colombians, who were likely to extradite him to the United States.

The Colombian government presented a formal request for extradition on November 20, 2004, approximately five months after the Cubans had arrested Rasguño at the Havana airport. According to the Colombian news sources, the steps to transfer Rasguño became complicated after the arrest since Colombia and Cuba did not have an extradition treaty. Brigadier General Jesús

Becerra, chief of Cuba's antinarcotics agency, said, "He is detained, he has a defense lawyer, he enjoys the rights provided by our constitution."[28]

The Cuban government continues to push for a cooperation agreement with the United States, but to date the Bush administration has not moved from the case-by-case cooperation of the 1990s. Abelardo Moreno, Cuba's deputy minister of foreign affairs, has criticized the U.S. government's decision to turn down six Cuban proposals in this regard, in spite of the fact that "the U.S. population would be the prime beneficiary."[29] In private, U.S. drug agents are furious at the way in which the issue of U.S.-Cuban cooperation has been politicized. Because of the anti-Castro politics of South Florida, the U.S. Coast Guard District 7 headquarters in Miami purposely says very little about its liaison office in Havana, even though the intelligence passed along by the Cubans has become increasingly reliable and specific (Kitfield 2002, 2698). As a result, the U.S. public remains largely unaware that Cuba has helped the United States track drug smugglers and that the Cuban government has arrested dangerous drug traffickers and drug lords.

The U.S. Naval Station at Guantánamo Bay and U.S.-Cuban Cooperation

The U.S. Naval Station at Guantánamo Bay (Gitmo) has been a major irritant to Cuban nationalists since its establishment at the beginning of the twentieth century. A victorious United States claimed control of the strategically located property at the end of the Spanish-American War in 1898. The base, formally established in 1901, is the oldest of all U.S. overseas military bases. In addition, Gitmo is the only U.S. base located in a Communist country and is the only U.S. base that operates with an infinite lease. Fidel Castro, who has not cashed any of the U.S. rent checks since 1960, has described the naval base as "a dagger plunged into the heart of Cuban soil."[1]

This chapter begins by reviewing the early history associated with the U.S. naval base at Guantánamo Bay. A second section pays particular attention to the numerous U.S.-Cuban conflicts related to the base that have arisen since the beginning of the Cuban revolution. The third section focuses specifically on the U.S. and Cuban unilateral and bilateral efforts in the 1990s that resulted in a reduction of tension regarding the base and its operations. The following section of the chapter analyzes the cooperative efforts of the 1990s, and the final section considers the state of base relations during the George W. Bush administration.

Early Historical Background

In order to best understand the context of the long-standing tensions between the United States and Cuba with regard to the base, this chapter covers in greater depth historical events that were briefly presented in the introduction. It is important to keep in mind that the United States had its "eyes upon Cuba" long before the triumph of Castro's revolution in 1959 (Smith 2000, 22). As far back as 1783 President John Adams articulated U.S. long-term aims regarding the island. He noted that Cuba should remain in Spanish hands until that time when the United States could seize the island. In a letter dated June 23, 1783, Adams wrote that Cuba was a natural extension of the American continent and that annexation of Cuba was indispensable for the continuation of the Union (Ricardo 1994, 10).

Thomas Jefferson became the first of four U.S. presidents who subsequently attempted to purchase Cuba from Spain. After the Louisiana Purchase in 1803, Jefferson recognized the strategic importance of Cuba's location in the Gulf of Mexico. In 1809 Jefferson wrote of Cuba: "I candidly confess that I have ever looked upon Cuba as the most interesting addition that can be made to our system of States, the possession of which would give us control over the Gulf of Mexico and the countries and isthmus bordering upon it" (Baker 1997, 31). Jefferson even suggested that he would withhold aid to Latin American revolutionaries if Napoleon would give Cuba to the United States (McCoy 1995, 15–16).[2]

Secretary of State John Quincy Adams argued in 1823 that Cuba would eventually be drawn to the United States by the laws of political gravitation:

... there are laws of political as well as physical gravitation; and if an apple severed by the tempest from its native tree cannot choose but fall to the ground, Cuba, forcibly disjoined from its own unnatural connection with Spain, and incapable of self-support, can gravitate only towards the North American Union, which by the same law of nature cannot cast her off from her bosom. (Smith 2000, 23)

During the same year, the Monroe Doctrine proclaimed U.S. opposition to future colonization of the American continents by any European power, thereby underscoring U.S. claims to hemispheric hegemony.

In 1848, shortly after the end of the U.S. expansionist war with Mexico, President Polk, fully imbued with the spirit of manifest destiny, authorized negotiations for the purchase of Cuba, but England and France strongly protested the transfer of the island from Spain. In the interest of maintaining cordial U.S.-European relations, U.S. negotiations for the purchase of Cuba were subsequently put on hold.

In 1854 the Pierce administration made yet another attempt to purchase the island for $130 million. At this time the U.S. ministers to Spain, England, and France drafted the infamous Ostend Manifesto, which justified wresting Cuba from Spain on the grounds that the United States needed to protect itself from potential problems that could result if a slave revolt were ever to occur in Cuba as had occurred on the island of Haiti. According to the crafters of the manifesto, a slave rebellion in nearby Cuba could spread its contagion to the United States:

> We should be recreant to our duty, be unworthy of our gallant forefathers, and commit base treason against posterity, should we permit Cuba to be Africanized and become a second St. Domingo, with all its attendant horrors to the white race, and suffer the flames to enter our own neighborhood shores, seriously endanger or actually to consume the fair fabric of our Union. (Smith 2000, 24)

The Buchanan administration tried twice unsuccessfully to purchase Cuba from Spain for $130 million. However, interest in the Cuba question receded in the late 1850s as the United States became increasingly absorbed with its own complicated domestic issues. The heated debate over slavery eventually foreclosed the possibility of admitting any new slave territory into the Union.

During the Civil War, President Lincoln's naval blockade of the Confederacy demonstrated the need for coaling stations in the Caribbean, and Secretary of the Navy Gideon Welles listed Guantánamo Bay as one of several possibilities. This was the first time that anyone had mentioned Guantánamo specifically as a base (McCoy 1995, 19). Within three years after the end of the U.S. Civil War, a conflict erupted in Cuba that was a war for independence, a civil war, and a race war.

From 1868 to 1878, Cubans of all colors joined forces and fought the bitter first war of independence, the Ten Years War. The violent upheaval during these years made it impossible for the United States to pursue any deal with Spain for a naval station. By constructing the *trocha*, a defensive line across the middle of the island, the Spanish army was able to keep the Cuban rebels from crossing over into the western half of Cuba, thereby containing the rebellion. After struggling for a decade, Cubans not only failed to achieve their goal of independence, but the island's economy was reduced to a shambles, and the institution of slavery remained intact. In fact, slavery on the island would not be abolished until 1886. It would take another war before the United States would be able to acquire a base at Guantánamo.

José Martí came of age during the first war of independence, and from his exile in the United States he formed the Cuban Revolutionary Party in 1892 and rallied support for another movement to break from Spain. Martí's initial admiration of the United States had faded during his exile, and he feared that a U.S. intervention in the struggle would ultimately lead to a protectorate status for the island. He wrote of his concern to his brother:

> Every day my life is in danger. I am in danger of giving up my life for my country, for my duty—as I understand it and must execute it—so that Cuba's independence will prevent the expansion of the United States throughout the Antilles, allowing that nation to fall, ever more powerfully, upon our American lands. Everything I have done, everything I will do, is toward this end. It has been a silent and indirect process, for there are things which must be kept hidden if they are to take place. . . . I have lived inside the monster and know its entrails—and my weapon is only the slingshot of David. (Smith 2000, 108)

When hostilities between Cuba and Spain resumed in 1895, Martí became an early martyr to the cause. Within two years, the renewed struggle degenerated into a bloody war of attrition. The American public followed news of the war and identified with the Cubans, who, like the American colonists, were fighting for independence against a European power. Popular sentiment to join in the struggle was further inflamed by the yellow journalism of the U.S. press, which sensationalized the atrocities in order to increase readership. U.S. sugar and business interests also favored intervention (Baker 1997, 34). However, President McKinley, who did not want to upset recovery from the recent economic depression, skillfully resisted the popular sentiment for war.

Assistant Secretary of the Navy Theodore Roosevelt had been preparing for war for many years and was anxious to showcase U.S. naval power. Along with Roosevelt, many Democrats and Republicans were determined to establish naval dominance in the Caribbean, especially after the French began building a canal in Panama and the British had disputed the boundary between Venezuela and British Guiana. Cuba dominated both entrances to the Gulf of Mexico and was strategically positioned on the route to the proposed Panamanian canal.

When the USS *Maine* mysteriously blew up in Havana harbor on February 5, 1898, Roosevelt intensified the pressure for the United States to enter the war.[3] After McKinley failed to respond immediately, Roosevelt privately declared that McKinley had "no more backbone than a chocolate éclair" (Frederick 2003, 594). Soon after, the public adopted the jingoism of newspaper editor William Randolph Hearst and began shouting, "Remember the *Maine*, to hell with Spain!" Succumbing to the combined pressures of "politics, profits, patriotism and piety," President McKinley yielded to the drumbeat for war (Frederick 2003, 593). On April 24, 1898, Congress authorized sending troops against Spain and recognized the independence of Cuba.

The U.S. government claimed that it was entering the war to help in liberating Cuba, and the Teller Amendment was crafted to underscore the altruistic motives of the United States: "The United States hereby disclaims any disposition or intention to exercise sovereignty, jurisdiction, or control over said island except for the pacification thereof, and asserts its determination, when that is accomplished, to leave the government and control of the island to its people" (Gott 2004, 102).

The Cuban general Máximo Gómez, however, never requested U.S. troops and instead only requested a supply of arms and ammunition. In fact, many Cuban leaders believed in April 1898 that they were finally on the verge of victory. Once the Americans entered the conflict, the Cubans soon found themselves forced to the periphery of the fighting (Baker 1997, 35). In public, U.S. general William Shafter noted that the Cuban rebels lacked shoes and adequate weapons, but in private, U.S. soldiers were appalled that so many were blacks and mulattoes. Stephen Crane, who had come to Cuba as a news reporter, referred to the rebels as "real tropical savages," and General Shafter recommended that the Cubans be kept in the rear, digging ditches and latrines (Perrottet 1995, 31).

When victory came on July 17, 1898, the Spanish flag was lowered, but instead of the Cuban flag, the U.S. flag flew over Cuba. Mark Twain, who opposed nascent U.S. imperialism and was the vice president of the Anti-Imperialist League, caustically suggested that the Stars and Stripes be replaced with the skull and crossbones. The conflict, which Secretary of State John Hay dubbed a "splendid little war," ended with a bitter insult to Cuban pride.

Establishing the U.S. Naval Station at Guantánamo Bay

U.S. military occupation of Cuba formally began on January 1, 1899, and Washington dictated the terms of the peace and wrote the new Cuban constitution. Humiliated Cuban nationalists were further incensed by an addendum to the constitution called the Platt Amendment, which gave the United States the right to intervene in Cuba "for the preservation of Cuban independence, and the maintenance of a government adequate for the protection of life, property, and individual liberty." Additionally, the terms of the Platt Amendment required Cuba "to sell or lease to the United States land necessary for coaling or naval stations at certain specified points, to be agreed upon with the President of the United States." News of this concession caused rioting around Cuba, but the United States made it clear that if the Cubans did not accept the Platt Amendment, there would be no end to U.S. military occupation (Pérez 1988, 187). Even the governor-general, U.S. Army general Leonard Wood, wrote President McKinley that "there is, of course, little or no independence left in Cuba under the Platt Amendment" (Baker 1997, 36).

Guantánamo was not directly mentioned in the Platt Amendment, because the amendment's crafters feared that its inclusion as a specific location would further infuriate the Cubans, who were already incensed over the whole idea of U.S. bases on the island. In addition, there was concern that southern members of Congress, who were interested in preserving funding for the naval yards in their own districts, might refuse to support the amendment (McCoy 1995, 48). In November 1902 the U.S. Navy negotiated the specific sites with Cuban president Tomás Estrada Palma. Estrada Palma held firm to leasing the land rather than selling it to the United States, and he agreed to only two locations, Bahía Honda and Guantánamo.

The United States recognized Cuba's ultimate sovereignty over the approximately forty-five-square-mile area at Guantánamo that would comprise the base and its surrounding waters; however, Cuba was forced to concede that as long as the United States occupied the base, the United States would retain complete control. The word *ultimate* was interpreted to mean that Cuban sovereignty would be interrupted during U.S. occupancy (McCoy 1995, 51). If the United States ever gave up the area, Guantánamo would ultimately revert to Cuba.

On December 10, 1903, control of the Cuban territory on Guantánamo Bay was officially handed over to the United States. The Cuban government sent a note to the United States requesting that the ceremony be kept low key, because the Cuban people were protesting against the lease. Soon after the ceremony, 600 U.S. troops landed. Theodore Roosevelt immediately celebrated the importance of Guantánamo and described it as the "absolutely necessary strategic base" for controlling the Caribbean and the route to the Panama Canal (Ricardo 1994, 17).

Nationalist tensions continued to simmer beneath the surface of the new republic of Cuba. Given that context, it is not surprising that results of the

1906 presidential election in Cuba were contested, resulting in political unrest on the island and a second U.S. occupation that lasted until 1909. During these years, the U.S. Navy became focused on enlarging Guantánamo in order to improve its defenses by obtaining the high ground to the north and east of the base and to gain easier access to the water supply of the Yateras River. In response, the Cuban government resorted to diplomatic stall tactics to avoid ceding additional sovereign territory to the United States. Hoping to break the impasse in 1910, the navy offered to trade the lease at Bahía Honda for the desired extension of Guantánamo. However, the negotiations between the United States and Cuba to finalize the trade dragged on for two more years, as the Cuban secretary of state continually slowed the process by raising other serious concerns such as future U.S. interventions, rumored U.S. claims against Cuba for property damages, and the status of the Isle of Pines, where U.S. citizens there were threatening to hoist their own flag (McCoy 1995, 65).

Cuba's internal dynamics became even more complicated on May 20, 1912. Frustrated Afro-Cubans chose that very day, Cuba's Independence Day, to launch an armed protest movement. After fighting valiantly against the Spanish, they had received no real independence in the new republic, because the racist character of colonial society had remained unchanged. In response to the racial unrest on the island, the U.S. government reinforced Guantánamo and deployed marines to protect U.S. sugar estates. However, U.S. troops were under orders not to intervene in the racial conflict, and some 3,000 Afro-Cubans were killed in the carnage that followed.

The United States was able to force Cuba into an arrangement for extending the water boundaries of Guantánamo. In exchange for Bahía Honda, which no longer held its original strategic importance, the United States took control of almost the entire bay surrounding the Guantánamo Naval Base. According to the original agreement, the access channel was to have been shared so as to guarantee free trade by the Cuban ports of Caimanera and Boquerón (Ricardo 1994, 18).[4]

Cuba's presidential elections continued to generate internal conflict, and in 1917 President Wilson found it necessary to send 220 marines to the base in order to protect U.S. properties from the civil unrest that erupted after the disputed presidential election of 1916. Wilson's primary concern was that Germany might take advantage of Cuba's continuing political instability by establishing submarine bases around the island's well-hidden coves or by convincing the rebels to collaborate with German agents. For Wilson, it was important to first stabilize Cuba and then to pressure the Cuban government to end its neutral position with respect to World War I. In the end, Cuba duly followed Wilson's wishes and declared war on Germany one day after the United States made its own declaration.

Throughout World War I, Cuba's sugar supply to the United States was even more important than the naval base at Guantánamo Bay. During the war years, the base underwent some development, but its most significant role was that of a refueling station. For the next twenty years after the war, Guantá-namo changed very little, and military life on the base moved at a slow pace. A short story reflecting life on the base and entitled "Guantanamo Blues" was published in 1930. The author, a "navy wife," depicted the base as a boring American outpost where sex and drinking were the chief diversions.[5]

The despised Platt Amendment held until 1934, when President Franklin D. Roosevelt proclaimed the Good Neighbor policy, which promised to usher in a less-interventionist era in U.S.–Latin American relations. With the repeal of the Platt Amendment, it was hoped that Cuban nationalists would no longer be able to use the amendment to rally others to the cause. By timing the demise of the amendment to coincide with the demise of the Cuban revolution of 1933, Washington also hoped to confer legitimacy on a more acceptable Cuban government dominated by Fulgencio Batista. Although the United States did abrogate the Platt Amendment, it did not relinquish control of Guantánamo, and a new treaty formalized the agreement on the base by adding that "so long as the United States shall not abandon the said naval station of Guantánamo, or the two Governments shall not agree to a modification of its present limits, the station shall continue to have the territorial area that it now has." Annual rent was changed from the original of $2,000 in gold coins to $4,085, or about 14 cents an acre (Baker 1997, 656).

As the possibility of another war in Europe grew, the base underwent extensive development to give it all the facilities of a domestic port, and some $34 million were invested toward that end. Thousands of Cubans came to work on the base during this period, providing the contract labor for the construction projects. While a few hundred Cuban employees lived in trailer camps on the base, most had to commute (McCoy 1995, 123). As they had done in past years, Cubans frequently complained that naval authorities on the base violated Cuban labor laws by hiring nonunion workers. One Cuban wrote to the Office of Inter-American Affairs in Washington, D.C., and complained bitterly about the low wages ranging from $15 to $21 per week. Moreover, many employees had to deduct $3 per week from their wages in order to pay for transportation to the base. Rising at 4 a.m. to catch the train, they did not return home until 8 p.m. each night (McCoy 1995, 136). Cubans were desperate for jobs, but many resented their base employers nonetheless.

During World War II, the base's population reached its high of 10,000 personnel, and they provided logistics services and support for the U.S. Atlantic Fleet, rescued survivors of ships torpedoed in the area, protected merchant shipping threatened by German submarines, and patrolled for German U-boats. After the war, the base's operations were greatly curtailed (Coe 1995, 296). Some 2,200 to 2,500 Cubans were employed permanently by the base, and approximately 1,200 lived on the base itself. In 1946 the Cuban workers continued to push for a labor union, a demand that was ultimately granted, and a union formed in December 1950 (McCoy 1995, 142).

The presence of a large U.S. naval base transformed the daily life of the communities surrounding the installation. The impact was most notable in the city of Caimanera, on the western side of Guantánamo Bay, and in the city of Guantánamo, north of the base. Meeting the needs of U.S. service personnel became the principal economic activity of both cities. Hundreds of dependents of base personnel established residence in the city of Guantánamo, and North American ways took a firm hold. In 1958 the *Times of Havana* declared that Guantánamo was "the most Americanized city in the whole of Cuba" (Pérez 1999, 239).

By the early 1950s, about 2,000 residents of the city of Guantánamo worked on the base as carpenters, mechanics, electricians, plumbers, painters, welders, truck drivers, gardeners, seamstresses, cooks, and maids. The base generated a Cuban payroll of almost $4 million annually (Pérez 1999, 241–42). Among the 7,000 Cuban residents of Caimanera there were also hustlers, gamblers, pimps, and bootleggers, as well as a community of retired naval personnel who remained to operate bars and cafés.

An average of 2,000 to 3,000 servicemen visited Caimanera weekly and frequented the gambling houses, casinos, bars, and brothels. George Wally wrote, "Caimanera is the Barbary Coast of Cuba, where American sailors on pass from only across the bay . . . stay overnight to make whoopee in sailor fashion" (Wally 1946, 40). Rear Admiral Gene LaRocque, who first visited Guantánamo Bay in 1940 aboard the USS *Arkansas*, put it more bluntly, stating that Caimanera was "a place all the sailors wanted to visit. It was a giant whorehouse . . . and all the sailors took advantage of it" (McCoy 1995, 95).

The Cuban Revolution and Guantánamo

Fidel Castro and his revolutionaries began operations in the Sierra Maestra, just west of Guantánamo Bay, in 1956, and on several occasions the base itself figured prominently in the conflict. The 1903 treaty between the United States and Cuba clearly stated that "no material, merchandise, or munitions are to be transported into Cuban territory" (Mason 1984, 148). However, the United States had violated the agreement in 1952 by supplying Batista with munitions from the base (Mason 1984, 14). In 1958 Raúl Castro accused the United States of once again using the base to supply fuel and ammunition to Batista's planes. Photographs taken on the base landing strips while planes took on those supplies were published in the U.S. press and in newspapers in other parts of the world as irrefutable proof of the support that the United States was giving to the Batista regime (Ricardo 1994, 24).

On June 27, 1958, Raúl Castro retaliated by detaining forty-nine sailors and marines who were returning to the base from liberty on the island. Fidel Castro deftly used the detention as a way to affirm his own leadership, placate the United States, and demonstrate his support for his brother. On July 18 Fidel noted that his brother had been unable to contact him in advance since Raúl's forces had no access to radio transmitters. Then Fidel grandly announced that "despite all this, today I am publicly ordering [the sailors' and marines'] release. . . . I believe that these North American citizens cannot be blamed for the shipment of bombs to Batista by the government of their country" (Szulc 1986, 450). Although the existence of a U.S. base on Cuban soil was an affront and antithetical to Castro's vision for the revolution, he did not want to provoke the ire of the United States, and the release of the U.S. soldiers reflected a pragmatic and politically skillful move. After the kidnapping incident, the U.S. military declared Cuban territory off limits to personnel on leave, and the marines increased their posts along the fence line and refined their security procedures (Mason 1984, 14).

Fidel Castro again showed his ability to deflect U.S. concerns about his intentions regarding the base later in the month. As the rebel force gained ground, Batista removed Cuban army guards protecting the aqueduct that was the only source of water for the base. Batista feared that the guards had become "sitting ducks" for rebel attack, and as a result, U.S. Marines were moved into Cuban territory to assume guard duty. Castro immediately responded by issuing a formal declaration stating that "the presence of North American forces

. . . is illegal and constitutes aggression against Cuban national territory," but "we are ready to give guarantees that the water supply will not be interfered with because our objective is not to attack that facility" (Szulc 1986, 450). Castro's carefully crafted statement both asserted Cuba's sovereignty and at the same time assured the United States that rebel forces posed no threat to the operations of the base.

Cubans who worked on the base posed yet another problem for the United States during the conflict. In response to Castro's numerous radio pleas for support, many Cuban workers on the base began smuggling fuel, bullets, spare parts, blankets, shoes, food, and first-aid kits right through the base gate (McCoy 1995, 202). They managed to do so for the most part by plying the U.S. soldiers with rum, and once the soldiers became drunk, the Cubans made off with the goods. Cubans who commuted to the base via car or truck emptied their gas tanks each morning into storage vats and refilled them on the base each night before departure (Cruz Díaz 1977, 130; Dougherty and Bahía 1990, 85).

The gates between the base and Cuba were permanently closed to U.S. service personnel and civilians on January 1, 1959, the day of Castro's triumph. On January 2 Castro made his first speech from a balcony in Santiago and announced, "This time it will not be like 1898, when the North Americans came and made themselves masters of our country. This time, fortunately, the Revolution will truly come to power" (Gott 2004, 165). In the United States, Assistant Secretary of State for Inter-American Affairs Roy Rubottom expressed grave doubts about Castro's motivations and worried about U.S. interests on the island, especially with regard to the U.S. naval base. Ambassador Peter Bonsal believed that the treaty would hold in spite of the tensions, but he advised the development of a plan for the base that would give Cuba a role in its operations (McCoy 1995, 205).

In the months that followed, tensions between Havana and Washington increased as Castro accused the United States of trying to undermine his government while condemning the North American presence at the base (Mason 1984, 15). Cubans who continued to work at the base found themselves caught in the middle. Family members and friends accused them of being too friendly with the Yankees, and the new government enforced a new bank rule that required them to convert their wages from dollars to pesos. Other Cuban workers complained of poor treatment on the base that ranged from insults to being shoved and roughed up by marines. Federico Figueras Larrazábal, general secretary of the Cuban workers' union on the base, was fired for stating that the United States was looking for an excuse "again to enslave" the island and for making "unfounded statements and charges" on the radio and in newspapers (McCoy 1995, 210).

U.S. officials also viewed with suspicion the sweeping social changes that were taking place on the island, as well as the Castro government's friendly overtures to the Soviet Union. During the 1960 presidential campaign, candidates Kennedy and Nixon both took hard-line public stands on Cuba, and President Eisenhower issued a press release on November 1 in which he reaffirmed U.S. rights to the base and stated that "because of its importance to the defense of the entire hemisphere, particularly in the light of intimate relations which now exist between the present Government of Cuba and the Sino-Soviet bloc, it is essential that our position in Guantánamo be clearly understood" (McCoy 1995, 225). Finally, on January 3, 1961, the United States broke off diplomatic relations with the Castro government, and the Central Intelligence Agency (CIA) refined plans for an exile invasion of the island.

The CIA-orchestrated Bay of Pigs invasion on April 17, 1961, was a disaster for the Cuban exiles and the United States, and soon rumors spread of Castro's plans for retaliation against the base at Guantánamo (Mason 1984, 16). Castro, however, made no threatening moves and instead ordered that a large number of Nopalea cactus plants with particularly prickly spines be planted along eight miles of the base's fence line (Mason 1984, 16). The creation of a "cactus curtain" served to discourage Cubans from fleeing to Guantánamo, which by 1961 had become a common occurrence. Under terms of the base's lease, the United States was obliged to return all fugitives; however, no such returns took place, because the United States would neither confirm nor deny the existence of any such refugees on the base (Coe 1995, 270).

In *Guantánamo: The Bay of Discord*, Roger Ricardo (1994, 26) claims that between 1959 and 1962, before a more effective system of vigilance and defense was established on the border, the U.S. military enclave became an important center of counterrevolutionary operations directed by the CIA through the Naval Intelligence Service. Liaison agents were sent out from the base to meet with the counterrevolutionary organizations that operated in some parts of Cuban territory. Weapons and other supplies for insurrectional groups and means for sabotaging the economy were sent from Guantánamo into the eastern part of the country. Meanwhile, the CIA hatched plans for assassinating leaders of the revolution.

When Castro became convinced that the United States was planning to attempt another invasion, he appealed to the Soviet Union for protection, and the secret installation of Soviet missiles in Cuba led to the missile crisis of October 1962 (Beschloss 1991, 362). During the crisis, the Cubans stepped up patrols along their side of the fence at Guantánamo and tightened procedures for the Cuban employees of the base to pass to the other side. Each morning and night, workers were searched as they walked between a set of parallel wire fences that became known as the cattle chute. In response, the United States placed a 735-acre minefield on its side of the base, thereby creating the largest U.S. minefield in the world. In the years after the crisis, an average of 137 Cuban "fence-jumpers" annually risked death to reach the "paradise" promised by radio and television stations broadcasting from the base (Baker 1997, 656).

In April 1963 it was revealed that the Pentagon had requested $18 million to expand navy facilities in Puerto Rico, and rumors soon spread that the United States was planning to abandon Guantánamo. Almost concurrently, Jack Anderson wrote a column in the *Washington Post* in which he exposed a two-year-old cover-up related to the 1961 murder of Rubén López Sabariego, a Cuban worker at Guantánamo suspected of being a spy (McCoy 1995, 261). Shortly after the incident occurred in 1961, the Cuban government had sent the United States a note informing U.S. officials that the mutilated and beaten body of López Sabariego had been unearthed in a shallow grave at Guantánamo. The Cuban government, as stipulated by Article IV of the treaty, demanded that the participants in the murder be delivered up by U.S. authorities. In the tense days of 1961, the United States acknowledged the death but refused any explanation and likewise refused to turn over any U.S. personnel to Cuban authorities.

Jack Anderson's revelations, coupled with the rumors about abandoning the base, kept Washington abuzz. Senator Gordon Allott (R-Colo.) went so far as to call for the United States to establish a provisional government at Guantánamo and to continue to train free Cubans into armed forces, thus converting Guantánamo into a base of operations for overthrowing Castro. Allott's suggestion drew a blistering response from Senator Frank Church (D-Idaho). Church noted that many of the exile leaders who would form the provisional government represented a "few families who owned or controlled nearly all of the land and wealth of Cuba. Those men were not likely to be greeted on the shores of Cuba as liberators, but, rather as those who would reinstate the plantation-and-peon economy that existed in Cuba under the Batista regime."[6]

The debate about establishing a provisional government on the base carried on throughout the summer, and by October Castro weighed in as well. He announced that given U.S. hostility toward his government, Cuba would not sign the Nuclear Test Ban Treaty unless the United States prohibited nuclear weapons in the Panama Canal Zone, Puerto Rico, and all U.S. bases in the Western Hemisphere outside the U.S. mainland. Moreover, the United States must relinquish the base at Guantánamo, a source of spies and saboteurs (McCoy 1995, 274).

The 1964 Water Crisis

The Cuban threat not to sign the Nuclear Test Ban Treaty and the U.S. threat to establish a U.S.-backed provisional government on Guantánamo Bay were contentious and serious issues, yet ironically it was water that led to a real crisis on the base. Ever since its establishment, the primary drawback to Guantánamo had been its lack of access to fresh water. In 1934 the navy contracted an agreement with the Cuban government for permission to extract water from the Yateras River, ten miles north of the base, and five years later the water began flowing into two treatment plants on the base. The U.S. government paid a monthly rate of about $14,000 and received about 2.5 million gallons per day (Mason 1984, 19).

The water supply to the base remained secure from 1934 until February 6, 1964, when the Cuban foreign minister Raúl Roa informed the Swiss embassy in Havana that the Revolutionary Council of Cuba had decided to cut off the supply of water to the naval base until the United States released twenty-nine Cuban fishermen who had been seized by the U.S. Navy four days earlier for fishing illegally in U.S. territorial waters (McCoy 1995, 281).

Navy planes had spotted four Cuban fishing trawlers off the Dry Tortugas Islands seventy miles from Key West. The Cubans claimed that they had been blown off course and that they were unaware that they had entered into the U.S. three-mile limit. The Cubans were handed over to state authorities in Florida and jailed under a law passed in 1963 that prohibited fishing in Florida waters without a license and that denied licenses for citizens of Communist countries (McCoy 1995, 280).

Castro had cut off the water in protest of what he believed to be an illegal arrest and jailing of Cuban nationals. U.S. officials, however, became convinced that Castro was using the trivial incident of the arrest as an excuse to reopen the question as to the legality of the base treaty. Meanwhile, President Johnson responded to the water crisis by ordering the base to become as self-sufficient as possible, and over $10 million was spent to disassemble and transport a desalination plant and to reassemble it at Guantánamo (Mason 1984, 19–20). Additionally, Cuban workers were told that they could work on the base hereafter only if they went into exile and lived permanently on the base. Seventy-five decided to remain.

Throughout this period and afterward, both Cuban and U.S. soldiers complained about provocative fence-line incidents. The U.S. side accused the Cubans of throwing rocks and using slingshots against them, while Cuban complaints against the United States were even more serious. U.S. Marines shot and killed two Cuban border guards, one in 1964 and one in 1966. Other acts of aggression against Cuban sentry boxes resulted in the wounding of two Cuban guards (Ricardo 1994, 25). In response, the Cuban sentry boxes were moved farther back from the dividing line.

Throughout the 1970s there was a gradual lessening of tensions between the governments of the United States and Cuba. The 1977 debate over the Panama Canal Treaty raised questions about the future status of Guantánamo, and Secretary of the Navy W. Graham Claytor Jr. proposed closing the base. Although Claytor's recommendation was ultimately reversed, the base was consolidated and there was an overall reduction in personnel by some 30 percent (Mason 1984, 31).

As the 1980s began, however, tensions between the two governments increased yet again as the Cold War reheated between the United States and the Soviet Union. The Reagan administration considered the guerrilla movements in Central America to be Communist inspired and linked to Soviet and Cuban interference. Secretary of State Alexander Haig noted in February 1981 that the guerrilla resistance in El Salvador was an effort that involved "close coordination by Moscow, satellite capitals and Havana, with the cooperation of Hanoi and Managua" (Smith 2000, 179).

According to President Reagan, the Cuban-Soviet threat was not limited to Central America, and he pointed to another Cuban-Soviet threat in the tiny Caribbean country of Grenada. In a television address to the nation on March 24, 1983, President Reagan displayed reconnaissance photographs of increased Russian activity in Cuba. He also showed another aerial photograph of a military airfield in western Cuba and referred to the Soviet-Cuban militarization of Grenada as "a power projection into the region through which much more than half of all American oil imports now pass" (Mason 1984, 26–27). Less than seven months after Reagan's address to the American people, U.S. Marines invaded Grenada, and some sixty Cubans were captured or killed. The Cuban government responded to the hostilities by spreading its own haphazard mine-fields on the Cuban side of the fence surrounding the base at Guantánamo.[7]

In 1984 the Defense Department announced that it planned on spending $43.4 million to improve the base, the greatest investment since World War II. Some journalists who participated in a rare visit to the base reported that the United States would not receive a worthwhile return on the investment. They tagged the base a "28,000-acre amusement park" and a "paradise for alcoholics and sports lovers among the Navy's lifers" (Mason 1984, 32).

For the remainder of the decade, relations were frozen between Washington and Havana, as the U.S. government continued to accuse the Cuban government of supporting leftist insurgencies in El Salvador and Nicaragua. At the same time, dissent began sweeping through the Soviet Union and Eastern Europe. By the end of the decade, Cuba suddenly found itself adrift, a lone socialist island in a capitalist sea (Baker 1996, 57).

The U.S. Naval Base in the 1990s

As the 1990s began, Cuba faced a massive security dilemma. It no longer could depend on support from the Soviet Union, and fears of a U.S. invasion of the island resurfaced. In an interview published in the April 15, 1991, issue of *Navy Times*, General Colin Powell, chairman of the Joint Chiefs of Staff, said, "I am running out of villains. I'm down to Castro and Kim Il Sung" (Ricardo 1994, 35). As the highest-ranking military officer to ever visit the Guantánamo Naval Base, he was even more explicit upon his arrival at the base. On that occasion, Powell said that danger still existed in the world, which was why the United States had 1,700 young men and women stationed on the base and why they had a mission to fulfill (Ricardo 1994, 35). In a similar vein, Admiral Leon A. Edney, chief of the Atlantic Command, stated on March 4, 1992, that Cuba posed the greatest threat to the security of the United States in the Atlantic. He emphasized that his command was keeping close tabs on the situation and was preparing to meet any eventuality (Ricardo 1994, 36).

A few days later, on March 8, 1992, an article appeared in the *New York Times* that revealed the main contents of a draft for a broad new policy statement on the U.S. mission in the post–Cold War era. The classified document, supervised by Undersecretary for Policy Paul D. Wolfowitz, warned of an impending internal crisis in Cuba. This period of crisis implied new challenges for the United States that would require a contingency plan for handling everything from a massive exodus of Cubans to the United States, to a military provocation by Cuba, to a war on the island. The United States must be prepared for "irrational acts from Cuba."[8]

Others in the George H. W. Bush administration, however, wanted to avoid an accidental or avoidable turn toward a military confrontation. Specific measures were discussed within the administration but were put on hold as the 1992 presidential election approached. Their implementation, for the most part, would begin in 1993 under the new administration of Bill Clinton (Domínguez 1997, 67).

Starting in 1993, when U.S. forces were scheduled to engage in a military exercise around the base at Guantánamo, the U.S. base commander began to give advance notification to his counterpart on the Cuban side, communicating some aspect of the exercise that the Cubans would have typically observed anyway. The information was operationally useless to the Cuban forces, but the procedure opened a communication channel that would expand and become useful in time. Cuba's Revolutionary Armed Forces responded in kind, providing the U.S. command at Guantánamo advance notification of their live-ammunition exercises (Domínguez 1997, 67). In other words, the symbolic notifications became a courteous type of tit for tat.

Flight safety was another area of U.S. concern. The runway approaches for the base had become difficult for U.S. pilots as more modern and demanding aircraft began using the facility. In 1994 the United States asked Cuba for a changed route into the airfield. The changes were granted a short time afterward, even though they required an increase in the Cuban airspace required by U.S. aircraft to approach the base. Later, the United States asked for even further changes, and these were also granted. The two armed forces appeared to be able to cooperate relatively easily on practical military matters, despite the poor overall state of relations between the countries (Klepak 2000, 20–21).

As part of the 1994 migration crisis, U.S. and Cuban military authorities developed a constructive relationship in order to deal with the complexities related to housing 30,000 refugees on the base. Meetings were held every four to six weeks between high-ranking Cuban and U.S. military authorities to deal with practical matters and to make certain there were no misunderstandings. The meetings continued even after the crisis subsided (Domínguez 1997, 69).

When a video of a December 1995 meeting between General John Sheehan, the U.S. Atlantic Command's commander, and Cuban general Carlos Pérez Pérez was shown on local television in Miami, parts of the Cuban American community were aghast. "It is shocking to observe top U.S. officials of an institution dedicated to defending our freedom fraternizing with the military leader of a regime which is a sworn enemy of the United States," fumed Representative Ileana Ros-Lehtinen (R-Fla.).[9]

A State Department source countered:

The Cuban government is not going to disappear. It's going to be there after Castro. It might well be the [next Cuban] government. . . . We don't want them [the Cubans] making a mistake and shooting at our guys, or us making a mistake and shooting at their guys, because of a plane taking off the wrong way, or a helicopter over the minefields—or a Cuban or U.S. patrol trying to rescue somebody risking death among the mines. Is that unreasonable? To me, it's eminently sensible.[10]

After General Sheehan's retirement in 1997, he maintained his contacts with Cuban officials. In March 1998 he toured the island and later urged the Clinton administration to "regularize contacts" between Cuban and American military chiefs.[11] During the visit, Sheehan traveled to eastern Cuba with Raúl Castro and noted, contrary to some accounts that claimed that the younger Castro did not inspire loyalty among the troops, "There clearly is an affection for him. . . . You can see the admiration in the young kids' eyes."[12] Sheehan's dovish stance toward Cuba was not that surprising given that the Defense Department wanted to avoid being drawn into a Cuban civil war or an eventual occupation of the island. Many U.S. military officers were uncomfortable with a U.S. policy that in some way was predicated on provoking a popular uprising or economic ruin.[13]

During the Kosovo crisis in April 1999, the United States once again considered using the base at Guantánamo as a refugee center. On April 6, 1999, White House spokesman Joe Lockhart stated that the United States had informed Cuba of its plans.[14] At first the Cuban foreign ministry remained silent, but then in a surprising gesture of cooperation, it signaled agreement to the plan to house the refugees at Guantánamo.[15] The main points of the statement were reiterated by Foreign Minister Roberto Robaina. He condemned NATO's military campaign against Yugoslavia but said that Cuba supported all humanitarian assistance for victims of the conflict.

Another Cuban government statement on January 11, 2002, explained:

The government of the United States of America, in accordance with previous commitments, made the decision to use the military base to shelter a number of them [Kosovars]. Such decisions are always made unilaterally; our views were never previously asked; and, we were never informed. However, on that occasion, for the first time, we were informed of the decision and the rational [sic] behind it. We then gave a constructive response.[16]

The Cuban government reciprocated the cooperative gesture that the United States had made of informing the Cubans prior to taking action by offering "to provide medical care or any other services that might be required."[17]

In June 1999 the United States completed the unilateral removal of the U.S. minefield that protected the base from Castro's troops. President Clinton had issued the order on May 16, 1996, with a triple purpose. First, the removal was a symbolic gesture to the international community after the United States had refused to sign the global treaty prohibiting the use of antipersonnel mines, since national security experts had argued that land mines were critical to peacekeeping between North Korea and South Korea.[18] Another purpose in removing the mines was to send a signal to Castro. General Sheehan explained: "How do you demonstrate to the Cubans that it is a different world? Taking away the minefield is one of them."[19] A third reason concerned the risk factor if the current trickle of refugees ever turned into a flood. "How would you channel them to safety?" asked Bob Cowles, a Pentagon official in charge of removing the mines. "Clearly, the humanitarian dimension was a major part of the president's decision."[20]

Ironically, over the years, more Americans than Cubans had been casualties of the U.S. minefield, according to official U.S. records. The marines lost thirteen members of crews who did regular replacement of old land mines. In fact, the job was so dangerous that the troops had their Social Security numbers tattooed in their armpits for posthumous identification. Five sailors died in 1964 when they accidentally wandered into the area. In addition, five Cuban asylum seekers lost their lives trying to cross to the U.S. side.[21]

Although the United States wanted the good public relations from announcing the removal of the land mines, officials did not do so, fearing that more Cubans might become emboldened to try and reach the base and ask for political asylum. Given that the Cuban side still retained its own minefield, Colonel Vincent Ogilvie, the spokesman for the Pentagon's Miami-based Southern Command, noted, "We don't now want to broadcast that it is fair game to run across the field." Ogilvie predicted that the topic of Cubans trying to sneak through the minefields would be discussed during the periodic talks between Cuban and U.S. military commanders at the naval base's border.[22] After forty years of tensions surrounding the Guantánamo Naval Base, the decade of the 1990s drew to a close on a note of cooperation.

Getting along at Gitmo

U.S. military officials such as General John Sheehan became increasingly concerned in the 1990s that the politics surrounding U.S.-Cuban relations were counterproductive and actually undermining U.S. national security. In fact, the U.S. Defense Department feared being drawn into a Cuban civil war or an occupation of the island. Many U.S. military officers were concerned that U.S. policies might actually provoke a popular uprising or an economic catastrophe, which in turn would lead to a massive exodus from the island or a serious military conflict. With these concerns at the fore, the U.S. commanding officer at Guantánamo Naval Base initiated efforts to open communications channels and to meet periodically with Cuban officers in order to avoid conflict. These measures were welcomed by the Cubans and similarly reciprocated.

At the U.S. Naval Station at Guantánamo Bay, U.S. and Cuban forces exist in close proximity—two unfriendly neighbors peering across the fence at each other. As a result, issues relating to the base and its operations reflect the highest of high politics. U.S. soldiers stand ready to protect the base from possible attack by Cuban forces. At the same time, the Cuban military has experienced the threat of a hostile foreign presence on the island for over forty years.

Throughout the 1990s efforts were made at reducing the tensions around the base. First, the U.S. base command began to give advance notification to the Cubans of some aspect of U.S. military exercises, and Cuba's Revolutionary Armed Forces then responded in kind by providing the U.S. command advance notification of their own live-ammunition exercises. Second, the United States asked Cuba for a changed route into the airfield in order to improve flight safety since the more modern U.S. airplanes needed more room to maneuver. The changes were granted a short time afterward, even though they required an increase in the Cuban airspace used by U.S. aircraft approaching the base. Third, regular meetings between the base commander and Cuban officers initiated during the rafter crisis of 1994 also served to reduce tensions, since the Cubans were informed as to operations on the base related to the housing of refugees. Furthermore, when U.S. spokesperson Joe Lockhart gave advance notification to the Cuban government that the United States was planning to house Kosovar refugees on the base, the Cuban government responded positively by offering medical assistance. Another important political outcome in 1999 was the U.S. removal of its minefield around the base. The decision was unilateral but sent Castro the message that the United States was interested in reducing tensions.

In sum, all of the above interactions can best be described as confidence-building measures (CBMs), because they were incremental and limited in their scope. Quiet diplomacy was essential in order to avoid a political backlash from the Cuban American community. Although the decade ended without any formalized political agreements between the United States and Cuba regarding the base, the U.S. decision to remove its minefield was a strong indicator that the United States wanted to reduce tensions and avoid conflict. Given the long and contentious history surrounding the base, these small steps at U.S.-Cuban cooperation were remarkable achievements. However, the events following September 11, 2001, would soon place the base on the forefront of the war on terror.

The George W. Bush Administration and Guantánamo Naval Base

On January 10, 2002, the U.S. government began to transfer captured illegal combatants of al-Qaida and the Taliban to the U.S. Naval Station at Guantánamo Bay. Since the Cuban government had protested U.S. occupation of its sovereign soil for decades, many observers expected to hear Fidel Castro express both his strong opposition and nationalist outrage. As recently as 2000 there had been vociferous protests and massive mobilizations during which the Cuban leadership had rallied in support of the release of the young shipwreck survivor Elián González after his Florida relatives had refused to return him to his father in Cuba. Wasn't the transfer of alleged foreign terrorists to Cuba an even greater affront to all Cubans? After all, the U.S. government did not want dangerous combatants on U.S. sovereign territory, and Defense Secretary Donald Rumsfeld had ruefully admitted as much when he stated that Guantánamo was "the least worst place."

On January 12 *Granma* ran a front-page official declaration outlining the government's position, which lacked the stinging invective usually featured in statements about U.S. policy.[23] The declaration instead offered a brief history of the base's existence and its changing role in U.S.-Cuban relations, including its most recent usage as an emergency refugee camp and detention center during the Haitian and Cuban rafter crisis. The tone was both moderated and subdued and claimed that the hostilities that once characterized U.S.-Cuban discussions about the base had since given way to "a climate of mutual respect" on both sides of Guantánamo's fences. In short, Cuba would not object to U.S. plans to hold suspected terrorists there: "We will not create any obstacles to the development of the [U.S. military] operation, though the transfer of prisoners of war by the U.S. government to the base—located on a space in our territory upon which we have been deprived of any jurisdiction—was not part of the agreement that the base was founded upon."[24]

The government's statement went beyond the initial expressions of compliance by offering medical assistance and a promise to maintain the sanitary conditions of the areas surrounding the base: "Should it become necessary, we're willing to cooperate with any medical assistance, and pledge to maintain the sanitary conditions in the areas surrounding the base under our control against plagues and diseases, in addition to any other useful, constructive, and humanitarian way possible."[25]

On January 19 Raúl Castro, head of the Cuban armed forces, hosted a press conference overlooking the U.S. base. He reiterated most of what was contained in the declaration and added a promise that Cuba would immediately return to U.S. custody any prisoners who might escape from the base. He also emphasized that Cuba was confident in the tight security at Guantánamo. After all, the base was surrounded by armed soldiers of both countries, a Cuban minefield, and the "cactus curtain."

This cooperative tone was all the more surprising considering that Cuba had designated 2002 "The Year of the Heroes Held Prisoner by the Empire." In late 2001, after a six-month trial in a Miami federal courtroom, a group of five Cuban agents were convicted of spearheading a spy ring known as the "Wasp Network."[26] The five agents allegedly had been sent in the mid-1990s to infiltrate U.S.-based Cuban exile groups, such as the Cuban American National Foundation (CANF) and Brothers to the Rescue.

There are two interpretations as to why the Castro regime did not criticize the transfer of the prisoners to the base. U.S. diplomats in Havana interpreted Castro's gestures as a calculated response to the Bush administration that had recently filled its key Latin American policy posts with hard-line anti-Castro officials like Otto Reich, Elliot Abrams, and John Negroponte. Vicki Huddleston, principal officer of the U.S. Interests Section, was dismissive of Castro's cooperation, saying, "It's all a façade. It's all cosmetic. Castro is very clever. And his number one goal is staying in power."[27]

On the other hand, the Cuban interpretation of Castro's motives pointed directly to the CBMs that had been put into place on Guantánamo during the 1990s. Felipe Pérez Roque, the Cuban foreign minister, noted that the collaboration reflected the fact that the base had been transformed in recent years from hostile territory to a symbol of détente. "We hope that one day the relations on all official matters can be handled with the respect and collaboration that is happening at Guantánamo," Pérez Roque said, and he noted that U.S. officials had advised Cuba in advance about the prisoner flights and that they had discussed issues of security around the base.[28]

In spite of its harsh rhetoric to the contrary, the Bush administration continued to contact and coordinate with the Cuban government. Shortly after the arrival of the prisoners, U.S. medical officers met with Cuban doctors to reassure the Cubans that the prisoners were not reintroducing malaria to the island, which had been free from the disease for fifty years.[29] The Cubans also discussed their efforts to control dengue fever, which had been detected in nearby Santiago Province. The medical discussions were part of the regular, monthly "fence-line" that had been held since 1995 just across the northeast gate on Cuban territory.

Since malaria and dengue fever posed a potentially dangerous threat to U.S. military personnel, their families, and the general Cuban population, it would seem unlikely that anyone could possibly object to communication between Cuban and U.S. authorities. In fact, the officials at Guantánamo had not publicly reported the exchange. They were forced to brief reporters only after Representative Ileana Ros-Lehtinen made a formal inquiry expressing her concern about increasing medical contacts between Cuba and the United States.[30] The inquiry by Ros-Lehtinen serves to illustrate clearly how Cuban exile politics continues to be a formidable obstacle to establishing CBMs between the United States and Cuba, and even the threat of tropical diseases spreading to or from Guantánamo Naval Base has not lessened the anti-Castro fever of hard-line Cuban American politicians.

U.S.-Cuban Cooperative Efforts
at Reducing the Threat of Accidental War

Forty-six years have passed since the triumph of Castro's revolution, yet continuing tensions and the possibility of armed conflict between the United States and Cuba remain serious concerns for policy makers in both countries. Both sides point to the other as the provocateur. The United States throughout the decades has been deeply suspicious of Cuba's foreign policy in support of "wars of national liberation" in Latin America and other parts of the Third World (Blight and Kornbluh 1998, 63). In the early years of the Castro regime, Ché Guevara articulated Cuban foreign policy and boldly called for the creation of "two, three Vietnams" in order to confront and weaken the United States and its allies (Domínguez 1997, 49). The reference to Vietnam certainly reverberated among U.S. officials.

From its perspective, the Cuban government bristled at U.S. attempts over the years to incite counterrevolution and the overthrow of Castro. Indeed, during the Cuban missile crisis in October 1962, the escalating hostilities between the United States, the Soviet Union, and Cuba nearly erupted into World War III. Although the thirteen days of the Cuban missile crisis marked the highest level of tensions between the United States and Cuba, in the decades since there have been numerous other hostile incidents. Domínguez argues that after the end of the Cold War, U.S.-Cuban relations evolved into an even colder war, and he notes that, after reviewing the history of U.S.-Cuban relations, it is difficult to understand why a major military clash between the two has not occurred already (Domínguez 1997, 65). However, there has not been a major clash, and this chapter offers evidence of cooperation between the United States and Cuba that helps to explain why the colder war between the two countries has not erupted into a hot war.

The chapter begins with a synopsis of U.S. anti-Castro activities from 1959 to the demise of the Soviet Union. Although the United States never attempted an invasion of Cuba after 1961, it never abandoned its efforts to destabilize the

Cuban government either. In fact, various government agencies subsequently orchestrated numerous assassination attempts against Castro and funded his enemies both inside and outside Cuba.

The second section traces Cuba's internationalist foreign policy toward the Third World during the same period. Cuba's revolutionary vision, always hostile to the U.S. government, was at the heart of both its domestic and foreign policies. Once the revolution was secured at home, the Castro government attempted "to make a world safe for its revolution" (Domínguez 1989, 6). As part of this goal, Cuba gave high priority to its support for other revolutionary governments in the Third World and often committed its own troops in order to strengthen other regimes and movements. However, once the Soviet Union collapsed, Cuba was forced to reevaluate its foreign policy goals and to refocus attention on an economy that would no longer receive subsidies from its former patron.

The decade of the 1990s became a roller coaster in terms of ups and downs with regard to U.S.-Cuban cooperation at reducing the risk of accidental war. Because of the numerous twists and turns, it is helpful to divide the decade into two periods. Section three therefore covers the first half of the decade, a five-year period that began with escalating threats but ended in cooperation and the signing of the immigration accords of 1994–1995. As a result of the momentous transformations in the Communist world, hard-line Cuban exile groups in the United States felt certain that the Castro regime would be the next domino to fall. In order to hasten Castro's defeat, these influential groups successfully lobbied the U.S. government to increase economic pressure on Cuba and to further tighten the trade embargo. The severely stressed Cuban economy caused major deprivations on the island, but the Castro regime did not collapse. As the economic crisis deepened, scores of desperate Cubans took to the high seas in small, makeshift rafts, and policy makers in the United States began to focus on how to avoid another Mariel migration crisis. In order to stem the rising flood of refugees, the U.S. government decided to cooperate with the Cuban government to create the migration agreements of 1994–1995, which drastically altered U.S. immigration policy toward Cuba. By 1995, it appeared that the United States was embarking upon a new post–Cold War Cuban policy that would treat Cuban migrants in much the same way as migrants from other countries.

Section four begins by describing how the cooperation between the United

States and Cuba on the migration issue was met with a strong Cuban American backlash in the United States. Not surprisingly, many Cuban Americans did not approve of the new agreements, which undermined the welcoming embrace that Cuban migrants intercepted on the high seas had received after Castro's revolution in 1959. Brothers to the Rescue and the Democracy Movement, two Cuban American organizations established during the rafter crisis, were radicalized by this change in U.S.-Cuban relations, and they began to pursue their own political agenda of provoking confrontation with the Castro regime by flying into Cuban airspace or sailing into Cuban territorial waters. Both groups maintained close ties to dissident groups on the island, and Castro viewed their behavior as an illegal intervention in Cuban domestic affairs.

On February 24, 1996, an unfortunate confrontation occurred when Cuban forces shot down two Brothers planes off the coast of Cuba. Tensions between the United States and Cuba returned to high levels as the two countries argued whether the planes had been flying in international or Cuban air space. The tragedy increased pressure for retaliatory measures, and President Clinton responded by signing into law the controversial Helms-Burton Act. The backlash continued into 1997, when Senator Bob Graham (D-Fla.) attached an amendment to a defense appropriations bill. The Graham amendment declared Cuba to be an enemy of the United States and required the Pentagon to produce a report explaining the level of threat posed by the Castro government.

During this same period, many U.S. military officers and White House officials came to view hard-line Cuban exile groups as loose cannons, whose stepped-up anti-Castro activities increasingly threatened to drag the United States and Cuba into an unwanted armed conflict. These officials believed that conflict with Cuba was not in the national interest of the United States, given the changes in the post–Cold War world. Accordingly, in 1998 the Pentagon published a report stating that Cuba no longer posed a military threat to the United States. The two governments moved quietly to restore cooperative efforts in order to better monitor the provocative activities of Cuban exile organizations, because both governments worried that the exiles might cause yet another unwanted confrontation. In section four, the two countries' joint efforts to reduce the likelihood of accidental war are subsequently examined, and the chapter closes with a review of the stance of the Bush administration regarding reducing the threat of accidental war.

U.S. Anti-Castro Activities, 1959–1990

As early as January 1960 the Central Intelligence Agency (CIA) undertook measures to destabilize the revolution and to eliminate Castro and other important Cuban leaders. CIA planes from Florida attacked and burned sugarcane fields in Pinar del Río and Camagüey (Baker 1997, 44). The agency also began providing arms, money, transportation, and supplies to anti-Castro rebels operating in the Escambray Sierra and elsewhere in Cuba (Matthews 1989, 332). In its desperation to bring down Castro, the CIA considered a number of schemes that now seem harebrained and unprofessional. One idea under serious consideration in 1960 involved impregnating cigars with a depilatory that would make Castro's body hair and beard fall out. Another plot involved the idea of contracting the Mafia to have Joe Bonano assassinate Castro (Gup 2000, 115–16). Most ominously, in March 1960 President Eisenhower authorized the CIA to begin planning an invasion to bring about Castro's removal.[1] Eisenhower explained his decision to British prime minister Harold Macmillan by noting that Castro had carried out "a precipitate revolution against the existing social order, and is far more internationalist in his pretensions to spread his revolution to surrounding countries than the usual type of nationalist whom the Communists court" (Gaddis 1997, 182). Soon after, the CIA set up exile training camps in Guatemala, where the CIA had overthrown the leftist government of Jacobo Arbenz in 1954. Tensions between Havana and Washington increased over the next several months once the U.S. canceled the sugar quota and after Texaco, Shell, and Standard Oil refused to refine Soviet crude petroleum and the Cuban government responded by confiscating their holdings (Pérez-Stable 1999, 80). A few days before leaving office, President Eisenhower severed U.S. diplomatic relations with the Castro government.

President-elect Kennedy had campaigned hard on the Cuban issue and in so doing had ostensibly committed himself to helping the exiles and domestic Cuban opposition in overthrowing Castro. At the Musgrove Conference on the Bay of Pigs in spring 1996, Arthur Schlesinger recalled that Kennedy thought that Castro was the prize exhibit in Khrushchev's threatening vision of wars of national liberation, even though the Soviet Union had not, to any serious extent, committed itself to Castro (Kornbluh 1998, 64). Even so, Kennedy inherited the existing invasion plan from the previous administration and was trapped into following through with it for two important reasons. First, when briefing the young new president about the invasion plan, CIA director

Allen Dulles repeatedly focused on the "disposal problem," since cancellation of the venture would result in the dispersal of 1,200 exiles in training throughout all of Latin America. In other words, the exiles would most certainly spread the word around the continent that the United States had softened its policy toward Castro. Dulles maintained and Kennedy understood that a poor disposal of the existing plan would be a serious blow to the balance of force in the hemisphere.

Kennedy also implicitly understood the domestic implications of canceling an invasion plan that had been previously approved by Eisenhower, the general who had commanded the largest successful amphibious landing in history. Kennedy knew that he would be portrayed by the Right as a lightweight who was "soft" on Communism. From the moment he first learned of the operation, Kennedy decided that it needed to be transformed into a neat little infiltration in which U.S. involvement could be plausibly denied. However, the CIA simply did not believe Kennedy when he said that he would not approve any direct American military involvement. Richard Bissell, the CIA's deputy director for plans, believed that the operation had to succeed no matter what the costs, and if the invasion were ever on the verge of failure, Kennedy would, in fact, reconsider his decision and send in the marines.

The CIA's assessment of Cuba was based in part on its previous successful operation in Guatemala in 1954, which easily removed Arbenz from power, and the agency therefore grossly underestimated Castro's strength and popularity (Blight and Kornbluh 1998, 79). As a result, the size, equipment, and training of the invasion force were inadequate. For the sake of secrecy, the landing site was moved from Trinidad to Playa Girón, a flat, swampy area far removed from the Escambray Mountains, which essentially foreclosed a viable escape route into the mountains. The preinvasion bombing runs conducted by the exiles failed to knock out Castro's air power, and Kennedy, true to his earlier assertions, withheld U.S. air support. The invasion failed miserably, but it convinced Castro of the United States' unrelenting hostility, and that realization drove Castro further into the Soviet camp. Partly to forestall another U.S. invasion, Castro ultimately decided to accept the installation of Soviet missiles on Cuban soil (Welch 2001, 69).

President Kennedy accepted responsibility for the fiasco at the Bay of Pigs, although the CIA's own internal investigation, declassified and released on February 18, 1998, noted that "it is essential to avoid grasping immediately, as many persons have done, at the explanation that the President's order canceling the D-day air strikes was the chief cause of failure." The report also noted that "it is essential to keep in mind the possibility that the invasion was doomed in advance, that an initially successful landing by 1,500 men would eventually have been crushed by Castro's combined military resources strengthened by Soviet Bloc–supplied materiel." Finally, the report underscored that "the fundamental cause of the disaster was the Agency's failure to give the project appropriate organization, staffing throughout by highly qualified personnel, and full-time direction and control of the highest quality" (Kornbluh 1998, 41).

In the aftermath of the defeat, General Maxwell Taylor presented President Kennedy an evaluation of the Bay of Pigs operation. The Taylor Report concluded that coexistence with the Cuban revolution was impossible for the United States and contained an outline for a covert plan named Operation Mongoose (Arboleya 2000, 104). Using methods that in today's language would be referred to as state-sponsored terrorism, the covert operation consisted of at least thirty-three different schemes intended to culminate in Castro's removal, including paramilitary raids, espionage, the counterfeiting of money and ration books, and attacks on oil refineries and farms. As part of the operation, the CIA subsequently contaminated Cuban sugar fields, detonated bombs in department stores, and set factories aflame (Beschloss 1991, 6).

Added to these covert efforts were diplomatic and economic measures that were designed to undermine the Castro government. As the result of U.S. pressures, Cuba's active membership in the Organization of American States (OAS) was suspended at the end of January 1962 (Domínguez 1989, 116), and Kennedy widened the 1960 trade embargo to include foreign products containing Cuban materials. Moreover, U.S. ports were barred to vessels trading with Cuba (Baker 1997, 44). President Kennedy pointed out that an expanded embargo would reduce the capacity of the Castro regime to engage in acts of aggression and subversion or other activities endangering the security of the United States and other nations of the hemisphere.[2]

On March 13, 1962, the Joint Chiefs of Staff provided Secretary of Defense Robert McNamara a top secret document entitled "Justification for U.S. Military Intervention in Cuba." The document, which was declassified in 2001, described U.S. plans to covertly create various pretexts that would justify a U.S. invasion of Cuba. These proposals, referred to as Operation Northwoods, formed the domestic component of Operation Mongoose. Incredibly, the pretexts included staging the assassinations of Cubans living in the United States and developing a fake "Communist Cuban terror campaign in the Miami area, in other Florida cities and even in Washington." Other pretexts considered the sinking of "a boatload of Cuban refugees (real or simulated)," faking a Cuban air force attack on a civilian jetliner, and creating a "Remember the *Maine*" incident by blowing up a U.S. ship in Cuban waters and subsequently blaming the incident on Cuban sabotage. The memorandum further explained that "the desired resultant execution of this plan would be to place the United States in the apparent position of suffering defensible grievances from a rash and ir-responsible government of Cuba and to develop an international image of a Cuban threat to peace in the Western Hemisphere."[3] In the end, McNamara rejected the outrageous proposals, but they clearly demonstrated the frighten-ing extremes to which those in the highest levels of the U.S. government seri-ously considered going in order to oust Castro.

U.S. military maneuvers in the Caribbean during the spring and summer of 1962 also went well beyond the ordinary. McNamara acknowledged that "if I had been a Cuban leader, I think I might have expected a U.S. invasion" (Blight et al. 1993, 41). Based on the precedent of the Bay of Pigs, Soviet premier Khrushchev and Castro both became convinced that the Americans "would try again to organize an aggression against Cuba" (Gaddis 1997, 262). In his memoirs, Khrushchev recalls that he thought that the installation of defensive missiles in Cuba would restrain the United States from precipitous military action against Castro's government (Khrushchev 1971, 547).

The Cuban missile crisis that resulted had a sobering impact on both super-powers, and afterward U.S. policy toward Cuba shifted from further consid-erations of military confrontation to focusing efforts on politically and eco-nomically isolating Castro's regime. As part of these efforts, U.S. citizens were banned from traveling to the island. The ban was ultimately challenged as an infringement on the rights of U.S. citizens to travel freely. The U.S. Supreme Court overturned the travel restraint but ruled that U.S. citizens uphold Trea-sury Department restrictions on spending money in Cuba. The end result was the same, as Americans did not choose to travel to a destination where they were unable to spend U.S. currency. Moreover, in the absence of direct flights, travel to Cuba was difficult and costly. The Castro regime considered all of these measures economic warfare against the island.

Meanwhile, many Cuban exiles now felt betrayed by the Bay of Pigs fiasco and believed that they could no longer count on the U.S. government as a reli-able military ally in their fight against Castro. Some exile paramilitary groups, such as Alpha 66 and Omega 7, resorted to extremist tactics and became actively involved in mounting commando raids against Castro's regime. By the end of the 1960s their strategy changed from planning an invasion to landing small parties that were armed on the island with the hope of sparking guerrilla warfare (Antón and Hernández 2002, 179).

One of the most controversial figures to ever emerge from these exile groups was the former pediatrician Orlando Bosch. Bosch had trained with the CIA, and, according to the U.S. Justice Department, between January 1961 and May 1968 "more than 30 violent acts were either claimed by or attributed to Bosch. These activities included bombings, armed incursions, and aerial attacks against targets in Cuba, Panama, and the United States" (Antón and Hernández 2002, 199). Although arrested by U.S. federal authorities at least five times, Bosch was always acquitted until 1968, when he was finally found guilty of firing a bazooka at a Cuba-bound Polish freighter in the port of Miami. He served four years of a ten-year sentence in federal prison before being released on parole.

Bosch soon fled the United States and began moving from country to country throughout Latin America. In June 1976, while in the Dominican Republic, he founded United Coordination of Revolutionary Organizations (CORU), which acted as an umbrella group for the most militant exile groups that executed anti-Castro terrorist acts on both foreign and U.S. soil. Later in 1976 Bosch was charged in Venezuela (along with Luis Posada Carriles) with masterminding the October 1976 bombing of the Cubana airliner in which seventy-three civilians died, and he spent eleven years in Venezuelan prisons, until he was released under suspicious circumstances in 1987. After his release, Bosch returned to the United States and was subsequently arrested for his earlier parole violation. However, exile groups and prominent Cuban American politicians pressured the Reagan administration to allow Bosch to remain in the United States. When the George H. W. Bush administration granted Bosch a presidential parole in July 1990, the Cuban government was outraged and maintained that the U.S. government only made symbolic gestures at reining in the hard-line exile groups, essentially ignoring most of their terrorist activities (Antón and Hernández 2002, 199).

Over the decades, prosecutions of anti-Castro plotters have been rare indeed, and some ninety Miami-area bombings remain unsolved from as far back as the mid-1960s.[4] The lack of prosecutions for their acts of violence led many militant exiles to believe that they had a free pass from U.S. law enforcement agencies. Exiles who received prison terms were often paroled or released. Most recently, Florida representatives Lincoln Díaz-Balart and Ileana Ros-Lehtinen and Florida governor Jeb Bush wrote letters on behalf of exile militants held in U.S. prisons, and in 2001 several were released, including José Dionisio Suárez Esquivel and Virgilio Paz Romero, who had been convicted of the 1976 car-bomb murder in Washington, D.C., of Chilean diplomat Orlando Letelier and his American assistant, Ronnie Moffitt. Once released, they were not deported as were other noncitizen criminals. Instead, they were permitted to stay in Miami, where they settled into the good life.[5] In the end, juries and the U.S. government itself have remained sympathetic to anti-Castro exiles, and today Miami remains a hotbed of anti-Castro plots.

Cuba's Anti-U.S. Foreign Policy in the Third World throughout the Decades

After the triumph of Castro's revolution, the United States quickly concluded that Castro was ready to act boldly to assist other revolutionaries in seizing power. In fact, the level of Cuba's support for revolutionary movements varied over the years but was more consistent than the support of the Soviet Union, China, or other Communist states (Domínguez 1989, 113). This revolutionary stance was cause for alarm for U.S. officials. In 1984 Kenneth Skoug, the director of the Office of Cuban Affairs, summarized the view that Washington had long held with regard to Cuba's role in the world:

> U.S. policy toward Cuba is shaped primarily by our perception of Cuban conduct in international affairs. Despite its size, it acts in world affairs in both a political and a military sense as a major power, with a large and well-equipped armed force—second largest in Latin America—and a history of a quarter century of foreign engagement. The Cuban Armed Forces are relatively rich in combat experience, almost all of it far from Cuban shores. Almost alone among Latin American states, Cuba involves itself intensively with the affairs of every state and virtually every political movement in the hemisphere and many even beyond. Havana is not merely aware of other states, but it knows about them in depth. It has a policy for each of them and for the region. It is one of the few states in Latin America with a sense of mission for the region as a whole, as well as a policy for Africa. (Skoug 1989, 349)

LeoGrande (1982, 169) has noted that Cuban internationalist foreign policy evolved over the years from an early "romantic phase," lasting until the death of Ché Guevara in 1967, to a policy that was more pragmatic. Initially, Cuba's attitude was embodied in a romantic and relatively unsophisticated policy aimed at expanding the family of revolutionary states among the underdeveloped nations. Cuba provided physical and political support to guerrilla movements in both Africa and Latin America. By so doing, it hoped to create a "third force" within the socialist camp that would promote a more militant strain of proletarian internationalism.

One illustrative example of a guerrilla organization that has survived into the twenty-first century that was directly influenced by Cuba during the early internationalist period is Colombia's Ejército de Liberación Nacional (ELN). In mid-1962 the José Galán International Brigade was formed in Cuba, and after returning to Colombia, the brigade members established a rural base in the Department of Santander. Eventually, members of the Galán Brigade were able to control the ELN (Safford and Palacios 2002, 358).

A second phase of the ELN began in 1965. After returning from Cuba, Fabio Vélasquez, pressured by his Cuban mentors, led an assault on the small town of Simacota in Santander in January 1965. From that moment on the focus of the ELN moved from clandestine urban activity to the effort to establish a rural Guevarist guerrilla *foco* of small groups of fast-moving guerrillas (Safford and Palacios 2002, 358–59).

In contrast to the Cuban regime's proletarian internationalism as illustrated by the case of the ELN, the Soviets pursued the conservative and cautious policy of peaceful coexistence. As a result, Cuba's activist foreign policy caused tensions in the Cuban-Soviet relationship. Castro maintained that peaceful coexistence was a fraud, because it failed to give proper support to wars of national liberation. For Castro, there could be no peaceful coexistence with U.S. imperialism, and he was willing to pursue foreign policy objectives that were not agreeable to the Soviets.

Once the United States successfully pressured the OAS to exclude Cuba from its ranks in 1962, Cuba was economically and politically isolated from the rest of the hemisphere. Cuba attempted to export revolution throughout Latin America in the hopes of creating other revolutionary governments that would establish ties with it. Mexico, with its own history of revolution, was the only Latin American country that did not sever its relations with Cuba, and the two countries maintained normal state-to-state relations. Cuba, even during the romantic phase, was willing to forgo efforts to overthrow those governments that were willing to maintain relations with it (LeoGrande 1982, 170).

Eventually, the majority of insurrectionary offensives of the 1960s were smashed. When Ché Guevara was captured and killed in Bolivia in October 1967, the Cuban regime began to reconsider its strategies. By 1969, Cuba moved away from indiscriminately providing support to any emergent guerrilla movement, and the strategy of exporting revolution was for all intents and purposes defunct by the end of the decade (LeoGrande 1982, 171).

As the 1970s began, Cuba sought to reintegrate itself into the hemisphere through diplomatic efforts rather than by fomenting and/or supporting revolution. Cuba was able to reestablish state-to-state relations with Argentina, Chile, and Peru, all of which in the early 1970s had left-of-center governments. The OAS sanctions began to erode and were finally relaxed in 1975. The Nixon administration even demonstrated an interest in renewing normal diplomatic and economic ties with Cuba. As far back as 1970, after discovering a Soviet submarine base at Cienfuegos, President Nixon showed that he preferred to deal with the Cuban issue through quiet diplomacy rather than brinkmanship (Haney 1997, 5).

In 1975 Secretary of State Henry Kissinger proposed that the time might be right to improve relations with Cuba. After all, Soviet-American détente was in full bloom, and Kissinger had reason to believe that Castro would also be interested in détente after a series of confidential conversations with Cuban diplomats at the United Nations (UN). In a speech in March of that year, Kissinger noted that there was "no virtue in perpetual antagonism" with Cuba (Szulc 1986, 640). In May Kissinger approved a "secret advance probe" policy through which Castro was informed that the United States was considering lifting sanctions against Cuba selectively and would suspend spy-plane flights over the island during preliminary contacts (Szulc 1986, 640).

In July the Cubans informed Assistant Secretary of State for Inter-American Affairs William D. Rogers that Castro would not insist that the United States end the economic embargo before negotiations began, a major change in his previous stand. Rogers told the Cubans that even the fate of Guantánamo was negotiable as well.

Late in September Rogers announced that the United States was prepared "to improve our relations with Cuba" and "to enter into a dialogue," but suddenly the whole effort went off track (Szulc 1986, 641). In Angola, a previously small Cuban presence began to assume much larger proportions. This increased Cuban presence elicited public criticism by Kissinger. Meanwhile, in Havana, Castro sponsored the Puerto Rican Solidarity Conference, urging Puerto Rican independence as "a matter of principle" (Szulc 1986, 641). Diplomacy collapsed, and the old hostility returned. In late 1985 Castro admitted that the Kissinger effort was the closest that the two countries ever came to a real breakthrough in the history of postrevolutionary relations (Szulc 1986, 641).

Cuba's commitments in Africa greatly intensified the suspicions of the United States. Havana had begun to offer extensive conventional military assistance, including logistics support and training, to established governments. The Cubans provided advisory and training missions in Sierra Leone, Equatorial Guinea, and Somalia. They also sent large numbers of combat troops to Angola and Ethiopia, and smaller contingents to Libya and the Congo. By 1978, Cuba had some 38,000 to 40,000 military troops in Africa, up from about 750 to 1,000 a decade earlier. In the 1980s the number rose even higher, with about 50,000 troops stationed for some years in Angola alone. By the decade's end, half a million troops had served in Africa, some 377,000 in Angola (Eckstein 1994, 172).

Eckstein notes that the Angolan mission had the greatest impact. The Cubans helped Agostinho Neto's Popular Movement for the Liberation of Angola (MPLA) consolidate power when the Portuguese pulled out, and they helped the MPLA fend off U.S.- and South Africa–backed rebels (Eckstein 1994, 172). In 1988 massive Cuban aid resulted in a decisive military victory in Cuito Carnavale, which changed the military, political, and diplomatic balance in the region (Campbell 2001, 187).

As the 1970s drew to a close, socialist governments gained power in Nicaragua and Grenada, and a leftist movement in El Salvador also gained in strength. Castro began to believe that revolution in Latin America was inevitable, and he stated as much: "Cuba cannot export revolution. Neither can the USA prevent it" (Eckstein 1994, 173). In 1978 Cuba offered training, advice, and military equipment to the Sandinistas in Nicaragua, although in real terms Cuba contributed less aid than did some other Latin American countries. Only after the Sandinista victory did Havana increase its assistance substantially. Castro both assisted and sympathized with the Sandinistas, but he proved to be a restraining force as well. In order for them to avoid the problems that Cuba had experienced, Castro urged the Sandinistas to maintain good relations with as many countries as possible, to avoid excessive dependence on the Soviet Union, to minimize conflicts with the United States, and to gradually build a socialist economy in order to limit the flight of U.S. capital and skilled cadre (Evans 1990, 111).

In El Salvador, Cuba aided the rebels, and Castro helped unify guerrilla factions, thereby contributing to the formation of the Farabundo Martí Front for National Liberation (FMLN). Cuba trained and armed guerrillas battling the government of El Salvador, but it provided the rebels with minimal weaponry after the failure of the "final offensive" of January 1981. Castro advocated a negotiated settlement, which helped pave the way to the 1992 ceasefire (Eckstein 1994, 174–75).

On March 13, 1979, the leftist New Jewel Movement (NJM) conducted a successful coup in Grenada. Although there was no evidence that Cuba had a direct role in bringing the NJM to power, Cuba quickly supported the new government, whose leader, Maurice Bishop, had spent time in Cuba and was on friendly terms with Castro. By September 1979, the Cuban government said publicly that it had sent medical and technical assistance to the new government and its people (Domínguez 1989, 163).

In addition to medical and technical assistance, Grenada also secretly received rifles, other light weapons, and ammunition from Cuba. More weapons began arriving from the Soviet Union in 1981, and by 1983 Grenada had become the Eastern Caribbean's premier military power (Domínguez 1989, 163). The United States became concerned that the Soviets and Cubans were grabbing small, vulnerable states in the Caribbean region and concluded that something had to be done before Grenada developed into "another Cuba" (Smith 2000, 180).

On October 13, 1983, Maurice Bishop was overthrown by an internal faction, and within the week he and three former cabinet ministers were executed. Castro was taken off guard by the precipitous events, but Cuba announced that it would honor existing agreements, including the joint Cuban-Grenadian construction of an airport. The Reagan administration maintained, however, that the airport was being built for military usage and not for tourism, as Bishop had previously asserted. In an address to the nation, Reagan stated that the airport facility "looks suspiciously suitable for military aircraft including Soviet-built long-range bombers" (Smith 2000, 181). Reagan also expressed his concern for the safety of American medical students who were living on Grenada.

Early on the morning of October 25, 1983, a detachment of 1,900 U.S. Marines and army airborne troops launched an assault on the island. Cubans and Americans faced each other in combat, although there were only 784 Cubans on the island, and 636 of them were there as construction workers. Not all of the Cubans had been issued weapons, since the Cuban commanding officer, Colonel Pedró Tortoló, only expected a U.S. rescue operation. He later said that "I never thought that they were going to launch an invasion" (Domínguez 1989, 168). Nevertheless, the lesson of the Grenada invasion was not lost on Fidel Castro, who decided that in a total crisis, the United States would try to annihilate him. In an interview with Tad Szulc, Castro said, "We have made great efforts to strengthen our defenses. After Grenada, we have made even greater efforts. We are increasing considerably our defense and resistance capability, including the preparation of the people for a prolonged, indefinite war" (Szulc 1986, 647).

In sum, from 1975 to 1990 Cuba sent over 300,000 troops to overseas military missions. Unlike the U.S. troops in Vietnam and Soviet troops in Afghanistan, Cuban troops were at times on the winning side in Africa. The Soviet Union had no more reliable military ally during the Cold War, even though at times Castro seemed to push for more revolutionary behavior than the cautious Soviets were willing to accommodate (Domínguez 2001, 185). By the 1990s, however, the Soviet Union would disappear, changing the international equation and leaving Cuba without its superpower ally.

From Confrontation to Cooperation, 1990–1995

Given the reconfiguration of power in the international system and the loss of Soviet support, Cuba modified its foreign policy behavior in the 1990s and curtailed its commitments in other countries. In March 1990 all Cuban military personnel in Nicaragua were brought back to Cuba, and in May 1991 Cuba's last troops were repatriated from Angola (Domínguez 2001, 186). By early 1992, all of the Cuban international behavior to which the United States historically had objected had now ceased. No longer did the Soviet-Cuban alliance exist, Cuban troops had been repatriated from other countries, and Cuban support for revolutionary movements had long since faded away. Although Cuba posed no threat to U.S. national security, the fact that Castro and his socialist regime had survived the demise of the Soviet Union and retained power came to drive U.S. post–Cold War policy toward the island. To a large degree, this focus on Cuba's internal politics and on Castro himself was generated by the Cuban American National Foundation (CANF) and/or its congressional allies.

During the decade since its creation, CANF had learned how to work the U.S. political system in order to push its own anti-Castro concerns onto the U.S. government's agenda, culminating in the 1992 passage of the Cuban Democracy Act (CDA). The loss of Soviet subsidies and the further tightening of the embargo with the passage of the CDA contributed to the staggering economic malaise on the island, and increasing numbers of rafters attempted to migrate illegally. When he witnessed the large numbers of rafters in distress on the high seas, José Basulto, a well-known veteran of the Bay of Pigs, founded Brothers to the Rescue. This group of Cuban Americans began flying single-engine planes over the Straits of Florida in order to search for and rescue desperate Cubans on rafts or small boats.

In 1994 U.S. officials began looking for ways to halt the flow of Cuban rafters who were washing up on Florida shores. Pentagon officials were especially concerned since many believed that U.S. military involvement in Cuba could be provoked by a mass exodus from the island (Fernández 2000, 187). At the same time, Castro was concerned about the increasing numbers of hijackings of Cuban vessels by Cubans seeking to leave the island. The coinciding of interests among influential sectors of the White House and the Pentagon and among Cuban government officials led to secret talks, which culminated in the historic migration agreements.

Backlash, Confrontation, and a Return to Cooperation, 1995–1999

Once the immigration accords were signed in 1994–1995, large numbers of rafters stopped appearing on the high seas, and Brothers to the Rescue no longer had a cause célèbre.[6] The group was angered by the agreements, which, according to Basulto, were "repugnant and tragic" (Fernández 2000, 187). Brothers decided to change its role, and instead of flying missions of mercy, it began flying into Cuban airspace and dropping leaflets over Havana urging Cubans to exercise civil disobedience against the Castro regime. "We are in favor of confrontation. The difference is we confront without weapons," Basulto told one interviewer (Collins 1996, 38). Havana took the incursions seriously and warned that if the Brothers to the Rescue planes violated Cuban airspace or Cuban waters, the planes would be attacked.[7]

Three weeks before the Brothers planes were shot down, a delegation of former U.S. diplomats and retired senior military officers visited Cuba on a fact-finding mission, and they were warned that the Cubans would not tolerate airspace incursions. Upon returning from the mission, Admiral Eugene Carroll notified officials at the State Department and U.S. intelligence agencies about the Cubans' concerns. Carroll's information, however, came as no surprise, because the Cuban government had previously filed numerous protests at the State Department (Center for Defense Information 1996). It appeared that the U.S. government, although aware of the problem, had not effectively tried to halt or investigate the incursions.

In reality, both the U.S. government and the Castro regime had reasons to worry about the methods of Basulto and Brothers to the Rescue. For decades, Basulto had remained completely dedicated to the overthrow of Castro and had a deep bond with his comrades in the Bay of Pigs exile force, saying, "The common cause made us brothers" (Wyden 1979, 38). Felix Rodríguez, the CIA operative who was present at the execution of Ché Guevara, wrote of the past anti-Castro exploits of Basulto: "On August 24, 1962, Basulto and half a dozen friends, all of them in their early twenties, sailed from Miami into Havana harbor and staged a raid on the waterfront Hotel Rosita de Hornedo, where scores of Soviet advisors lived" (Rodríguez and Weisman 1989, 111).

Rodríguez also explained Basulto's willingness to pursue his own objectives, even when they diverged from those of the U.S. government: "I was happy to be working with the Agency in 1962. Basulto was not. He felt—and still feels—that the CIA was more interested in promoting the U.S. national interest than it was in seeing a free and democratic Cuba . . . So Basulto quit working with the CIA and decided to strike out on his own" (Rodríguez and Weisman 1989, 110).

Basulto and Brothers to the Rescue became involved with Concilio Cubano, a network of 160 opposition groups in Cuba that had been formed in 1995. Concilio Cubano had asked the Cuban government for authorization to hold its first national meeting on February 24, 1996. In order to spread the word about Concilio Cubano that January, Brothers planes dropped leaflets over Havana that were printed with the thirty articles of the UN Universal Declaration of Human Rights. Castro subsequently arrested over a hundred members of Concilio Cubano and canceled the national meeting (Antón and Hernández 2002, 242).

The timing of the shoot-down of the Brothers to the Rescue planes and the death of four pilots on February 24, 1996, coincided with what was supposed to have been the start of the Concilio Cubano meeting. The Cuban Foreign Ministry later accused the group of being "organized, conceived, officiated, fomented, and financed by the U.S. government" (Watson 1996, 38). For Castro, the appearance of the Brothers planes precisely on February 24 confirmed the unacceptable linkage between internal dissent and its backing by anti-Castro groups in Miami. Three weeks later, President Clinton reacted to the tragedy by signing the Helms-Burton Act.

After the shoot-down, relations between the United States and Cuba were nearly as tense as they had been in the aftermath of the Bay of Pigs. In an interview published in *Business Week* on October 27, 1999, Richard Nuccio, Clinton's former special adviser, explained that after the shoot-down, the president had considered options for attacking Cuban air force units and defense structures. Clinton ultimately decided to increase economic sanctions rather than resort to military action. Meanwhile, in 1997 Senator Bob Graham (D-Fla.) was still inclined to consider military options. The senator added an amendment to the defense bill that declared Cuba an enemy of the United States and ordered the Pentagon to study Cuban military capabilities and to assess the threat Cuba posed to the United States.[8] Whereas the White House and the Pentagon were pulling away from confrontation, the hard-line Cuban American members of Congress and their allies were still pushing for a fight.

The shoot-down of the Brothers planes was a frightening wake-up call for both the United States and Cuba, and in spite of the public rhetoric of hostility in the aftermath of the shoot-down and the enactment of the Helms-Burton Act, bilateral cooperation between the two governments actually deepened as they quietly began to work behind the scenes to avoid being drawn into a conflict provoked by Cuban American organizations (Domínguez 2001, 194). The U.S. and Cuban governments cooperated in order to better monitor the activities of the Democracy Movement. Members of the Democracy Movement participated in yearly flotillas to commemorate the lives lost at sea during the rafter crisis and specifically to commemorate the forty-one lives lost as a result of the sinking of the *Trece de Marzo* tugboat on July 13, 1994.[9] Each year beginning in 1995, a flotilla of twenty to forty boats departed from Key West and traveled to the twelve-mile limit in front of Varadero Beach, Cuba. Ramón Saúl Sánchez, a member of Alpha 66 and founder of the Democracy Movement, explained that the commemoration was really only one goal of the organization and that the Democracy Movement would love nothing more than to force Fidel Castro to deploy his forces against the flotilla: "Our purpose is to have Castro be concerned, to bring a message of solidarity to the Cuban people, and to show that we are willing to take risks."[10] Whereas Brothers to the Rescue had tried to provoke Castro from the air, the members of the Democracy Movement hoped to provoke an incident at sea.

Both governments recognized the threat posed by the Democracy Movement, and they cooperated by setting down clear rules for the flotillas. The respective coast guards, supported by the air forces, established close communications, and U.S. Coast Guard officers even traveled to Havana in advance of each flotilla episode to discuss how each side was planning to prevent an incident (Domínguez 2001, 194). Domínguez writes that he was in Havana on July 13, 1996, and he watched on Cuban television the Cuban American flotilla just outside Cuban territorial waters. The flotilla was surrounded by collaborating U.S. and Cuban coast guard vessels (Domínguez 2001, 205).

Another area of bilateral cooperation involved unofficial visits to Cuba by high-ranking retired U.S. military officers, who met with Cuban military officers to discuss issues of mutual concern. These retired officers, such as General John Sheehan, Admiral Eugene Carroll, and General Charles Wilhelm, enjoyed a great deal of prestige among the Cuban public (Klepak 2000, 23). Beginning in the early 1990s, the Center for Defense Information (CDI), a nonpartisan, nonprofit organization committed to independent research related to global security, organized the meetings. CDI delegations gained access to many secure sites in Cuba, including a mothballed nuclear power plant, secret military tunnels, a Border Guard command center, a former Soviet submarine base, a munitions factory, and biotechnology production facilities (Baker 2003). The Cubans even created their own version of the CDI, Centro de Estudios para Información de Defensa (CEID), so that they could further build upon the collaborative efforts involving these unofficial military-to-military contacts. The visits to Havana allowed active Cuban and retired U.S. military officers to openly discuss issues related to migration, drug trafficking, operating procedures at the U.S. naval base at Guantánamo Bay, U.S. military maneuvers, and other regional threats (Center for Defense Information 2001). During these meetings, the Americans generally focused closely on migration and drug issues, while the Cubans officers expressed concerns related to U.S. military exercises near the island and Cuban American provocations as illustrated by the following statement of one of the Cuban officers:

> I would like to make a comment concerning the flotilla. In a previous meeting, it is something we have discussed with the U.S. Coast Guard

representatives. And even though the topic was discussed this morning, and seemingly it is a peaceful activity, we have to understand from the very moment the flotilla sails off from U.S. shores, they are violating international maritime law. There are provocations, even though they are conducted off Cuban territory waters. In other locations, they have violated the jurisdictional water of Cuba. They use the maritime salvage channels and they use international waters to establish communication through the channels of a sovereign country, something which is not allowed by the international maritime law. Besides there is the item that we discussed this morning, namely the danger it means as a provocation—the danger it brings as a provocation. We do know that the U.S. Coast Guard has made great efforts to force them to keep themselves off Cuban territory waters because we have monitored the conversations over the radio between the U.S. Coast Guard and the organizers of this flotilla. (Center for Defense Information 2001)

This statement is significant in that it underscores that the Cuban military officers recognized and appreciated the cooperation that they had received from the U.S. Coast Guard. When I participated as a member of the CDI delegation in November 2003, I questioned one Cuban official in the Foreign Ministry about cooperation between the two coast guards in monitoring the flotilla. The official explained that the cooperation was indeed working well, but that a greater concern for his ministry was the embedded position of Cuban Americans in all levels of the U.S. government's bureaucracy, because these Cuban Americans were driving perspectives on Cuba. He noted that there were thirty-four Cuban Americans in influential positions, not counting the Cuban American members of Congress. At the top of a list were Mel Martínez (U.S. secretary of Housing and Urban Development), Otto Reich (assistant secretary of state for Western Hemisphere Affairs), Adolfo Franco (assistant administrator for Latin America and the Caribbean United States Agency for International Development [USAID]), Mauricio Tamargo (Foreign Claims Settlement Commission), and Lino Gutiérrez (principal deputy assistant secretary for Western Hemisphere Affairs).

Explaining U.S.-Cuban Cooperation at Reducing the Threat of War

The shoot-down of the Brothers planes served to remind both U.S. and Cuban officials that a crisis could easily spiral out of control and that hard-liners within the Cuban American community could push the two countries into an unwanted war. Prior to the shoot-down, a number of Cuban Americans and Cuban American organizations had publicly admitted that they actually hoped to provoke a confrontation with the Cuban government. Brothers to the Rescue leader José Basulto may not have entered into Cuban airspace on the fateful day of the shoot-down, but he had established a pattern of incursions beginning in 1995 that motivated the Cuban government to file detailed diplomatic notes of protest with the U.S. government in the hopes of avoiding conflict. The State Department subsequently forwarded the complaints to the Federal Aviation Administration (FAA), whose officials ordered Basulto to stop.[11] Basulto did not stop, and on July 13, 1995, in conjunction with the Democracy Movement flotilla, Basulto flew a few hundred feet over the Malecón and dropped religious medals and bumper stickers. Upon his return to Miami that day, he announced that he did not care that he was violating Cuban airspace.[12]

On January 13, 1996, Cubans in Havana found their streets littered with leaflets that had been tossed in bundles from Basulto's plane. According to Brigadier General Rubén Martínez Puente, the chief of the Cuban Anti-Aircraft Defense and Air Force, this incident convinced the Cuban government that Brothers to the Rescue was beyond the control of the U.S. government.[13]

After the shoot-down, General John Shalikashvili, chairman of the Joint Chiefs of Staff, described the military contingency plans to President Clinton but argued against an attack on Cuban targets.[14] This approach was in keeping with the Pentagon's expressed desire to avoid conflict with Cuba. The Pentagon's case for avoiding conflict with Cuba was furthered in 1998. In fulfillment of the Graham amendment's requirement of assessing the threat posed by Cuba, the Pentagon concluded that Cuba "does not pose a significant military threat to the U.S. or to other countries in the region."[15] General Charles Wilhelm played an important role in the final report, and in an interview with this author in Havana in November 2003, he stated his concern that the United States and Cuba avoid being drawn into "signal events" like the 1996 shoot-down.

In order to avoid another incident, the two governments were forced to cooperate and did so by coordinating the supervision of the Democracy Movement flotilla. As part of the cooperative efforts, the U.S. Coast Guard seized the movement's *Democracia* vessel on July 13, 1997, after its leader, Ramón Saúl Sánchez, insisted that he would enter Cuban waters to pay homage to the forty-one people who died when the tugboat *Trece de Marzo* was rammed by Cuban fireboats. The U.S. Coast Guard justified the seizure by citing a presidential order requiring boat captains bound for Cuba from South Florida ports to obtain a permit. The Coast Guard subsequently seized the Democracy Movement boat *Human Rights* on December 19, 1998, after Sánchez set sail for Cuba, declaring his intent to distribute in Cuba copies of the Universal Declaration of Human Rights.[16]

Implementation of conflict avoidance over the flotilla was made possible through contacts between the two countries' coast guards and through unofficial meetings between retired U.S. military personnel and Cuban military officers. Since the United States and Cuba did not have formal diplomatic relations, the military-to-military contacts did not involve active-duty U.S. military officers. However, the participating retired U.S. officers were high ranking and had active-duty experience in dealing with Cuba.

Domínguez (2001, 194) has noted that the relationship between the two coast guards is professional and regular and that the two governments keep these political arrangements free from the contamination of the hostility that plagues their countries. The collaboration has worked to improve the sense of security that is necessary for dealing with issues of high politics related to war, even though the collaboration is quite limited in scope, dealing only with staged events on the high seas.

U.S. officials need to look more closely at this form of limited cooperation, because it can serve as a model for additional confidence-building measures (CBMs) between the United States and Cuba in the twenty-first century. In the case of the flotilla, U.S. officials were willing put ideological concerns aside in order to avoid being drawn into an unnecessary conflict with Cuba, even though it meant that they had to face down the pressure of a Cuban American group. This type of thinking involved moving away from old Cold War ideology.

If U.S. policy makers and the Pentagon continue to reorient their thinking about Cuba away from the old Cold War mindset, there are a number of CBMs that can be useful in further reducing the threat of accidental war. For example, the case of India and Pakistan illustrates how hostile neighbors can decide to implement CBMs in order to move away from conflict. Both India and Pakistan have agreed to maintain a hotline between commanders governing troop maneuvers and to jointly patrol common borders. Moreover, they have pledged not to launch preemptive attacks against each other. With regard to the case of the United States and Cuba, U.S. and Cuban officials could start by developing emergency safety procedures for crisis situations resulting from accidental air and sea intrusions. Had such procedures been in place in 1996, the tragic shoot-down might have been avoided, as well as the fall-out that followed.

Fall-out from the Shoot-Down, 1998–2005

In 1998 five Cubans were arrested in Miami on charges of conducting espionage on behalf of Cuba. One of the five, Gerardo Hernández, was additionally accused of conspiracy to commit murder related to the shoot-down of the Brothers to the Rescue planes. Between their arrest and trial, the five were held without bail for thirty-three months, and during seventeen of those months they were held in solitary confinement.[17] Moreover, their families complained that they were denied their rights to visitation.

As to the serious allegations, the five maintained that they had never spied on the U.S. government or U.S. military installations. Rather, they had infiltrated some Miami-based exile organizations after U.S. law enforcement failed to act on evidence turned over by Cuban authorities that demonstrated that the organizations posed a serious threat of terrorism against Cuba. In fact, on June 17, 1998, the Cuban government did submit to U.S. law enforcement officials a memorandum noting that several organizations in Miami were concerned that support for the embargo was eroding and that Cuba's economy was recovering from the collapse of the Soviet Union.[18] As a result of their concerns, the groups hoped to provoke a crisis between the United States and Cuba so as to increase hostility toward Cuba that would culminate in a U.S. attack or an invasion.

In order to counteract this serious national security threat to Cuba, the defendants admitted that they had been tracking the activities of José Basulto and Brothers to the Rescue as well as the activities of Orlando Bosch, Luis Posada Carriles, and associated paramilitary organizations. The five argued that the monitoring had been necessary, because during the twenty months before the shoot-down there had been at least twenty-five deliberate illegal flights into Cuban airspace.[19]

Prosecutors argued that Hernández, who alerted the Cuban government about the plans of Basulto and the other pilots, was guilty of conspiracy to commit premeditated murder, even though he was actually in Miami when the February 24 shoot-down took place. However, the trial judge ruled that in order to prove the conspiracy charge, the prosecution had to present evidence that Hernández was aware of a prearranged agreement to shoot down the planes before they reached Cuba. Merely informing the Cuban authorities of the threat was not enough to uphold a conspiracy charge.

Retired admiral Eugene Carroll testified for the defense and told of his experience in Havana three weeks before the shoot-down, during which time Cuban officials had alerted him about Basulto's incursions into Cuban airspace. Upon his return to the United States, Admiral Carroll notified the U.S. State Department and the Defense Intelligence Agency of the Cubans' concerns. Richard Nuccio, the Clinton administration official who "made Cuba policy on behalf of the President," read a memo from an assistant in the State Department that expressed the agency's awareness of the danger posed by the Brothers to the Rescue incursions prior to the shoot-down: "This latest over-flight can only be seen as further taunting of the Cuban Government. State is increasingly concerned about Cuban reactions to these flagrant violations. . . . [The] worst case scenario, is that one of these days the Cubans will shoot down one of these planes and the FAA better have all its ducks in a row."[20]

In the end, the prosecution carried the day by arguing that the five Cubans were in the country "for the purpose of destroying the United States." After very little deliberation, the Miami jury found all five Cubans guilty as charged. The five were sentenced to prison terms that ranged from fifteen years to life. They were separated from each other and placed in various federal maximum security penitentiaries throughout the United States.

At his 2001 sentencing, Gerardo Hernández defended his actions before the judge:

> Cuba has the right to defend itself from the terrorist acts that are pre-pared in Florida with total impunity, despite the fact that they have been consistently denounced by the Cuban authorities. This is the same right that the United States has to try to neutralize the plans of terrorist Osama Bin Laden's organization, which has caused so much damage to this country and threatens to continue doing so. I am certain that the sons and daughters in this country who are carrying out this mission are considered patriots, and their objective is not that of threatening the national security of any of the countries where these people are being sheltered.[21]

The Cuban government, along with other overseas government officials and international law specialists, criticized the unfairness of the trial. Grassroots community activists created an international campaign that was spearheaded by the San Francisco–based National Committee to Free the Five. In Cuba, the five became national heroes, whose sacrifice and dedication to the revolution were praised by state television and newspapers.

On May 20, 2005, Fidel Castro delivered a speech entitled "A Different Behavior" before a gathering of 200,000 in front of the U.S. Interests Section in Havana. In the speech, he revealed for the first time how the five had been uncovered in the United States. In 1998 Colombian author Gabriel García Márquez traveled to Washington, D.C., in the wake of terrorist attacks on hotels in Cuba. At Castro's behest, García Márquez delivered a message to President Clinton that briefed the U.S. president about additional terrorist plans that Cuba had uncovered, which implicated Cuban exiles living in the United States. As a result of García Márquez's message, U.S. authorities asked to meet with Cuban officials in Havana, and on June 16 and 17, 1998, several joint meetings of Cuban experts and U.S. Federal Bureau of Investigation (FBI) agents were held on the subject of plans for terrorist attacks against Cuba. The U.S. delegation acknowledged the value of the information and made a commitment to give a reply with an analysis of the materials as soon as possible. However, the Cuban government never received any additional input from the United States until the arrest of the five, who had been the undercover sources of the information on the terrorist activities. For Castro, the ultimate irony was that rather than use the Cuban intelligence to halt exile terrorists, the U.S. government had instead used it to arrest the five on charges of espionage.

In July 2005 a human rights body of the UN condemned the sentences for the five as arbitrary and unduly harsh. Less than one month later, on August 9, 2005, the Eleventh U.S. Circuit Court of Appeals threw out the convictions, noting that the pervasive prejudice against the Castro government had precluded a fair trial in Miami. In other words, the five would be retried but not in Miami. The appeals court judges referred to the first trial a "perfect storm," with widespread anti-Castro sentiment, extensive publicity in Miami, and improper comments by the prosecution and witness José Basulto, who implied from the stand that one of the defense lawyers worked for Castro.[22]

Lisandro Pérez, an expert on the Cuban exile phenomenon, noted that "the possibility of selecting twelve citizens of Miami–Dade County who can be impartial in a case involving acknowledged agents of the Cuban government is virtually zero." Pérez further noted that Miami itself is permeated by an "exile ideology" that favors U.S. intervention to topple Castro.[23] Additionally, the trial of the five took place within months of the Elián González controversy that rocked Miami, heightening passions and creating a state-of-siege mentality within the Cuban American community.

Ricardo Alarcón hailed the decision by the court of appeals as "a victory against those who promote terrorism, against hypocrites who tout a supposed war on terror and in reality protect terrorists and jail young men who only acted to oppose terrorism in the United States."[24] The Cuban government felt vindicated, and Alarcón noted that no one could say any longer "that our claim that the judicial process was filled with prejudice . . . has no basis."[25] However, the Cuban government's euphoria was tempered by the lack of widespread coverage that the case had been given by the mainstream media. The regime had witnessed the important effect of U.S. public opinion on the outcome of the Elián case and the resulting backlash in the Cuban American community. In contrast, public dissemination of the Cuban five's trial in 2001 and the circuit court ruling in 2005 were largely confined to the Miami media market. From 2000 to 2005, the case garnered precious little national media attention, and the few headlines that did appear, such as "Spies Among Us," were inflammatory.[26] Alarcón criticized the media for covering "the adventures of Kobe Bryant, the attire of Martha Stewart and the goings-on in Michael Jackson's bed," while the case of the Cuban five "was conveniently ignored by the big corporations trying to monopolize global information."[27] As it turned out, the U.S. appeals court decision was announced just days before Castro's seventy-ninth birthday on August 13, and the newspaper *Granma* pointed out that one of the five, René González, even shared Castro's birthday. In the end, the spy scandal of the Cuban Five had become the gift that just kept on giving, and on his seventy-ninth birthday Castro managed to still look like a winner in "the battle of ideas."

Conclusion

International relations theorists note that in an anarchic world with no central authority to mediate or settle interstate disputes, states themselves are forced to find ways to manage the conflicts that arise between them. States determine whether to achieve their security goals through cooperation or conflict. Although all states face the security dilemma, this dilemma does not often lead to major armed violence; war is an inherently infrequent event (Weede 1992, 377). In fact, states often do find ways to cooperate in order to settle their disputes. Therefore anarchy does not necessarily condemn international society to perpetual war, and the study of efforts at cooperation offers valuable insights for improving our knowledge about whether and how states can resolve their disputes without going to war.

This book has examined post–Cold War cooperative efforts undertaken by two long-standing enemies, the United States and Cuba. In the post–Cold War period, U.S.-Cuban cooperation has been recorded in areas of mutual interest, including illegal migration, drug trafficking, decreasing the tensions around the U.S. naval base at Guantánamo Bay, and reducing the threat of accidental war. This concluding chapter compares the findings from the four cases on the type and level of cooperation. The first section reviews the cooperation undertaken during the 1990s. The second section looks to the future in light of the current state of relations between the United States and Cuba, takes note of suggestions that have been made to improve the existing cooperative efforts, and points to areas for future research.

Review of Confidence-Building Measures and the Four Cases

Confidence-building measures (CBMs) presuppose the existence of differences of interests and of mutually low confidence in the relations between hostile states. Political and military leaders have utilized CBMs frequently in strife-ridden parts of the world to prevent conflict, to warn various parties of troubling developments, and to negotiate and/or strengthen agreements. The process begins by identifying common interests and by developing cooperation over time in incremental steps. Perhaps the most well known CBM was the installation of the hotline between the United States and the Soviet Union at the end of the Cuban missile crisis of 1962. Although the two superpowers were ideological opponents and were intensely suspicious of each other's military capabilities and intentions, they nevertheless were motivated to cooperate by fear of nuclear war. The hotline therefore was a small step in beginning to diminish tensions between the two hostile superpowers. Given the long history of distrust between the United States and Cuba, CBMs are practical tools for policy makers who are interested in lessening tensions between the two.

Case 1. Migration

The 1994–1995 migration agreements provide a clear case of U.S.-Cuban cooperation designed to avoid further conflicts over illegal immigration. For more than thirty years each side used illegal migration as a weapon against the other. The United States pointed to illegal migration as proof of the failures of Castro and Communism. The Cuban Adjustment Act of 1965, which essentially allowed those Cubans who arrived illegally in the United States to adjust their status and become U.S. citizens, increased the motivation of Cubans to migrate illegally. Castro, for his part, used illegal migration as a safety valve to export dissent by pushing Cubans opposed to his regime to leave the island. He also used illegal migration to pressure the United States by threatening to unleash waves of Cuban refugees.

During the 1994 rafter crisis, both sides realized that illegal migration was causing more pain than gain, and secret negotiations were initiated after former president Jimmy Carter contacted Fidel Castro on behalf of the Clinton administration. The United States did not want to deal with another exodus along the proportions of the Mariel crisis of 1980, and Castro wanted, at the very least, to end the hijackings of Cuban government vessels by Cubans fleeing the island. The two governments resorted to secret talks that ultimately culminated in two political agreements to better control illegal migration. These agreements dramatically altered U.S. immigration policy toward Cuba, with the United States pledging to repatriate Cubans intercepted at sea. However, the agreements of 1994–1995 dealt only with migration and did not attempt to address deeper problems in the relationship. During the George W. Bush administration, the United States canceled biannual migration talks in January 2004, after stating that the Cuban government was unwilling to discuss five key issues that were on the U.S. agenda related to exit permits, a new registration for the lottery that was used to determine which Cubans would receive exit permits, a deeper port in Cuba for repatriations by the U.S. Coast Guard, permission for U.S. diplomatic personnel to monitor the Cuban government's treatment of repatriated Cubans, and Cuba's acceptance of deported Cuban nationals. In spite of canceling the talks, the Bush administration continued to honor the accords in practice by returning Cuban migrants intercepted at sea.

Case 2. Drug Trafficking

Shortly after the fall of the Berlin wall, Cuban officials watched as the United States invaded Panama and removed Manuel Noriega from power. The George H. W. Bush administration justified the invasion in part on the grounds that Noriega had ties to international drug trafficking. In the absence of the superpower standoff, the United States showed, with the removal and arrest of Noriega, that it was free to move boldly on the world stage to exact regime change.

Cuba's leaders were sobered by the U.S. invasion of Panama and by Noriega's removal from power, and realized that they could not afford to be tied in any way to drug trafficking, since that would give the United States a plausible pretext to invade Cuba. At the same time, Cuba's leaders had a domestic concern about illegal drugs. Increasing numbers of foreign tourists on the island had brought with them an increasing influx of drugs. Drugs were damaging to the social fabric of Cuba, thereby threatening the survival of the revolution. As a result of both domestic and international concerns, Castro was motivated to promote cooperation in drug interdiction efforts.

The United States, however, severely restricted Cuban efforts at any regional cooperation and refused to consider Cuba's expressed interest in an official U.S.-Cuban agreement to formalize collaboration on counternarcotics. Cuban Americans strongly opposed any agreement that might rehabilitate Castro's image. Nevertheless, the Clinton administration did authorize small, limited steps toward cooperation on a case-by-case basis only.

U.S.-Cuban relations on drug trafficking reached a turning point on October 1, 1996, with the joint U.S.-Cuban search and seizure of the Colombian vessel *Limerick*. Cooperation on the *Limerick* yielded one of the largest cocaine drug busts in the history of counternarcotics operations. Moreover, a Cuban intelligence officer and three Cuban border guards were authorized to appear in U.S. District Court in Miami in order to testify at the criminal trials of the

Limerick's captain and chief engineer. Additionally, the Drug Enforcement Agency (DEA), the U.S. Coast Guard, and European authorities recognized several other achievements of the Cuban authorities during the 1990s in their efforts to fight drug traffickers. In February 1996 Cuban authorities seized the freighter *Spiritus* and confiscated 180 kilograms of cocaine, and in November 1998 Cuban authorities broke up an international smuggling ring of eighteen foreigners trafficking in drugs from Jamaica to Britain via Havana.

In response to these positive developments, in 1999 U.S. Coast Guard officials offered a number of specific suggestions to the White House to improve U.S.-Cuban counternarcotics operations. The proposals were to upgrade the fax connection between the two countries to a telephone connection, to coordinate radio frequencies, to station a counternarcotics specialist in Havana who would coordinate with Cuban law enforcement, and to provide technical expertise to assist in the joint boarding and searches of commercial vessels on a case-by-case basis. After meeting with a U.S. delegation in Havana in June 1999, the Cuban government passed a diplomatic note through the U.S. Interests Section saying that it accepted all of the U.S. proposals.

Since 2002 the Cubans have made several high-profile arrests of drug kingpins, and they have touted their successful efforts as proof that the United States and Cuba should deepen their cooperation by signing a drug agreement. However, the Bush administration has continued the Clinton administration's policy of cooperating with Cuba on a case-by-case basis only, and the U.S. Coast Guard District 7 headquarters in Miami purposely says very little about its liaison office in Havana in order to avoid public outcry from the Cuban American community.

Case 3. Decreasing Tensions at the U.S. naval base at Guantánamo Bay

Starting in 1993, the U.S. base commander at Guantánamo took the initiative of giving advance notification to his Cuban counterpart whenever U.S. forces were scheduled to engage in a military exercise around the base. Cuba's Revolutionary Armed Forces responded in kind, providing U.S. base command advance notification of their own live-ammunition exercises. Cooperative measures were also taken in the area of flight safety, even though the new safety measures resulted in greater U.S. use of Cuban airspace.

Tension at Guantánamo was linked to the contentious issue of migration also. In response to the 1994 migration crisis, U.S. and Cuban military authorities developed a constructive relationship in order to deal with the complexities of housing a large number of refugees on the base. Regular meetings between U.S. military officers and Cuban officers were initiated by U.S. base commander General John Sheehan. Every four to six weeks, the military officers of both countries discussed practical matters related to refugee-related base operations. The meetings eased tensions at the base and continued well after the refugee crisis subsided.

After General Sheehan's retirement in 1997, he maintained contact with Cuban officials, toured the island, and urged the Clinton administration to "regularize contacts" between Cuban and U.S. military chiefs. General Sheehan reflected a growing consensus within the Pentagon that the U.S. military should avoid being drawn into a Cuban civil war or an eventual U.S. occupation of the island.

During the Kosovo crisis in April 1999, the United States informed Cuba in advance of its plans to house Kosovar refugees at the base. In a surprising gesture of cooperation, the Cuban government responded by signaling its agreement to the plan. Finally, in June 1999 the United States completed its unilateral removal of the U.S. minefield that protected the base from Castro's troops, a gesture meant for both the international community and for Castro's government.

The Bush administration benefited from the climate of cooperation around the base during the early months of the war on terror. When the Bush administration decided to transfer illegal combatants from the war on terror to the base for detention, administration officials advised Cuba in advance about the prisoner flights and discussed issues of security around the base with Cuban authorities. Fidel Castro expressed condemnation of the terrorist attacks of September 11, 2001, and assured the United States of continued cooperation around the base by offering medical assistance and assurances that Cuba would return any detainees should they escape.

Case 4. Reducing the Threat of Accidental War

As the Cold War ended and Cuba lost the economic support that it had received from its Soviet benefactor, the Castro regime appeared to be destined for the dustbin of history. In spite of the many predictions to the contrary, however, Castro and his socialist regime managed to survive. In order to oust Castro from power, hard-line Cuban American organizations and their congressional allies pushed to tighten the U.S. embargo on Cuba with new punitive legislation such as the Cuban Democracy Act and the Helms-Burton Act.

Cuban American organizations also began pursuing independent agendas for destabilizing the Castro regime. José Basulto and Brothers to the Rescue pilots began flying into Cuban airspace in order to drop anti-Castro leaflets and also communicated with and gave support to dissident groups on the island. The Democracy Movement staged yearly flotillas in the international waters off the Cuban coast and admitted publicly that the organization hoped to provoke a violent confrontation by pushing Fidel Castro to deploy his forces against them.

The 1996 shoot-down of the Brothers planes was a wake-up call for both the U.S. and Cuban governments, and in spite of their publicly hostile rhetoric, bilateral cooperation between the two governments deepened as they began to work together to avoid being drawn into a conflict provoked by hard-line Cuban American organizations. Both governments set down clear rules for future flotillas, and the respective coast guards, supported by the air forces, established close communications. Moreover, U.S. Coast Guard officers traveled to Havana in advance of each flotilla episode to discuss how the two governments might prevent a confrontation between the flotilla participants and the Cuban armed forces.

Another avenue of bilateral cooperation involved unofficial visits to Cuba by retired U.S. military officers. These visits to Havana allow Cuban and retired U.S. military officers to openly discuss issues related to migration, drug trafficking, operating procedures at the U.S. naval base at Guantánamo Bay, U.S. military maneuvers, and other regional threats. Since the United States and Cuba do not maintain diplomatic relations, these meetings continue to serve as an indirect form of quiet diplomacy. The cordial ties that exist between retired U.S. military officers and the Cuban military officers may help to lay the groundwork for future cooperation and a more peaceful transition in U.S.-Cuban relations.

Comparing the Cases as to Levels of Cooperation

Table 6.1 summarizes and compares the four cases of cooperation. Although all four cases fit within a CBM framework, there are distinct variations between the cases with regard to the different levels of implementation. Only the immigration case resulted in a formalized political agreement or treaty. Chapter 3 noted the low level of case-by-case cooperation in controlling drug traffic and suggests that the measures undertaken by the United States and Cuba might better be described as mini-CBMs rather than full-fledged CBMs. The other two cases likewise exhibited very low levels of cooperation that were not at all formalized or regularized, in contrast to the precision of the migration agreements, which established biannual meetings.

Skeptics might ask whether the limited cooperative efforts in the other cases should even be termed CBMs. Can we seriously speak of cooperation between the two countries as long as Cuba maintains that the United States seeks to overthrow Castro and as long as the United States retains Cuba on its list of terrorist nations? Klepak argues for greater nuance in considering confidence building between Cuba and the United States (Klepak 2000, iv). Even if many of the decision makers in both countries still cling to decades-old hostile perceptions, there is compelling evidence of sectoral confidence building involving important U.S. citizens on the one hand and Cuban bureaucracies and some influential parts of the decision-making elites on the other. Interestingly enough, members of the U.S. military and their counterparts in Cuba have shown themselves to be very receptive to CBMs (Klepak 2000, 28). This represents a seismic shift in U.S. military perceptions in that the Pentagon has come to see the Castro government as an unfortunate but nonthreatening hangover from the Cold War (Klepak 2000, 25). The Pentagon report of 1998 that addressed the threat posed to the United States by Cuba concluded that Cuba "does not pose a significant military threat to the United States or to other countries in the region."[1] This was a forceful confirmation of a metamorphosis in the Pentagon's perceptions.

This shift can perhaps best be understood in light of the fact that two of the issues that have assumed greater importance for the Pentagon during the post–Cold War period are the struggle against the illegal international narcotics trade and the growing phenomenon of illegal migration (Klepak 2000, 25). In order to better address these concerns, Cuban cooperation was deemed necessary by U.S. officials, and Cuba proved itself willing to cooperate since it did not want to give the remaining superpower any excuse to intervene in Cuba's domestic affairs or to invade the island.

Since the United States considers illegal migration and drug trafficking to be serious threats to its national security, it has proved to be most willing to cooperate with Cuba in those areas. Cubans, however, are more deeply con-

Table 6.1. Comparison of the Four Cases of Cooperation

CBMs	Immigration	Drugs	Gitmo Naval Base	Avoiding Accidental War
Goals: Conflict/ Avoidance	Pentagon did not want to be forced into military conflict resulting from a mass exodus from Cuba center.	Pentagon concerned that a crisis in Cuba could result in Cuba be coming a drug transit center.	Housing Cuban refugees on U.S. base in Cuba increased tensions between the two countries. Gen. Sheehan worked to reduce those tensions.	Pentagon concerned that another incident like the shoot-down of Brothers could lead to an unwanted military confrontation.
Implementation: Quiet/unofficial diplomacy	Secret negotiations in New York	Secret talks in Havana	Military-to-military meetings at the naval base	Communication between coast guards and with retired U.S. military officers
Outcome: Political agreements	Immigration Accords 94–95	Memo passed via interests section in Havana	Improved channels of communication on operating procedures	Coordination of supervision of flotillas
Issues: High politics	High politics: Immigration had been used as a weapon by both countries	High politics: U.S. precedence of regime change in Panama	High politics: U.S. naval base on Cuban soil considered a violation of sovereignty	High politics: related to war
Scope: Incremental, small steps	Limited to immigration only	Limited to case-by-case	Limited to pragmatic, operational concerns	Limited to supervision of flotilla

cerned with lessening tensions around the U.S. naval base at Guantánamo Bay and with reducing the threat of accidental war caused by provocations of hardline Cuban American organizations. These concerns were clearly articulated in the transcript of the meeting that took place between retired U.S. military officers, a U.S. Coast Guard official, and Cuban officers in Havana in February 2001, when one Cuban official noted that the United States and Cuba have different perspectives on national security issues (Center for Defense Information 2001).

As the decade of the 1990s drew to a close, U.S. policy makers, military officials, and scholars reconsidered the most important U.S. national interests with regard to post–Cold War Cuba. As noted in this and the preceding chapters, many have argued that the principal threat for the United States was potential Cuban refugee flows triggered by economic, political, or social turmoil on the island. Secondarily, many have warned that Cuba could become a haven for drug dealers or terrorists who would use the island as a staging area, transshipment point, or training site.

Into the Twenty-first Century

Rothkopf (2000) has written that, aside from its proximity to the United States, the factors that gave Cuba disproportionate prominence, and warranted special and often costly U.S. policies, are now gone. The United States in the twenty-first century needs to recognize a new set of national interests vis-à-vis Cuba. Rothkopf urges close cooperation between U.S. and Cuban law enforcement authorities, immigration authorities, customs authorities, and others in recognition of the new security threats confronting both countries. Active inclusion of Cuba in regional programs in these areas and the expansion of existing programs should also be key focal points of future efforts. Recent progress in pilot efforts in these areas should be seen as even stronger evidence of the merits of such approaches (Rothkopf 2000, 110, 123). Modest cooperative efforts or CBMs between the United States and Cuba were established during the 1990s. Their existence and success support Rothkopf's "call for a post–Cold War Cuba policy."

Cuba and the United States Beat around the Bush, 2000–2005

The George W. Bush administration has adhered to the migration agreements, has continued to cooperate on drug interdiction, and has waived enforcement of Title III of the Helms-Burton Act. However, as of 2005 there has been no documented evidence of recent efforts at increased confidence building between the United States and Cuba. Instead, tensions between the two countries have risen to levels unmatched since the Cuban missile crisis, and tit-for-tat retaliatory measures threaten to undo much of the previous efforts at CBMs.

The first strong hint of a shift away from confidence building came early in the spring of Bush's first year in office, when the new president "reopened wounds" by nominating for top posts several controversial individuals who had been heavily involved in the U.S. interventions in Central America in the 1980s and 1990s.[2] These officials included Elliot Abrams, who had two convictions in 1991 for misleading Congress about the Iran-Contra scandal; John Negroponte, who as U.S. ambassador to Honduras had been accused of ignoring atrocities committed by the Honduran government; and Otto Reich, a hard-line Cuban American who made absolutely no secret that his key policy objective was to overthrow Castro. Cuban officials were most concerned by the return of Reich.[3]

Otto Reich had risen to prominence during the Reagan administration when he was appointed the head of the Office of Public Diplomacy within the State Department. According to the National Security Archives, Reich used his role to pursue his own agenda to such an extent that in 1987 the comptroller-general of the United States, a Republican appointee, found that some of the efforts of his office were "prohibited, covert propaganda activities . . . beyond the range of acceptable agency public information activities."[4] A letter of September 30, 1987, concluded that Reich's office had violated "a restriction on the State Department's annual appropriations prohibiting the use of federal funds for publicity or propaganda purposes not authorized by Congress." Moreover, Reich's office was discovered to have written bogus editorial pieces under the names of Nicaraguan Contras, which were submitted and subsequently published in the mainstream media.[5]

More ominous for U.S.-Cuban relations was Reich's widely accepted connection to Orlando Bosch and Bosch's numerous terrorist activities directed against Cuba. In her book *Cuba Confidential*, Ana Louise Bardach notes that "a half dozen declassified CIA and state department cables leave little doubt that Reich used his position to lobby for the pardon of Orlando Bosch, who the Bush Justice Department had concluded had participated in more than 30 terrorist actions" against the island.[6]

During the Clinton presidency, Reich moved into corporate lobbying and worked on behalf of Bacardi Rum, which had an enormous stake in overthrowing the Castro regime so that it could reclaim old distilleries on the island. Reich was a major architect in drawing up the Helms-Burton legislation in 1995, under which Bacardi would be able to sue its competitors for doing business in Cuba. These connections led to accusations of conflict of interest and also received a storm of protest from the Cuban government. Cuba subsequently responded to Reich's "recess appointment" by President George W. Bush by publishing "Orlando Bosch's terrorist curriculum vitae."[7] In linking Reich and Bosch, the Cuban government pointed to the hypocrisy of the U.S. government. After September 11, the Bush administration had condemned all terrorists, had criticized all countries that harbored terrorists, and yet Reich himself had connections to Cuban exile terrorists.

Another incident that sharply increased tensions between Havana and Washington was the arrest on September 21, 2001, of Ana Belén Montes, the Defense Intelligence Agency's senior analyst for matters involving Cuba. Montes, a Puerto Rican, stood accused of spying for Cuba after passing details about a particular Special Access Program related to the national defense of the United States.[8] Montes had been under FBI surveillance since May 2001, but the investigation was abruptly ended, and Montes was arrested after U.S. officials feared that Cuban intelligence agencies might pass along the information provided by Montes to other countries, "particularly some in the Middle East."[9] Montes subsequently was convicted of spying on March 19, 2002, and sentenced to a twenty-five-year term. According to her attorney and federal prosecutors, she had not been motivated by money but had "engaged in these activities because of her belief that U.S. policy does not afford Cubans respect, tolerance, and understanding. She was motivated instead by her desire to help the Cuban people and did not receive any compensation."[10]

Former U.S. drug czar General Barry McCaffrey interpreted the Montes case differently from those officials who focused on the possibility that Cuba might pass sensitive intelligence information on to Middle Eastern countries:

> Of course, it is clear that the Cuban intelligence services continue to aggressively conduct operations designed to penetrate U.S.-based Cuban exile groups and to infiltrate and monitor U.S. military capability. The

recent arrest of U.S. defense analyst Ana Belén Montes on spy charges and the earlier conviction of a Cuban espionage ring in South Florida underscore the fear of the Cuban leadership of terrorist attacks by Cuban exile groups on their island as well as their sense of paranoia and vulnerability to possible U.S. military attack. (McCaffrey 2002, 1)

During the first week of May 2002, a historic visit to Cuba by former president Carter dominated the news, and hopes were raised that perhaps a thaw between the two countries might result from the visit. Even before Carter's arrival, however, the State Department arms control chief, John R. Bolton, announced in a speech at the Heritage Foundation that the Bush administration believed that Cuba was pursuing weapons of mass destruction, particularly biological weapons.[11]

Within the next few weeks, Major General Gary Speer, the commander of U.S. forces in the Caribbean, cast doubt on the highly charged bioweapons accusation. On May 23 Speer noted that Cuba had an active biomedical research program but that there was no evidence that Cuba was actually producing bioweapons.[12] Former president Carter also noted that before undertaking his trip to Cuba, he had specifically asked Bush administration officials if they had evidence that Cuba had been sharing biotechnology with enemies of the United States, and they had told him no.[13]

On May 20, 2002, on the centennial celebration of Cuba's independence from Spain, President Bush announced that he would not lift the Cuban trade embargo unless Fidel Castro released political prisoners, conducted independently monitored elections, and accepted a list of U.S. conditions for a "new government that is fully democratic."[14] The president called this policy his Initiative for a New Cuba. The policy stemmed from a review directed by Reich. Bush also stated that he would veto further measures on trade that relaxed restrictions or that lifted the ban that empowered the Treasury Department to fine U.S. citizens traveling to Cuba. He concluded, "Well-intentioned ideas about trade will merely prop up this dictator."[15]

In response to Bush's Initiative for a New Cuba and defying calls for democratic reforms to his one-party system, on June 12, 2002, Fidel Castro led hundreds of thousands of people in a march in support of a constitutional amendment declaring Cuba's socialist state "untouchable." The massive march in Havana and in cities across the island in support of the amendment had been announced exactly one month after activists from Project Varela, whose cause had been embraced by Carter during his unprecedented television address to the Cuban people, submitted a proposed referendum for deep reforms in the socialist system. In comments to international media, several Communist officials accused project organizers of being on the U.S. government payroll (Cuba Source 2002).

The Cuban government's accusations were not without some basis, because U.S. diplomats in Cuba had been actively working inside the country to bring an end to Castro's rule. These activities had increased during the George W. Bush administration and included the encouragement of dissidents, such as Osvaldo Payá, the organizer of the Varela Project. U.S. diplomats also distributed more than 1,000 short-wave radios to Cubans and supported antigovernment journalists. As would be expected, Cuban government officials regarded these activities as improper intervention in their internal affairs.[16]

Almost concurrently, the State Department accused Cuba of deliberately subverting American efforts to fight terrorism by steadily providing Washington with erroneous tips and other false information about potential threats. According to Dan Fisk, the deputy assistant secretary in the Bureau for Western Hemisphere Affairs at the Department of State, the tips from Cuba, which began on the day of the September 11 attacks and had been arriving almost monthly, had led American investigators on "wild goose chases" and had diverted important resources. Fidel Castro and his government "are actually impeding our efforts to defeat the threat of terrorism," Fisk said, because prudence requires investigators to follow every lead. "This is not harmless game-playing," Fisk added. "It is a dangerous and unjustifiable action that damages our ability to assess real threats.[17] Fisk's accusations came as hundreds of Cuban Americans and others seeking to ease economic sanctions against Cuba converged in Washington, D.C., for two days of meetings and lobbying, and supporters of sanctions sought to muster a publicity counteroffensive.[18]

Cuba's foreign minister, Felipe Pérez Roque, angrily rebutted State Department charges that his government was providing the United States with false leads on terrorism, and he accused one American official of "lying with impudence." Pérez Roque said that Castro's government had repeatedly sought to cooperate with the United States since the September 11 attacks but that the Bush administration had rejected its overtures.[19]

By March 6, 2003, tensions regarding U.S. diplomats' activities in Cuba reached a boiling point. Fidel Castro criticized the United States, warning that Cuba did not need the U.S. foreign office or Interests Section. Castro's remark was an angry response to a public visit in February by the U.S. Interests

Section chief James Cason with Havana dissidents. "Anyone can see that this is a shameless and defiant provocation," Castro said of Cason's meeting with the dissidents (Cuba Source 2003). "Perhaps the numerous U.S. intelligence agents working at the Interests Section could explain to him that Cuba can easily do without this office—a breeding ground for counterrevolutionaries and a command post for the most offensive subversive actions against our country." Castro seemed to take special exception to Cason's earlier declaration that "the Cuban government is afraid, afraid of freedom of conscience, afraid of freedom of expression, afraid of human rights." "Actually," Castro said, "Cuba is so afraid that it will calmly take all the time needed to decide on its course of action regarding this bizarre official" (Cuba Source 2003).

In a move that shocked the international community, beginning March 18, 2003, the Castro government carried out its largest mass arrest of dissidents in years and again accused Cason of trying to foment counterrevolution. The Cuban government announced that it would put the dissidents, whom it called traitors, on trial for allegedly working with Cason. Through a statement read on state-run television, the Cuban government accused Cason of trying "to foment the internal counterrevolution," and further stated that "no nation, no matter how powerful, has the right to organize, finance and serve as the center for subverting the constitutional order."[20] The arrests appeared to target those dissidents who had met with Cason during his extensive travels around Cuba. Daniel P. Erikson, the director for Caribbean Projects at the Inter-American Dialogue research group in Washington, D.C., said that the Castro government may have seen Cason's activism as a provocation—"as the United States thumbing its nose at them."[21]

An editorial in the *Washington Post* on April 3, 2003, noted that many of the almost eighty dissidents were associated with the Varela Project, but the crackdown may have had deeper reasons as well.[22] Over the previous few weeks there had been two skyjackings and a ferry hijacking in Havana. In all of these cases, the well-armed hijackers wanted to be taken to Miami or Key West, which had also been the destination of the hijackers of a Cuban government patrol boat. Further, the editorial noted, the Cuban church had blasted the regime, and the economy continued to be in crisis.

James Cason responded that the crackdown by Cuban officials on dissidents had helped to create the potential for large-scale exoduses similar to ones in 1980 and 1994, and that the actions taken by Cuba against activists were stoking renewed fear among the island's residents. Cason concluded: "The continued disintegration of Cuban society generates instability throughout the region and creates the threat of a mass migration to the United States. This undermines our security and the long-term potential for the Cuban nation" (Cuba Source 2003).

The next shocking event occurred on April 11, 2003, when Cuban authorities executed three men who had hijacked a ferry during the previous week in a failed attempt to reach the United States. Four other men who had used a gun and knives to help commandeer the boat were given life sentences. Although the death penalty had been infrequently applied in Cuba, the three faced a firing squad after being convicted of "very grave acts of terrorism."[23] The executions came at the end of the same week in which seventy-eight nonviolent dissidents received harsh prison terms of up to twenty-eight years for conspiring with U.S. diplomats.

Hijackings, of which there had been seven in seven months, greatly angered Cuban officials, who argued that U.S. policies, like the Cuban Adjustment Act, encouraged illegal migration. In fact, Cubans had lodged this complaint during their meeting with the Center for Defense Information (CDI) on February 14, 2001, when one Cuban official noted:

> Another commitment that was made through the '94/'95 agreements is that both nations fight the use of violence to migrate. Unfortunately, this part of the agreement has not been fulfilled by the U.S. government either because since '95 to the present, the hijacking or smuggling of several airplanes and vessels or boats has taken place. And sometimes the hijackers use firearms and those people are now roaming the streets in the United States—or are free in the United States, I'm sorry to say. (Center for Defense Information 2001)

Cuban officials were particularly indignant over the release on bail of several men who hijacked a plane to Miami in March 2003. Even so, the summary trials and the imposition of the death penalty for the three hijackers alienated many U.S. officials who had previously advocated dialogue with Cuba. "This about ends that discussion," Rep. Charles Rangel (D-N.Y.) told the *New York Times*. "I don't know how far they are going to go, but they know how to support their enemies and get rid of their friends."[24]

On April 27, 2003, Castro himself explained the executions of the three hijackers: "The wave of hijackings had to be stopped radically."[25] Castro further explained on Cuban television that Cuba had to apply the death sentence without hesitation to avoid further armed attempts by Cubans expecting to be received as heroes in the United States. Castro blamed the United States, saying that the U.S. authorities were tolerant of Cuban hijackers and that the U.S. government encouraged illegal migration by granting automatic residence to the Cubans who made it there. "The sinister idea is to provoke armed conflict between Cuba and the United States in the hope of ending the revolution," Castro affirmed.[26]

Given the jailing of the dissidents and the executions of the three hijackers, the Bush administration's inclination was to hammer Castro. However, with some 40,000 Cubans openly endorsing Osvaldo Payá's petition drive (Varela Project) calling for free speech, multiparty elections, and increased private enterprise, Bush did not want to provoke further retaliatory measures by Castro that might cripple the first real chance for democratic change on the island. For Bush, that meant walking a fine line between backing Payá and keeping U.S. support below Castro's radar (Padgett 2003, 46).

In a disappointment to some Cuban American activists, the White House decided after a few weeks of deliberation and after expelling fourteen Cuban diplomats for "inappropriate and unacceptable activities" not to take additional steps to punish Fidel Castro for cracking down on prodemocracy dissidents.[27] Many had expected Bush to use the 101st anniversary of Cuba's independence from Spain on May 20, 2003, to announce a toughening of U.S. policy. Still, Isabel Roque, sister of Marta Beatriz Roque, an independent economist and dissident who had received a twenty-year sentence, said that Cubans did not want Americans to go too far. "We don't want the Marines to invade our island."[28]

During the height of tensions resulting from the crackdown and executions, no one was sure what to expect from the Bush administration. Daniel P. Erikson noted that the politics of Cuba policy were increasingly uncertain but that Bush had time and again stopped short of going as far as some Cuban American activists had urged. Although Bush did not loosen the embargo, he also did not agree to tighten it or to take other tough steps. Erikson concluded that Bush's policy "is a mixed bag. Much of this is a continuation of the Clinton policy."[29]

President Bush showed that he was unwilling to bend to Cuban American pressures to back away from the migration agreement. A few weeks following the execution of the three hijackers, Bush decided to return twelve other suspected hijackers after he received assurances from the Cuban government that the twelve would not receive more than ten-year prison sentences.[30] Cuban American National Foundation executive director Joe García voiced outrage at the return of the twelve and accused Bush of cooperating with the Cuban government in a way that "goes far beyond" that of former president Clinton. García noted that under Clinton's migration policy, rafters caught on the high seas were returned to Cuba and set free on the island under U.S. supervision. However, Bush had negotiated "jail terms with a country that our own State Department lists as a terrorist state."[31] On August 30, 2003, García appeared on the Fox News program *The Beltway Boys* and alluded to a potential Cuban American voter backlash when he emphasized that if less than 1 percent of Cuban Americans had changed their vote in the 2000 presidential election, Bush would not be in the White House.

During the 2004 presidential campaign, Bush countered the criticism that he had not cracked down hard enough on Cuba. In June he announced stricter rules whereby Cuban Americans visiting their families on the island would be limited to one trip every three years, and they would now be required to apply for and receive approval from the Office of Foreign Assets Control (OFAC) prior to departure. The new restrictions provided no discretionary measures for additional family visits during the three-year period. In other words, if a Cuban American's grandmother suffered a heart attack, there was no possibility of an emergency trip to Cuba to visit her in the hospital.

In addition, the new regulations sharply narrowed the definition of family. In the past, family visits could be made to anyone related by a common great-grandparent, but under Bush's new policy, visits could only be made to immediate family members: spouse, children, parents, grandparents, and brothers-and sisters-in-law. Many Cuban Americans protested that the new definition of family was out of line with Cuban culture, which considered families to include cousins and more distant blood relatives. With the new policy, President Bush hoped to starve Castro of hard currency and to further tighten the economic squeeze on the regime.

The next month in Tampa, Florida, the president announced that Fidel Castro promoted sex tourism to Cuba. He told a gathering of law enforcement officials, "The dictator welcomes sex tourism. Here's how he bragged about the industry. This is his quote: 'Cuba has the cleanest and most educated prostitutes in the world.'"[32] It was later revealed that Bush's source for the quote was an undergraduate paper that did not provide proper citation for

Castro's remark. The student who wrote the paper explained that the president had taken the quote out of context, and he noted, "Castro was merely trying to emphasize the successes of the revolution by saying 'even our prostitutes are educated.'"[33] The State Department later released the original quote in its correct context. In a 1992 speech before the Cuban National Assembly, Castro had said: "There are hookers, but prostitution is not allowed in our country. There are no women forced to sell themselves to a man, to a foreigner, to a tourist. Those who do so do it on their own, voluntarily.... We can say that they are highly educated hookers and quite healthy, because we are the country with the lowest number of AIDS cases."[34]

Not only was the quote over ten years old, but its true context revealed that President Bush had completely misrepresented Castro's stance on prostitution. Nevertheless, the unfounded charge was welcomed by the Cuban American community, and by linking Castro with sexual tourism, the president showcased his anti-Castro credentials.

Since President Bush's reelection in November 2004, administration officials have paid close attention to the growing ties between Venezuelan president Hugo Chávez and Fidel Castro. In fact, concern in Washington has been growing steadily over the past five years. In 2000 Chávez and Castro signed the Integral Cooperation Accord, and U.S. officials began to suspect Cuba of reviving its mothballed internationalist foreign policy. For his part of the accord, Castro pledged to supply Venezuela with 20,000 medical professionals and educators in exchange for a pledge from Chávez to supply Cuba with 53,000 barrels of oil a day at preferential prices.[35] U.S. policy makers were concerned that Chávez and Castro were forming a strategic alliance, especially since Chávez frequently had expressed his open admiration for Castro and the path of the Cuban revolution. Moreover, the two men had a warm personal relationship that dated back to the early 1990s. In 1994 Castro had invited Chávez to Cuba to recuperate and make speeches, after Chávez was released from prison for his 1992 coup attempt.[36]

After Chávez was elected to the Venezuelan presidency in 1998, U.S. officials hoped that he would not long survive given the opposition of many sectors of Venezuelan society, including the wealthy, the oil sector, organized labor, and increasing numbers of military personnel. In April 2002 oil workers and other opposition groups launched anti-Chávez strikes and protests that culminated in Chávez's removal by a military coup, and when the military announced on April 12 that Chávez had resigned, U.S. officials openly expressed their satisfaction. In less than forty-eight hours, however, Chávez was reinstated after his supporters rioted in nearly every city of the country.

Chávez subsequently survived a referendum vote on his recall in 2004. U.S. officials expressed disappointment that the recall did not turn Chávez out of office, but his victory was celebrated in Havana. In December 2004 Chávez and Castro jointly poked Washington in the eye by forming the Bolivarian Alternative for the Americas (ALBA), a regional response to the U.S.-supported the Free Trade Area of the Americas (FTAA). In 2005 Chávez increased his rhetorical attacks on the United States. He embraced socialism, repeatedly denounced neoliberalism, trumpeted his Bolivarian vision of a unified continent independent of Washington, and further deepened his partnership with Cuba by signing some forty-nine agreements in commerce, energy and oil, finances, agriculture, communications, banking, health care, and education.[37]

U.S. policy makers noted warily that the Chávez-Castro partnership might factor into a growing swing to the left in Latin America that could become hostile to fundamental U.S. security interests. During a visit to Latin America in the spring of 2005, Secretary of State Condoleezza Rice referred to Chávez as a "destabilizing" influence in the region, and Secretary of Defense Donald Rumsfeld referred to Castro and Chávez as "troublemakers."[38]

Former assistant secretary of state for Western Hemisphere Affairs Otto Reich reflected the mood of the Bush administration in a cover story in the March 21, 2005, *National Review* in which he referred to Chávez and Castro as "Latin America's Terrible Two." "With the combination of Castro's evil genius, experience in political warfare, and economic desperation, and Chávez's unlimited money and recklessness, the peace of this region is in peril," he wrote. "The emerging axis of subversion forming between Cuba and Venezuela must be confronted before it can undermine democracy in Colombia, Nicaragua, Bolivia, or another vulnerable neighbor."[39]

The growing concern in Washington was that the much younger Chávez might become Castro's heir and the new continental leader of leftist revolution. Castro himself noted that President Bush and other U.S. officials were hanging their hopes on rumors of Castro's failing health, thinking that "if the dog dies, so does the rabies." To that sentiment, Castro noted, "But now Venezuela has turned into a [new] dog."[40]

During a quick trip to Peru and Paraguay in August 2005, Secretary of Defense Rumsfeld referred to the social uprisings in Bolivia that had forced out two presidents in two years and noted that Cuba and Venezuela had been "involved in the situation in Bolivia in unhelpful ways."[41] The next week Chávez made his thirteenth visit to Cuba since 1999 and spoke alongside Castro during his regular Sunday television and radio show, *Aló Presidente*.[42] He refuted Rumsfeld's remarks and noted that U.S. imperialism was the world's greatest threat and not Cuba or Venezuela.[43]

Within days the close relationship between Castro and Chávez was thrown into the headlines of U.S. media when television evangelist and founder of the Christian Coalition of America, Pat Robertson, suggested on August 22, 2005, that the United States assassinate Chávez. In the wake of the media uproar that followed Robertson's inflammatory suggestion, both Chávez and Castro benefited. Whereas U.S. policy makers had hoped to focus the public's attention on Castro and Chávez as trouble-making thugs, Robertson's outlandish remark instead put the U.S. government on the defensive. The image of Castro and Chávez as regional thugs was further eroded in the days following the devastation of Hurricane Katrina, when both leaders offered to send relief money and medical personnel and supplies to aid the victims.

The only relief that was of interest to Washington was relief from the winds that seemed to be blowing Latin American governments to the left. In December 2005 leftist presidential candidate Evo Morales won a landslide victory in Bolivia and quickly arranged a regional tour. During Morales's visit to Venezuela, Chávez declared, "The axis of evil—do you know who the axis of evil is? Washington—that's the axis of evil. And their allies in the world, who threaten, who invade, who kill, who assassinate." Chávez went on to propose that "we are creating the axis of good, the new axis of the new century." To that declaration Morales added, "The movement is not only in Bolivia. Fidel in Cuba and Hugo in Venezuela are logging triumphs in social movements and leftist policies."[44] Morales joined a growing list of leftists who had been elected to the presidency in Brazil, Uruguay, Paraguay, Argentina, and Chile.

During the Clinton administration, hostile policies toward Cuba were often followed by nascent cooperation, and the Bush administration, overburdened with the rebuilding of Iraq abroad and New Orleans at home, may yet find it more advantageous to move from confrontation to cooperation. If that is the case, practical ideas for future cooperation have already been generated based on the prior cooperation established during the 1990s.

Looking to the Future of U.S.-Cuban Cooperation

In 1999 a bipartisan, independent task force of the Council on Foreign Relations on U.S.-Cuban Relations in the 21st Century declared that "Cuban communism is dead as a potent political force in the Western Hemisphere today." Members of the task force recommended "military-to-military confidence building measures, and greater anti-drug cooperation" (Fisk 1999). With regard to increasing antidrug cooperation, Wayne Smith of the Center for International Policy has proposed some concrete steps for future implementation. First, the United States should drop all efforts to impede Cuba's access to intelligence sharing in the three existing regional organizations. Second, the U.S. Coast Guard should be authorized to begin a systematic exchange of information with its Cuban counterpart and to coordinate patrol areas and responsibilities on a continuing basis. Third, there should be frequent and periodic meetings between representatives of the Cuban Border Guard and the U.S. Coast Guard to discuss joint drug interdiction operations, problems, and ways to overcome them. Fourth, joint training exercises would enhance drug interdiction capabilities. And fifth, the U.S. should publicly acknowledge Cuba's cooperation in drug interdiction efforts (Smith 1998, 4–5).

Another area related to drug trafficking in which U.S.-Cuban cooperation would benefit the entire region involves working to resolve the Colombian civil war. In fact, further research about Cuba's efforts in helping to mediate between the Colombian government and the guerrillas could possibly shed light on the strength of Cuba's commitment to halting drug trafficking in the region. One of the items on the CDI agenda during the February 2001 meeting in Havana was a lengthy discussion about Colombia, and one Cuban official was quick to point out that Cuba was already playing a cooperative role in helping to peacefully resolve the conflict:

> I think the Cuban position regarding this Colombian conflict has been quite clear. Cuba has accepted to cooperate for the resolution of the Colombian conflict, taking into account, first of all, the historic links we have with the Colombians. The Cuban and Colombian peoples have had their close links practically from the very founding of the two nations. But what has been quite underscored in the Cuban policy is that in Colombia, as it happened in the case of Angola, Cuba is not seeking its own benefits. Our cooperation has been very noticed. And besides, it has been extremely careful and unselfish. And in this sense, something

which is key to us has been taken into account. Namely, it is an internal situation in the country.

Our government has always said and has always upheld the view that countries' internal conflicts should be solved by the countries themselves, even though in the Colombian case, due to the specific circumstances, certain international assistance may be required. (Center for Defense Information 2001)

As to improving confidence building with regard to illegal migration, Phillip Peters in his research for the Lexington Institute has provided suggestions for both the United States and Cuba. First, he notes that although it would be hard for a U.S. administration to break with the practice of granting permanent residence to all Cubans who reach U.S. shores, the practices associated with the Cuban Adjustment Act are at variance with the migration agreements and should be reversed. Second, both Cuba and the United States should cut the costs of consular fees charged to emigrants, since the fees are usually paid by U.S. relatives, and therefore disadvantage those Cubans without U.S. relatives. A third suggestion calls for Cuba to give U.S. officials access to Cuban media so that they can provide information about legal emigration procedures, because many Cubans remain unaware of the legal options that were granted under the agreements. Peters also notes that Cuba needs to implement broader economic reforms so as to increase incentives for young Cubans to live and work in Cuba (Peters 2001, 7).

By establishing cooperation in the field of biotechnology, the United States and Cuba could likewise lessen tensions related to Cuba's bioweapons capacity. On May 8, 2002, just two days after John Bolton, U.S. undersecretary of state for arms control, made his controversial speech about Cuba's capacity to produce bioweapons, Glenn Baker, Cuba project director of the CDI, spoke with a representative of the Cuban Interests Section about the possibility of bringing a group of experts to Cuba to learn more about the charges. As a result of that conversation, a CDI delegation including scientists, a former United Nations chief weapons inspector, military experts, and videographers was invited to Cuba, and the delegation toured nine biotechnology centers of their choosing from October 6 to 9, 2002 (Baker 2003).

The following year I was a participant in another CDI delegation that visited Cuba from November 3 to 6. On November 5 our delegation attended a working meeting with the Scientific Pole of West Havana at the Center for Genetics Engineering and Biotechnology. During the meeting, Cuban scientists proposed the collaboration of Cuban biotechnological institutes with U.S. scientific institutions. They noted that U.S. citizens and Cuban citizens both suffered similar rates of diabetes and cancer and that U.S. and Cuban scientists could conduct mutual studies in order to work for the health of the citizens in both countries and in order to build confidence within the scientific communities. These proposed studies could include collaboration and the exchange of specialists with the National Cancer Institute, the Centers for Disease Control and Prevention, and the Federal Drug Administration.

In a related vein, it was announced in July 2004 that the U.S. government had given permission to CancerVax, a California biotechnology company, for the licensing of three experimental cancer drugs from Cuba. CancerVax executives explained that it was the first time an American biotechnology company had obtained permission to license a drug from Cuba.[45] More recently, on August 31, 2005, the Bush administration announced that it was backing away from its prior claims that Cuba had an offensive biological weapons effort. The State Department report instead noted that Cuba has the "technical capability" to pursue biological weapons research and development.[46] The report marked the first time that the U.S. government had publicly softened its stance on the controversy.

Given that the George W. Bush administration is no longer insisting that Cuba is creating offensive bioweapons, perhaps there is now a crack in the door to the White House for those officials who hope to create more CBMs between the United States and Cuba. At the very least, CBMs offer a new pathway for U.S.-Cuban relations that would be an alternative to the tired policies of the past. The U.S. policy of undermining Castro with the U.S. embargo has punished both countries for over forty years, and the unofficial policy of waiting for the biological solution is likewise flawed. As former CIA director George Tenet on occasion remarked, "The bad news is Castro has a great gene pool, and he's stopped smoking cigars."[47]

On July 31, 2006, as this book was nearing completion, a statement written by Fidel Castro was read on Cuban television by Castro's personal secretary. In the statement Castro explained that his recent trip to Argentina and the previous week's anniversary of the Cuban Revolution had caused him "days and nights of non-stop work" and "extreme stress."[48] As a result, he was suffering from intestinal bleeding that would require hospitalization, invasive surgery, and several weeks of recuperation.

For the first time in 47 years Fidel Castro ceded his power and temporarily passed control of the government to his brother and designated successor, Raúl. With reference to the United States Fidel further noted, "In the Cuban situation, based on plans of the empire, my health becomes a secret of state that cannot be divulged constantly."[49] The news was indeed stunning for the Cuban people, most of whom had known only one leader. Meanwhile in Miami, Cuban Americans took to the streets in party atmosphere. They waved Cuban and American flags, shot off fireworks, and chanted "Cuba libre."

Castro's illness gives a new sense of urgency to the message of this book. Working to build confidence between the two countries serves the long-term interests of both. When the inevitable transition comes, an established pattern of cooperation will make it easier to reestablish healthier diplomatic ties between the United States and post–Fidel Castro Cuba.

Notes

Introduction

1. Vanessa Arrington, "U.S. Ignores Cuba's Christmas Warning," Cubanet, December 15, 2004 <www.cubanet.org>.

2. Arrington, "U.S. Ignores Cuba's Christmas Warning."

3. Arrington, "U.S. Ignores Cuba's Christmas Warning."

4. John Hughes, "Bush's Cuban Quandary," *Christian Science Monitor*, October 15, 2003.

Chapter 1. Cuban Exile Politics

1. "A Look at Luis Posada Carriles' Life," Associated Press, May 17, 2005.

2. Sue Anne Pressley, "Elián Case Casts Shadow on Legacy," *Washington Post*, April 29, 2000.

3. Pablo Bachelet, "New Lobby Kills Threats to the Embargo," *Miami Herald*, July 12, 2005.

Chapter 2. The Migration Agreements of 1994–1995

1. María de los Angeles Torres, "Uprooted by History, We Are Cuba's Lost Children in Search of Our Past," *Washington Post*, February 1, 1998.

2. Anne Rochell, "In the Dawn of Castro's Cuba, Fearful Parents Sent 14,000 Children to Freedom in America." *Atlantic Constitution*, February 21, 1998.

3. de los Angeles Torres, "Uprooted by History."

4. "Exiles Dock in Cuba, Ignore U.S. Warning," *Miami Herald*, October 9, 1965, cited in Engstrom 1997.

5. "Mariel: 25 Years Later," special publication of *Miami Herald/El Nuevo Herald*, April 3, 2005.

6. *The Cuban Émigrés: Was There a US Intelligence Failure?* Staff Report, Subcommittee on Oversight, Permanent Select Committee on Intelligence, U.S. House of Representatives.

7. "Cuba Assails Clinton on Guantánamo Detentions," *New York Times*, August 21, 1994.

8. "Agreement with U.S. on legal migration," *Caribbean and Central American Report*, Latin American Newsletters: London, October 6, 1994: 3.

9. *Caribbean and Central American Report*, October 6, 1994.

10. "U.S. Suspends Migration Talks with Cuba," Associated Press, January 7, 2004.

11. Kevin Sullivan, "U.S. Backs Out of Talks in Cuba on Immigration," *Washington Post*, January 7, 2004.

12. Christopher Marquis, "U.S. Halts Cuban Immigration Talks; Worsening of Ties Seen," *New York Times*, January 8, 2004.

13. Sullivan, "U.S. Backs Out of Talks in Cuba."

14. David Orvalle, "Let 'Truckonauts' Stay, Group Asks U.S. Court," *Miami Herald*, June 9, 2005.

Chapter 3. U.S.-Cuban Cooperative Efforts on Drug Interdiction

1. Lillian Riera, "U.S. Refusal to Collaborate with Cuba Will Incite Drug Trafficking," *Granma International*, October 15, 2004.

2. Alfonso Chardy, "Cuba Cancels Pact to Halt Drug Traffic," *Washington Post*, April 28, 1982.

3. A detailed account of the Ochoa case is included in Oppenheimer, *Castro's Final Hour*, 1992.

4. Cuba was excluded from active participation in the OAS in 1962.

5. Doug Farah, "Cuba Wages a Lonesome Drug War," *Washington Post*, May 25, 1999.

6. "Colombians Convicted in Drug Case with Cuba Tie," *Reuters*, March 13, 1997.

7. Farah, "Cuba Wages a Lonesome Drug War."

8. George Gedda, "U.S., Cuba Hold Counter-Narcotics Talk," Associated Press, June 21, 1999.

9. "Castro Urges Anti-drug Pact with U.S." *BBC Online Network*, July 27, 1999, <news.bbc.co.uk/2/hi/americas/405002.stm> (accessed in 2003).

10. "Statement on Drug Trafficking Made by Dr. Fidel Castro Ruz, President of the State Council of the Republic of Cuba, at the Commemoration of July 26, 1953," <www.cuba.cu/gobierno/discursos/1999/ing/n260799i.htm> (accessed in 2003).

11. "Statement on Drug Trafficking Made by Dr. Fidel Castro Ruz."

12. Latin American Working Group, <www.lawg.org./drugcert2.htm> (accessed in 2003).

13. Latin American Working Group.

14. Juan O. Tamayo, "Despite Concern, Clinton Omits Cuba as Major Drug Transit Point," *Miami Herald*, November 11, 1999.

15. Juan O. Tamayo, "What's Just Passing 'Through'?" *Miami Herald*, October 29, 1999.

16. Dan Burton and Ben Gilman, "The Compelling Case of Castro's Cocaine," <www.house.gov/burton/oped11.htm> (accessed in 2003).

17. Tamayo, "Clinton Omits Cuba."

18. Tamayo, "Clinton Omits Cuba."

19. Gillian Gunn Clissold, "Cooperate with Castro on Drugs," *Washington Post*, August 25, 1999.

20. Juan O. Tamayo, "Witnesses Link Castro, Drugs," *Miami Herald*, Jan. 4, 2000.

21. Juan O. Tamayo, "Cuban Drug Link Called Limited," *Miami Herald*, Jan. 5, 2000.

22. William Delahunt and Phillip Peters, "U.S. Needs to Enlist Cuba in War on Drugs," *Boston Herald*, January 27, 2002.

23. Carlos Batista, "Cuba Seeks Deals with U.S. to Fight Terror, Migrant Smuggling, Drugs," *Agence France Presse*, March 19, 2002, <ciponline.org/cuba/cubainthenews> (accessed in 2003).

24. Roundtable on Drug Dealer Arrested by Cuba, broadcast from the studios of Cuban Television, March 18, 2002.

25. Portia Siegelbaum, "The War on drugs in Cuba," *Havana Journal*, February 23, 2005, <havanajournal.com> (accessed in 2005).

26. Peter Sleven, "Cuba Urges Cooperation on Drug Interdiction," *Washington Post*, March 19, 2002.

27. Sleven, "Cuba Urges Cooperation."

28. "El misterio rodea caso de 'Rasguño' en Cuba," *El País*, May 6, 2005.

29. Riera, "U.S. Refusal to Collaborate with Cuba Will Incite Drug Trafficking."

Chapter 4. The U.S. Naval Station at Guantánamo Bay and U.S.-Cuban Cooperation

1. Steven Komarow, "Mine Removal Is Signal to Castro," *USA Today*, December 8, 1997.

2. One of the best sources that I found for information and the history of the naval base is the unpublished Ph.D. dissertation, "Guantánamo Bay: The United States Naval Base and Its Relationship with Cuba," by Mary Ellene Chenevey McCoy (University of Akron, 1995).

3. In 1998 the National Geographic Society funded a study that used modern computer-based modeling systems to analyze which was a more likely cause for the *Maine*'s loss—a coal bunker fire igniting a magazine or an external mine igniting a magazine. The result of the extensive analysis indicated that either cause could have been the source. The analysis is available in the February 1998 *National Geographic*, "A Special Report—What Really Sank the MAINE," by Thomas B. Allen.

4. I was unable to find any U.S. documentation referring to this agreement. According to the U.S. Navy, some confusion has always existed regarding terms of the original lease itself. The terms of the lease are contained in three documents—two agreements and a treaty. The contents of these documents are not well known. At times they have been misunderstood locally and also in Havana and Washington. It is small wonder that such has been the case. It was reported officially in 1936 that the Naval Station did not even possess a copy of the original lease agreement.

5. Robert L. Muse, "Is the U.S. Naval Base at Guantanamo Bay, Cuba, U.S. Sovereign Territory, and if so, What Difference Does It Make?" Presentation at the Center for International Policy Conference, Washington, D.C., March 5, 2003.

6. Congressional Record, 88th Congress, 1st session, June 17, 1963, 109, cited in McCoy 1995, 270.

7. Carol Rosenberg, "Guantanamo Base Free of Land Mines," *Miami Herald*, June 29, 1999.

8. Patrick E. Tyler, "U.S. Strategy Plan Calls for Insuring No Rivals Develop," *New York Times*, March 8, 1992.

9. Jim Hampton, "U.S., Cuban Generals Should Talk," *Miami Herald*, June 30, 1996.

10. Hampton, "U.S., Cuban Generals Should Talk."

11. Christopher Marquis, "Pentagon: Cuban Military Not a Threat," *Miami Herald*, March 29, 1998.

12. Marquis, "Cuban Military Not a Threat."

13. Ibid.

14. Randall Mikkelsen, "U.S. to Bring Kosovo Refugees to Cuba Base," *Cubanet News*, April 7, 1999, <64.21.33.164./CNews/y99/apr99/07e2.htm> (accessed in 2003).

15. Pascual Fletcher, "Cuba Signals Agreement to U.S. Base Refugee Plan," *Cubanet News*, April 9, 1999, <64.21.33.164/CNews/y99/apr99/09el.htm> (accessed in 2003).

16. "Statement by the Government of Cuba to National and International Public Opinion," *Granma*, January 14, 2002.

17. "Statement by the Government of Cuba to National and International Public Opinion."

18. Rosenberg, "Guantanamo Base Free of Land Mines."

19. Komarow, "Mine Removal Is Signal to Castro."

20. Ibid.

21. Ibid.

22. Rosenberg, "Guantanamo Base Free of Land Mines."

23. Nick Miroff, "Guantánamo's New Guests Get Little Attention in Havana," *World Press Review*, January 8, 2002.

24. Miroff, "Guantánamo's New Guests."

25. Ibid.

26. Nick Miroff, "The Tale of Five Cuban Spies," *World Press Review*, January 8, 2002.

27. Ginger Thompson, "Cuba, Too, Felt the Sept. 11 Shock Waves, with a More Genial Castro Offering Help," *New York Times*, February 7, 2002.

28. Thompson, "Cuba, Too, Felt the Sept.11 Shock Waves."

29. Carol Rosenberg, "U.S., Cuba Talk about Malaria." *Miami Herald*, February 22, 2002.

30. Rosenberg, "U.S., Cuba Talk about Malaria."

Chapter 5. U.S.-Cuban Cooperative Efforts at Reducing the Threat of Accidental War

1. For a detailed account of the planning for the Bay of Pigs invasion, see Wyden 1979. For the CIA's own evaluation of the operation's failure, see Kornbluh 1998.

2. Department of State, *Bulletin*, February 19, 1962.

3. The entire text of the memorandum is available on the National Security Archive Web page <www.gwu.edu/nsarchiv/news/20010430/northwoods.pdf>.

4. Juan O. Tamayo, "Anti-Castro Plots Seldom Lead to Jail in U.S.," *Miami Herald*, July 23, 1998.

5. Ann Louise Bardach, "Our Man's in Miami: Patriot or Terrorist?" *Miami Herald*, April 17, 2005.

6. Jefferson Morley, "Shoot Down," *Washington Post*, May 25, 1997.

7. I was in Cuba in March 1995, and several Cubans complained about leaflets that had been dropped from small planes.

8. Christopher Marquis, "Cuba Still No Threat, Pentagon Insists," *Miami Herald*, May 7, 1998.

9. The *Trece de Marzo* was a Ministry of Transport tugboat that was hijacked by a group of Cubans trying to migrate illegally to the United States. The tug was rammed and sunk by pursuing Cuban vessels. Forty-one Cubans perished in the tragedy. The official Cuban government version of the sinking called the incident regrettable, but underscored that the Cuban Border Guard did save thirty-one passengers and that the tragedy demonstrated how unscrupulous elements had been willing to risk the lives of numerous people, among them women and children, in an attempt to immigrate illegally to the United States, whose authorities usually do not grant Cubans visas to travel.

10. David Lawrence, "The Day Is Coming When We Will All Go to Cuba," *Miami Herald*, July 7, 1996.

11. Morley, "Shoot Down."

12. Ibid.

13. Ibid.

14. Ibid.

15. Marquis, "Cuba Still No Threat."

16. Elaine De Valle, "Exiles Press On with Plan for Tie-ups," *Miami Herald*, May 24, 1999.

17. Linda Backiel and Leonard Weinglass, "An Analysis of the Case of the Cuban Five," <1www.freethefive.org> (accessed August 15, 2005).

18. Backiel and Weinglass, "Case of the Cuban Five," 6.

19. Ibid., 7.

20. Ibid.

21. Ibid., 6.

22. Scott Hiaasen, Luisa Yanez, and David Ovalle, "Court Overturns Spy Verdicts," *Miami Herald*, August 10, 2005.

23. Backiel and Weinglass, "Case of the Cuban Five," 2.

24. Hiaasen, Yanez, and Ovalle, "Court Overturns Spy Verdicts."

25. Vanessa Arrington, "Cuba Wants U.S. to Release Five Agents," Associated Press, August 10, 2005.

26. Backiel and Weinglass, "Case of the Cuban Five," 4.

27. "Top Cuban Lawmaker Says Spies, Not Michael Jackson, Deserve Foreign Media Coverage," *Caribbean Net News*, <www.caribbeannetnews.com> (accessed July 21, 2005).

Conclusion

1. Marquis, "Cuba Still No Threat."

2. Christopher Marquis, "Bush Latin American Nominations Reopen Old Wounds," *New York Times*, August 1, 2001.

3. Duncan Campbell, "Friends of Terrorism: Bush's Decision to Bring Back Otto Reich Exposes the Hypocrisy of the War on Terror," *Guardian* (London), February 8, 2002.

4. Quoted in Campbell, "Friends of Terrorism."

5. Campbell, "Friends of Terrorism."

6. Quoted in Campbell, "Friends of Terrorism."

7. "Orlando Bosch's Terrorist Curriculum Vitae to Refresh Otto Reich's Memory," *Granma*, January 31, 2002.

8. Walter Pincus and Bill Miller, "Attacks Expedited Arrest in Espionage Case," *Washington Post*, September 28, 2001.

9. Pincus and Miller, "Attacks Expedited Arrest."

10. Neely Tucker, "Defense Analyst Pleads Guilty to Spying for Cuba," *Washington Post*, March 20, 2002.

11. Peter Slevin, "Cuba Seeks Bioweapons, U.S. Say," *Washington Post*, May 7, 2002.

12. "More Doubt Is Cast on Cuba Bioweapons," *Washington Post*, May 25, 2002.

13. Kevin Sullivan, "Carter Urges Democracy for Cuba," *Washington Post*, May 15, 2002.

14. Karen DeYoung, "Bush: No Lifting of Cuba Policies; President Reaffirms U.S. Sanctions," *Washington Post*, May 21, 2002.

15. DeYoung, "No Lifting of Cuba Policies."

16. Bill Sternberg, "U.S. Works for a Regime Change in Cuba, Too," *USA Today*, October 23, 2002.

17. Christopher Marquis, "U.S. Accuses Cuba of Trying to Disrupt Antiterrorism Effort," *New York Times*, September 18, 2002.

18. Marquis, "U.S. Accuses Cuba."

19. Ibid.

20. Paul Richter, "U.S. Bristles at Cuba's Arrest of Dissidents," *Los Angeles Times*, March 20, 2003.

21. Richter, "U.S. Bristles at Cuba's Arrest of Dissidents."

22. "Cuba's Crackdown," *Washington Post*, April 3, 2003.

23. David González, "Cuba Executes 3 Who Tried to Reach U.S. in a Hijacking," *New York Times*, April 12, 2003.

24. González, "Cuba Executes 3."

25. "Three Hijackers Were Killed to Deter U.S.-Backed Exodus, Castro Says," *New York Times* (Reuters), April 27, 2003.

26. "Three Hijackers Were Killed."

27. Paul Richter, "Bush Stays Put on Cuba Policy," *Los Angeles Times*, May 21, 2003.

28. Ibid.

29. Ibid.

30. Andres Oppenheimer, "Bush's Honeymoon with Hispanics Has Faded," *Miami Herald*, July 31, 2003.

31. Oppenheimer, "Bush's Honeymoon."

32. Maura Reynolds, "Bush Took Quote Out of Context, Researcher Says," *Los Angeles Times*, July 20, 2004.

33. Ibid.

34. Ibid.

35. Hampden Macbeth, "Chávez and Castro Work in Tandem Infuriating United States," <www.canadiandemocratic movement.ca/Article667.html> (accessed August 2005).

36. Alexei Barrionuevo and José de Córdova, *Wall Street Journal*, February 2, 2004.

37. "Cuban Trade with Venezuela," Center for International Policy's Cuba Program, <www.cipoline.org/cuba/trade/Venezuelatrade.htm> (accessed August 2005).

38. Jim Lobe, "Bush's New 'Axis of Evil'-Castro and Chávez," <FinalCall.com> (accessed April 12, 2005).

39. Lobe, "Bush's New 'Axis of Evil.'"

40. Barrionuevo and de Córdova, "For Aging Castro Chavez Emerges as a Vital Crutch."

41. Vanessa Arrington, "Chávez Slams U.S. in Show with Castro," *Miami Herald*, August 22, 2005.

42. "Washington Worried by Venezuela, Cuban Socialism," *Yahoo News*, August 20, 2005.

43. Arrington, "Chávez Slams U.S."

44. "Bolivia 'to join Chavez's fight,'" *BBC News*, January 3, 2006 <newsvote.bbc.co.uk>.

45. Andrew Pollack, "U.S. Permits 3 Cancer Drugs from Cuba," *New York Times*, July 15, 2004.

46. Warren P. Strobel, "U.S. No Longer Insists that Cuba Is Creating Offensive Bio-weapons," *Miami Herald*, August 31, 2005.

47. Sternberg, "U.S. Works for a Regime Change in Cuba."

48. "Castro steps aside after surgery," *BBC News* (online), August 1, 2006.

49. "Cuban TV: Castro says health 'stable'" *CNN.com*, August 1, 2006.

References

"Agreement with U.S. on Legal Immigration." 1994. *Caribbean and Central American Report*, October.

Amaro, Nelson, and Alejandro Portes. 1972. "Una sociología del exilio: Situación de los grupos cubanos en los Estados Unidos." *Aportes* 23: 6–24. Quoted in Silvia Pedraza, "Cuba's Refugees: Manifold Migrations." In *Origins and Destinies: Immigration, Race, and Ethnicity in America*, ed. Rubén G. Rumbaut. Belmont, Calif.: Wadsworth, 1996.

Antón, Alex, and Roger, E. Hernández. 2002. *Cubans in America: A Vibrant History of a People in Exile*. New York: Kensington.

Arboleya, Jesús. 1996. *Havana-Miami: The U.S.-Cuba Migration Conflict*. Melbourne: Ocean Press.

———. 2000. *The Cuban Counterrevolution*. Athens: Ohio University Press.

Bach, Robert L. 1987. "The Cuban Exodus: Political and Economic Motivations." In *The Caribbean Exodus*. New York: Praeger. Quoted in Jesús Arboleya, *Havana-Miami: The U.S.-Cuba Migration Conflict*. Melbourne: Ocean Press, 1996.

Bach, Robert L., Jennifer B. Bach, and Timothy Triplett. 1981/1982. "The Flotilla Entrants: Latest and Most Controversial." *Cuban Studies* 11/12: 29–48.

Baker, Christopher P. 1997. *Cuba Handbook*. Chico, Calif.: Moon.

Baker, Glenn, ed. 2003. *Cuban Biotechnology*. Washington, D.C.: Center for Defense Information.

Bardach, Ann Louise. 2002. *Cuba Confidential: Love and Vengeance in Miami and Havana*. New York: Random House.

Beschloss, Michael R. 1991. *The Crisis Years: Kennedy and Khrushchev, 1960–1963*. New York: Harper Collins.

Blight, James G., and Peter Kornbluh, eds. 1993. *Politics of Illusion: The Bay of Pigs Invasion Reexamined*. Boulder, Colo.: Lynne Rienner.

Blight, James G., Bruce J. Allyn, and David Welch. 1993. *Cuba on the Brink: Castro, the Missile Crisis and the Soviet Collapse*. New York: W. W. Norton.

Booth, Cathy. 1992. "The Man Who Would Oust Castro." *Newsweek*, October 26, 56–58.

Brenner, Phillip, William LeoGrande, Donna Rich, and Daniel Siegel, eds. 1989. *The Cuba Reader: The Making of a Revolutionary Society*. New York: Grove Press.

Burton, Dan, and Ben Gilman. 1999. "The Compelling Case of Castro's Cocaine." http://www.house.gov/burton/oped11.htm (accessed in 2003).

Campbell, Horace. 2001. "Cuito Carnavale." In *The Oxford Companion to Politics of the World*, 2nd ed., ed. Joel Krieger. New York: Oxford University Press.

Center for Defense Information (CDI). 1996. "Ending the Cold War Freeze." Show Transcript. http://www.cdi.org/adm/937/transcript.html (accessed in 2003).

———. 2001. Unpublished transcript of meeting in Havana between CDI delegation and Cuban military officers.

Church, George J. 1994. "Cubans, Go Home." *Time*, September 5, 28–34.

Cirules, Enrique. *The Mafia in Havana*. Melbourne: Ocean Press, 2004.

Clinton, William Jefferson. 2004. *My Life*. New York: Alfred A. Knopf.

Coe, Andrew. 1995. *Cuba: Pearl of the Caribbean*. Chicago: NTC.

Collins, James. 1996. "Blown Out of the Sky." *Time*, March 4, 39.

Corbett, Ben. 2002. *This Is Cuba: An Outlaw Culture Survives*. Cambridge, Mass.: Westview Press.

Cruz Díaz, Rigoberto. 1977. *Guantánamo Bay*. Santiago de Cuba: Editorial Orient. Quoted in Mary Ellene Chenevey McCoy, "Guantánamo Bay: The United States Naval Base and Its Relationship with Cuba." Ph.D. diss., University of Akron, 1995.

"Cuba and Terrorism." Center for International Policy's Cuba Project. http://www.ciponline.org/cuba/cubaandterrorism/terrorismhome.htm (accessed in 2003).

The Cuban Émigrés: Was There a US Intelligence Failure? Staff Report, Subcommittee on Oversight, Permanent Select Committee on Intelligence, U.S. House of Representatives (Washington, D.C.: U.S. Government Printing Office, 1980), 3, cited in Zucker and Zucker 1996.

Cuba Source (summary of news items reported on Cuba). http://www.cubasource.org/chronicles/summary.htm (accessed 2003–2005).

Darilek, Richard. 1999. "East-West Confidence Building: Defusing the Cold War in Europe." In *Global Confidence Building: New Tools for Troubled Regions*, ed. Michael Krepon et al., 275–90. New York: St. Martin's Press.

De la Torre, Miguel A. 2003. *La Lucha for Cuba*. Berkeley: University of California Press.

Devabhaktuni, Sony, Matthew C. J. Rudolph, and Amit Sevak. 1999. "Key Developments in the Sino-Indian CBM Process." In *Global Confidence Building: New Tools for Troubled Regions*, ed. Michael Krepon et al. New York: St. Martin's Press.

Didion, Joan. 1987. *Miami*. New York: Simon and Schuster.

Domínguez, Jorge I. 1989. *To Make a World Safe for Revolution*. Cambridge, Mass.: Harvard University Press.

———. 1992. "Cooperating with the Enemy? U.S. Immigration Policies toward Cuba." In *Western Hemisphere Immigration and United States Foreign Policy*, ed. Christopher Mitchell. University Park: Pennsylvania University Press.

———. 1997. "U.S.-Cuban Relations: From the Cold War to the Colder War." *Journal of Interamerican Studies and World Affairs* 39, no. 3: 49–75.

———. 2001. "Cuban Foreign Policy and the International System." In *Latin America in the New International System*, ed. Joseph S. Tulchin and Ralph H. Espach. Boulder, Colo.: Lynne Rienner.

Dougherty, William F., and José Bahía. 1990. "Caught between Two Flags." Unpublished manuscript, Guantánamo Bay, Cuba. Quoted in Mary Ellene Chenevey McCoy, "Guantánamo Bay: The United States Naval Base and Its Relationship with Cuba." Ph.D. diss., University of Akron, 1995.

Eckstein, Susan. 1994. *Back from the Future: Cuba under Castro*. Princeton, N.J.: Princeton University Press.

Engstrom, David W. 1997. *Presidential Decision Making Adrift: The Carter Administration and the Mariel Boatlift*. Lanham, Md.: Rowman and Littlefield.

Esteban, Angel, and Stéphanie Panichelli. 2004. *Gabo y Fidel: El Paisaje de una Amistad*. Bogotá: Espasa Calpe.

Evans, Ernest. 1990. "Cuban Foreign Policy toward Latin America." In *Cuba: The International Dimension*, ed. George Fauriol and Eva Loser. New Brunswick, N.J.: Transaction.

Fernández, Alfredo A. 2000. *Adrift: The Cuban Raft People*. Houston: Arte Público Press.

Fisk, Daniel W. 1999. "Cuba Alert: New Policy Initiatives Reaffirm Fundamentals of U.S. Policy toward the Castro Regime." January 19. http://www.ciaonet.org/pbel/csis/hem01/fid01.html (accessed in 2003).

Franklin, Jane. 1997. *Cuba and the United States: A Chronological History*. Melbourne: Ocean Press.

Frederick, Peter J. 2003. "Becoming a World Power." In *The American People: Creating a Nation and a Society*, Vol. 2, ed. Gary B. Nash and Julie Roy Jeffery. New York: Longman.

Furiati, Claudia. 2003. *Fidel Castro*. Barcelona: Plaza Janés.

Fursenko, Aleksandr, and Timothy Naftali. 1997. *One Hell of a Gamble: Khrushchev, Castro and Kennedy 1958–1964*. New York: W. W. Norton.

Gaddis, John Lewis. 1997. *We Now Know: Rethinking Cold War History*. New York: Oxford University Press.

García, María Cristina. 1996. *Havana US: Cuban Exiles and Cuban Americans in South Florida 1959–1994*. Berkeley: University of California Press.

Gibbs, Nancy R. 1994. "Dire Straits." *Time*, August 29, 28–32.

Gilderhus, Mark T. 2000. *The Second Century*. Wilmington, Del.: Scholarly Resources.

González, Edward, and Kevin F. McCarthy. 2004. *Cuba after Castro: Legacies, Challenges and Impediments*. Santa Monica, Calif.: RAND.

González-Pando, Miguel. 1998. *The Cuban Americans*. Westport, Conn.: Greenwood Press.

Gott, Richard. 2004. *Cuba: A New History*. New Haven, Conn.: Yale University Press.

Gup, Ted. 2000. *The Book of Honor*. New York: Doubleday.

Haney, Patrick J. 1997. "Soccer Fields and Submarines in Cuba: The Politics of Problem Definition." *Naval War College Review* 50 (Autumn): 67–84.

Hernández, Rafael. 2002. "Frozen Relations: Washington and Cuba after the Cold War." *NACLA Report on the Americas* 35, no. 4 (January/February), 21–26.

Khrushchev, Nikita. 1971. *Khrushchev Remembers*. Trans and ed. Strobe Talbott. Boston: Little, Brown. Quoted in J. L. Gaddis, *We Now Know: Rethinking Cold War History*. Athens: Ohio University Press, 1997.

Kitfield, James. 2002. "Busted, on the High Seas." *National Journal*, 34, no. 8: 2698–2704.

Klepak, Hal. 2000. "Confidence Building and the Cuba–United States Confrontation." Ottawa, Ontario: Department of Foreign Affairs and Trade.

Kornbluh, Peter. 1998. *Bay of Pigs Declassified*. New York: New Press.

———. 2000. "Cuba, Counternarcotics, and Collaboration: A Security Issue in U.S.-Cuban Relations." The Caribbean Project, Center for Latin American Studies, Georgetown University, December.

Krepon, Michael, et al., eds. 1999. *Global Confidence Building: New Tools for Troubled Regions*. New York: St. Martin's Press.

Latin American Working Group. http:www.lawg.org./drugcert2.htm (accessed in 2003).

Lee, Rensselaer, III. 1997. "Cuba's Drug Transit Traffic." *Society* (March/April): 49–55.

LeoGrande, William M. 1982. "Foreign Policy: The Limits of Success." In *Cuba: Internal and International Affairs*. Beverly Hills: Sage.

———. 2000. "Conclusion: Cuba's Dilemma and Ours." In *Cuba: The Contours of Change*, ed. Susan Kaufmann Purcell and David Rothkopf. Boulder, Colo.: Lynne Rienner.

Levine, Robert M. 2002. *Secret Missions to Cuba: Fidel Castro, Benardo Benes, and Cuban Miami*. New York: Palgrave Macmillan.

Lievesley, Geraldine. 2004. *The Cuban Revolution*. New York: Palgrave MacMillan.

Mason, Theodore. 1984. *Across the Cactus Curtain*. New York: Dodd, Mead.

Masud-Piloto, Félix R. 1988. *With Open Arms*. Totowa, N.J.: Rowman and Littlefield. Quoted in Jesús Arboleya, *Havana-Miami: The U.S.-Cuba Migration Conflict*. Melbourne, Australia: Ocean Press, 1996.

Matthews, Herbert L. 1989. "The Bay of Pigs." In *The Cuba Reader: The Making of a Revolutionary Society*, ed. Phillip Brenner, William LeoGrande, Donna Rich, and Daniel Siegel. New York: Grove Press.

McCaffrey, Barry R. 2002. "Challenges to U.S. National Security." *Armed Forces Journal International*. May. http:// www.afji.com/AFJI/Mags/2001/May/viewpoint.html (accessed in 2003).

McCoy, Mary Ellene Chenevey. 1995. "Guantánamo Bay: The United States Naval Base and Its Relationship with Cuba." Ph.D. diss., University of Akron.

Molyneaux, Maxine. 1999. "The Politics of the Cuban Diaspora in the United States." In *The United States and Latin America: The New Agenda*, ed. Victor Bulmer-Thomas and James Dunkerley. Cambridge, Mass.: Harvard University Press.

Moody, John. 1994. "Splits in the Family." *Time*, September 5, 35.

Newhouse, John. 1992. "Socialism or Death." *New Yorker*, April 7, 52–83.

Nuccio, Richard. 1999. "U.S. Policy toward Cuba Is Schizophrenic." *Business Week Online*. October 27. http://www. fiu.edu/~fef/nuccio1099.html (accessed in 2003).

Oppenheimer, Andres. 1992. *Castro's Final Hour*. New York: Simon and Schuster.

Padgett, Tim. 2003. "Who's Bugging Castro?" *Time*, May 19, 46–48.

Pedraza, Silvia. 1996. "Cuba's Refugees: Manifold Migrations." In *Origins and Destinies: Immigration, Race, and Ethnicity in America*, ed. Silvia Pedraza and Rubén G. Rumbaut. Belmont, Calif.: Wadsworth.

Pérez, Louis A. 1999. *On Becoming Cuban: Identity, Nationality and Culture*. New York: Harper and Collins.

———. 2006. *Cuba: Between Reform and Revolution*. New York: Oxford University Press.

Pérez-Stable, Marfeli. 1999. *The Cuban Revolution: Origins, Course and Legacy*. New York: Oxford University Press.

Perrottet, Tony. 1995. "The Struggle against Colonialism." In *Cuba*, ed. Tony Perrottet and Joann Biondi. Boston: Houghton Mifflin.

Peters, Phillip. 2000. "U.S./Cuba Bilateral Relations: Cooperation at Arm's Length." Arlington, Va.: Lexington Institute, no. 24 (December). Georgetown University Cuba Briefing Paper Series. <www.lexingtoninstitute.org>

Portes, Alejandro, and Robert Bach. 1985. *Latin Journey: Cuban and Mexican Immigrants in the United States*. Berkeley: University of California Press.

"President Proclaims Embargo on Trade with Cuba." 1962. Department of State Bulletin, February 19. http://www.jkf-online.com/jpsj62tec.html (accessed in 2005).

Ricardo, Ricardo. 1994. *Guantánamo: The Bay of Discord*. Melbourne: Ocean Press.

Rodríguez, Felix I., and John Weisman. 1989. *Shadow Warrior*. New York: Simon and Schuster.

Rojas Aravena, Francisco. 1998. "Confidence Building Measures and Strategic Balance a Step Toward Expansion and Stability." In *Strategic Balance and Confidence Building Measures in the Americas*, ed. Joseph S. Tulchin and Francisco Rojas Aravena. Stanford, Calif.: Stanford University Press.

Rothkopf, David J. 2000. "A Call for a Post–Cold War Cuba Policy . . . Ten Years after the End of the Cold War." In *Cuba: The Contours of Change*, ed. Susan Kaufman Purcell and David Rothkopf. Boulder, Colo.: Lynne Rienner.

Safford, Frank, and Marco Palacios. 2002. *Colombia: Fragmented Land, Divided Society*. New York: Oxford University Press.

Schoultz, Lars. 1998. *Beneath the United States*. Cambridge, Mass.: Harvard University Press.

Shifter, Michael. 1998. "United States-Latin American Relations: Shunted to the Slow Track." *Current History*, 97, vol. 616: 49–54.

Skoug, Kenneth N. 1989. "The United States and Cuba." In *The Cuba Reader: The Making of a Revolutionary Society*, ed. Phillip Brenner, William LeoGrande, Donna Rich, and Daniel Siegel. New York: Grove Press.

Smith, Peter H. 2000. *Talons of the Eagle: Dynamics of U.S.–Latin American Relations*. New York: Oxford University Press.

Smith, Wayne S. 1987. *The Closest of Enemies*. New York: W. W. Norton.

———. 1998. "Cuba: Lost Opportunities for Cooperation on Drugs." Publication of the Center for International Policy. http://www.us.net/cip/cubadrug/htm (accessed in 2003).

Stafford, Frank, and Marco Palacios. 2002. *Colombia: Fragmented Land, Divided Society*. New York: Oxford University Press.

Staten, Clifford L. 2003. *The History of Cuba*. Westport, Conn.: Greenwood Press.

Szulc, Tad. 1986. *Fidel: A Critical Portrait*. New York: William Morrow.

Tierney, John T. 1994. "Congressional Activism in Foreign Policy: Its Varied Forms and Stimuli." In David A. Deese, ed., *The New Politics of American Foreign Policy*. New York: St. Martin's Press. Quoted in Walt Vanderbush and Patrick J. Haney, "Policy toward Cuba in the Clinton Administration." *Political Science Quarterly* 114 (1999): 387–408.

Torres, María de los Angeles. 1999. *In the Land of Mirrors: Cuban Exile Politics in the United States*. Ann Arbor: University of Michigan Press.

———. 2003. *The Lost Apple: Operation Pedro Pan, Cuban Children in the U.S., and the Promise of a Better Future*. Boston: Beacon Press.

Treaty of Relations between the United States and Cuba. 1934. http://www.hose-hulman.edu/~delacova/us-cuba/treaty-5-29-34.htm (accessed in 2003).

U.S. Congress. House. 1999. Subcommittee on Criminal Justice, Drug Policy, and Human Resources of the Committee On Government Reform. *Cuba's Link to Drug Trafficking*. 106th Cong. 1st sess., November 17. <www. gpo.gov/congress/house/> or <www.house.gov/reform> (accessed 2003).

Vanden, Harry, and Gary Prevost. 2002. *Politics of Latin America: The Power Game*. New York: Oxford University Press.

Vanderbush, Walt, and Patrick J. Haney. 1999. "Policy toward Cuba in the Clinton Administration." *Political Science Quarterly* 114: 387–408.

Wally, George B. 1946. *Vivan los cubanos*. Havana. In Pérez, *On Becomng Cuban: Identity, Nationality and Culture*. New York: HarperCollins, 1999.

Watson, Russell. 1996. "The Lost Brothers." *Newsweek*, March 4, 38.

Weede, Erich. 1992. "Some Calculations on Democracy and War Involvement." *Journal of Peace Research* 29: 377–83.

Welch, David. 2001. "Cuban Missile Crisis." In *The Oxford Companion to Politics of the World*, 2nd ed., ed. Joel Krieger. New York: Oxford University Press.

Williamson, Edwin. 1992. *The Penguin History of Latin America*. New York: Penguin Books.

Wyden, Peter. 1979. *Bay of Pigs: The Untold Story*. New York: Simon and Schuster.

Zucker, Norman L., and Naomi Flink Zucker. 1996. *Desperate Crossings: Seeking Refuge in America*. New York: M. E. Sharpe.

Index

Melanie M. Ziegler received her doctorate in political science from Miami University, Oxford, Ohio, in 2004. She currently teaches courses in comparative foreign policies, Latin American politics, and international studies at Miami University.